The
MUSE
in the
MACHINE

THE FREE PRESS
A Division of Macmillan, Inc.
NEW YORK

Maxwell Macmillan Canada
TORONTO

Maxwell Macmillan International
NEW YORK OXFORD SINGAPORE SYDNEY

The
MUSE
in the
MACHINE

Computerizing the
Poetry of
Human Thought

DAVID GELERNTER

The Free Press
A Division of Macmillan, Inc.
866 Third Avenue, New York, N. Y. 10022

Maxwell Macmillan Canada, Inc.
1200 Eglinton Avenue East
Suite 200
Don Mills, Ontario M3C 3N1

Macmillan, Inc. is part of the Maxwell Communication
Group of Companies.

Printed in the United States of America

printing number

1 2 3 4 5 6 7 8 9 10

Library of Congress Cataloging-in-Publication Data

Gelernter, David Hillel.
   The muse in the machine / David Gelernter.
      p. cm.
   ISBN 0–02–911602–3
   1. Artificial intelligence. 2. Consciousness. 3. Cognition.
   4. Emotions. I. Title.
   Q335.G366 1994
   006.3'01'9—dc20   93–49721
                                                           CIP

For my boys and my Jane

Contents

Acknowledgments

Acknowledgments are ordinarily a fairly cut-and-dried affair, but these are different. The summer of 1993, during which this book was completed, was the hardest of our lives. My wife and I needed lots of help, badly—and help was so generously forthcoming that I almost believe we will remember the summer more, in the end, for the kindness of family, friends, the community and total strangers than for the crime that occasioned it. If it in fact works out that way, isn't the only possible conclusion that good beats evil in the end?

Thanks are due first to our families—particularly to Cheri and Joel, to my parents and Jane's, Ed, Judy and other family members; and to our devoted dear friend Soledad Morales.

The manuscript would never have made it to the finish line without the extraordinary exertions of Nick Carriero and Chris Hatchell. I will always associate this book with their overwhelming generosity.

The Clemans, the Bialeks, Rabbi and Mrs. Benjamin Scolnic, the Agins, the Schwartzes, the Patkins and the Larrisons put themselves out repeatedly to help us with the children, which is the most important sort of help there is.

Among our friends and neighbors and my colleagues who helped us in innumerable ways, large and small, the Lermans, Jane Milberg, Bob King, Susan Shapiro, Ed Keegan and Martin and Beverly Schultz were particularly indispensable. We deeply appreciate the help and good wishes of our friends Steve Nowick, the Arangos and the Jaggannathans, of Patricia MacDougall and the Yale Architecture Class of '83 (a truly great vintage!), of the Hamenachems, of the loads of people who brought us food, of the Yale police and particularly Officer Joe Vitale, of Ruth Anne Levinson and the JCC summer program staff, of Gail Brand and the whole Ezra community, Rabbi Weinberg and the B'nai Jacobites, President Levin, Provost Rodin and the Yale community *en masse*. I'm tempted to round out this huge list by appending the entire community of computer science researchers. Nothing moved and cheered me more last summer than the outpouring of good wishes that sloshed in daily from colleagues all over the world. People often write these notes because they feel they ought, without a sense that they will do much good; but they do immense good.

My graduate students carried on splendidly and cheered me up enormously. Thanks to all of them, and particularly Susanne Hupfer and Eric Freeman.

An academic is in bad shape without his books. Many thanks to Winston Atkins, Ellen Belcher and Paul Conway, whose expert ministration resuscitated so many of my tattered, burnt and drenched books and journals.

Last but (obviously) not least, my profound thanks to the medical people who so patiently reassembled me. They are a cast of thousands, too many to list. But the three whose exertions were most heroic are Rhonda Laidlaw, Marsha Dymarczyk and Dr. Henry Spinelli.

A few "normal" acknowledgments . . .

The research discussed here owes a great deal to my graduate students, but Scott Fertig in particular is responsible for much of the work and virtually all of the software that figures in this story. Dr. Mitch Sklar laid the basis years earlier with his own fine work.

My editor Susan Arellano did a great job with this quirky book. I am indebted to her, particularly for her patience.

Many parts of this book have gained from my conversations over the years with Professors Ivan Fox and Drew McDermott. (But they are to be held wholly guiltless of any responsibility for the strange doctrines contained herein.)

Parts of Chapter 8 benefitted at an earlier stage from Barbara Harshav's superb editing and critical acumen. I'm only slightly ashamed to confess that if Mrs. Harshav liked this book and everyone else in the world hated it, I'd consider it a great success.

Every book I have written and every book I will write reflects, imperfectly, the wisdom of George McCorkle. He was an inspiring man.

And finally my wife Jane, from whom this summer I have learned the meaning of *eishet hayil. Ha-zorim b'dima, b'rina yiktsoru.*

Chapter One

A New Folk Psychology

It's hard to conceive offhand of a less promising consumer innovation than a computer that comes factory equipped with "emotions"—but here's a candidate: how about a "*spiritual*" computer? The spiritual computer spends its time pondering the mysteries of the universe, occasionally printing cryptic messages on its screen and otherwise ignoring the user altogether.

Here's what the "emotional" computer would do. You might describe a complicated medical case to it and ask for the diagnosis. The computer might give you a serious, telling answer, but add, ". . . still, I'm not happy with that; it doesn't feel right."

You might describe a complex legal case and ask for its advice. It's answered harder questions before, but on this occasion it might put you off with a comment about how the plaintiff reminds it of your sister.

You might describe an intricate stock deal and ask whether you should invest. In the past its advice has been solid—not infallible but better than any human's you've ever consulted, in part because it has billions of case histories down cold. But on this occasion it tells you, " 'Buzz off. I'm not in the mood. Let's talk about Jane Austen."

1

Who needs this kind of nonsense from a computer? Science does; in a broader sense we all do, because adding "emotions" to computers is the key to the biggest unsolved intellectual puzzle of our time: how thinking works. Oddly enough, our "emotional" computer will be capable of "spirituality" as well. No topic is further than spirituality from the interests of the researchers who are trying to understand the human mind. But as we will see, spirituality turns out to be central to cognitive psychology, and therefore to artificial intelligence, and therefore to computer science, and therefore to the whole history of science and technology.

————————

Why these dramatic pronouncements and radical claims? Surely the science of mind is making fine progress without them.

Of course it is, but at the same time it suffers from a large and important problem. Here's an analogy.

Until 1759 sailors faced a big obstacle at sea: they only half knew where they were. Latitude was easily determined, but longitude was a mystery. Only when a meticulously accurate portable clock emerged at the end of a massive international research effort did the mystery of the longitude finally come clear (Landes 1983). To sailors, this development was a revelation; knowing half your position wasn't always a lot better than not knowing it at all.

Thought scientists today have a similar problem. The study of how thinking works is a big field—it encompasses philosophers of mind, cognitive psychologists, neurophysiologists and legions of frantically intense computer scientists bent on carrying off the greatest conjuring trick of all time, building minds out of computers. But thought science today is at sea. Despite monumental exertions, it has achieved a good grasp of no more than half the problem before it. Reasoning is one big part of human thought, and thought science has reasoning decently under control. Philosophers and psychologists understand it and computers, up to a point, can fake it. But there is one other big piece of the picture, which goes by many names: creativity, intuition, insight, metaphoric thinking, "holistic thinking"; all these tricks boil down at base to *drawing analogies*. Inventing a new analogy—hitching two thoughts together, sometimes two superficially *unrelated* thoughts—brings about a new metaphor and, it is generally agreed, drives *creativity* as well. Studies (and intuition) suggest that creativity hinges on seeing an old problem in a new way, and this so-called "restructuring" process boils down at base to the discovery of new analogies. How analogical thinking works is the great unsolved problem, the unknowable longitude, of thought science. "It is striking that," as the philosopher Jerry Fodor remarks, "while everybody thinks analogical reasoning is an important ingredient in all sorts of cognitive achievements that we prize, nobody knows anything about how it works"—not even, Fodor adds (twisting the knife), in an "in the glass darkly sort of way" (1983, 107).

Thought scientists have exhausted themselves trying to solve the riddle. To cite only the most dramatic example, Roger Penrose (1989) posits by way of explanation an esoteric quantum mechanical freak of nature. Fodor (1983, 127) believes the answer is not merely unknown but unknowable—that such problems are just "bad candidates for scientific study."

I will present here a new model of human thought that puts analogy at the center of the action and offers what I claim is a direct, fairly simple explanation of how it works.

I'm about to tell a new and different story of human thought. But new and different does not mean concocted out of whole cloth. My method is more like the archeologist's who reconstructs an ancient vase out of its scattered shards. Most of my shards are important, intriguing, but (I claim) insufficiently appreciated results of experimental psychology. Some of my shards come from philosophy or computer science. Some—the most beautiful—are the work of poets, particularly the mind-obsessed English Romantics. A great poet has a more than average chance of possessing a mind that is, as William Wordsworth puts it, "haunted by herself." "In Egypt, Palestine, Greece and India the analysis of the mind had reached its noon and manhood," Samuel Taylor Coleridge writes in 1817, "while experimental research was still in its dawn and infancy" (Coleridge 1817/1975, 54). It's an overstatement, but an intriguing one. Modern thought science has no truck with poetry. But I am convinced that these poets can tell us deep, beautiful, *scientifically indispensable* facts about thought.

Like weathered pottery fragments, some of my pieces won't fit exactly; others are missing and will require what appear (at first) to be big leaps of faith to reconstruct. But when everything is in place and a smooth, coherent shape emerges, those leaps will seem merely inevitable.

The result will be, in essence, a new "folk psychology"—cognitive science's slightly snide term for prescientific, commonsense psychology, the sort that can be done before even a single grant proposal gets funded. I will marshal a fair amount of scientific data to support my argument, but I will appeal more frequently to intuition and common sense. The results might or might not be convincing to scientists. I hope they are, but my main goal is to reach those readers for whom the human mind is not a profession but a passion. These aficionados are as likely to be poets, priests, gossips, or truck drivers as cognitive scientists. If I can show these people anything at all that broadens or deepens their grasp of this boundlessly fascinating, all-consuming topic even a little, I will be satisfied.

Dinner parties and boat rides

Here is my argument. Human thought is laid out in a continuous spectrum. Every human mind is a spectrum; every human mind possesses a broad continuous range of different ways in which to think. The way in which a person happens to be thinking at any given moment depends on a characteristic I'll call "mental focus." Focus can be high or low or medium; it changes throughout the day, not because the thinker consciously changes it, as he might consciously raise his arm, but in subliminal response to his physiological state as a whole. Fatigue (for example) makes focus go lower. Wide-awakeness makes it go higher.

Mental focus might sound like another way of saying "degree of alertness"; what's new is the way *cognition as a whole* changes in response to changing focus. High focus puts the thinker at the high end of the cognitive spectrum, and certain consequences follow. At the high end, thought is analytic and penetrating. It deals in abstractions and displays a "demythologized intelligence"—as the poet Robert Bly (1991) calls it—"that moves in a straight line made up of tiny bright links and is thereby dominated by linked facts." If a person's briefcase is stuck, he needs to open it and is in a high-focus state, he will methodically run down the list of factors that cause briefcases to jam, plan a course of action and do it. His thoughts are well behaved. He has no doubt that they *are* (mere) thoughts; they do not impose themselves like hallucinations. Perceptions turn obediently into easily retrieved memories. In the future he will have no trouble recalling how he behaved during this particular stuck briefcase incident.

Almost all attempts to simulate thought on a computer have dealt exclusively with this narrow, high-focus band at the top of the spectrum.

As we set off down-spectrum, thinking becomes less penetrating and more diffuse, consciousness gradually "spreads out" and—this is a key point that I will spend much of the chapter explaining—emotion starts gradually to replace logical problem-solving as the glue of thought. The rest of the chapter pins down these vague pronouncements. When a briefcase jams and the owner's focus level is medium, instead of a cool logical analysis he is more likely to think "last time when I did this, it opened." Thought is less analytical, more concrete. He might simply give the thing a good whack. (Thought: a good whack usually helps out in situations like this.)

A few research efforts in artificial intelligence have attempted to reproduce this "medium-focus" type of thought—although, without noticing the spectrum itself.

Confronted with a stuck briefcase towards the bottom of the spectrum, the owner is likely not to solve the problem at all. He is more likely as he ponders the briefcase to find himself thinking "that was some hot muggy day when I bought this damned briefcase in Milford—did I overpay?—I pay more than I need to for most things. But I'm better than Bill Schwartz in that regard—Schwartz's dinner party last fall was sort of fun—Molly sure didn't want to go—she looked nice in that short midnight blue dress, though—Columbus Avenue, we got the thing in that shop around Seventy-sixth Street . . ."

Now suppose our thinker's focus is just a bit lower. His thought-stream might start off in the same way—might extend, say, through "Schwartz's dinner party last fall was sort of fun," and pause there for a while—various aspects of the party come to mind; and then, next thing he knows, the thinker might find himself contemplating

Long Island Sound as he crossed it on a ferry years ago, seated on the stern deck, admiring the glitter of the soft green water on a bright, hazy summer afternoon. That summer afternoon has no obvious connection of any kind with the Schwartz's dinner (which consisted, let's say, of an elaborate meal served on three end-to-end rickety card tables in a cramped SoHo apartment nowhere near Long Island Sound, and is memorable mainly for noise and the overwrought, grinning Schwartz's stories about the school board elections and Molly on her knees playing scrabble) but, for some reason or other, it comes to mind—

But this is a tremendously important phenomenon, this coming-to-mind seemingly out of thin air, when we are in a mental state that we might informally call "relaxed"—what I would call "low focus"—of thoughts bearing no evident relationship to their predecessors. Readers may doubt that it happens; just *because* it comes about in relaxed mental states only, the thinker rarely takes note of it, just passively experiences it. But psychologists have been aware of the phenomenon since at least 1823, when one Ludwig Börne (cited in Jones 1963, 160) wrote that, if you monitor your thinking uncritically for a few days, ". . . you will be amazed at what novel and startling thoughts have welled up in you." Modern studies that I will cite later back up this strange contention. Any reader who monitors his own thoughts for a while will discover the phenomenon for himself. Try it and you will see that it *does* happen.

Does it matter? Yes, enormously. These unexpected transitions from thought *A* to a seemingly unrelated thought *B* are (as I will discuss) exactly the occasions on which analogies are discovered and metaphors emerge. *A* and *B* don't *necessarily* make an analogy. The Schwartz affair and that trip across Long Island Sound might not be analogous in the least. But when analogies do emerge, they emerge in this way. It may be that, say, the Schwartz party and the ferry trip are two occasions on which our thinker had a wonderful time with a subtle undertone of anxiety, because of something that was going to happen the next day—

This mental leap from the noisy party to the placid boat ride is paradigmatic of the most significant unsolved problem of cognition. *Affect linking*, I will claim, is responsible for bringing these leaps about. They are not random (nor need they have anything to do with repressed Freudian angst); they come about exactly when *two recollections engender the same emotion*, and they only happen towards the low-focus end of the spectrum.

Towards the lower end of the spectrum, affect linking causes creativity, metaphor, and in some cases spiritual mind-states to emerge. Other cognitive events accompany affect linking: thought grows ever more concrete. Recollection grows broader, more tangible and full of ambience and all-inclusive until eventually, a recollection becomes indistinguishable from a hallucination; and other things being equal, the illogic of dreaming waits at the bottom.

No computer program of which the author is aware attempts to simulate low-focus thought.

The cognitive spectrum provides us with a vantage point from which we can survey and make sense of human thought as a whole. More: it tells us something about the *dynamics* of human thought—its history over multiple time scales. Over the course of a day fatigue sets in and the character of thought changes. Over the first decades of life maturity comes about, and the character of thought changes. Over the millennia of human existence the modern mind gradually emerges, and the character of thought changes. I'll call these the Big Three cognitive transitions. They differ radically in character and take place over radically different time scales. But it's a curious fact that, if we view these three transitions from the spectrum's vantage point, they all three seem to tell the same underlying story. It is the story of gradual transition across the spectrum, from high focus towards low in the daily passage from awake to asleep; from low towards high in the development of a child or the emergence of the modern mind. The three transitions remain radically different, but the *underlying theme* turns out to be the same.

Now let me fill out this picture, make it more precise, and attempt to convince you that it is true.

The spectrum

Children have short attention spans.

There's nothing remarkable about that, but it perfectly epitomizes the *sort* of fact that appears to be wholly unconnected to topics like computer science or the philosophy of mind. Most practitioners of those disciplines would agree: children have short attention spans . . . *so what*? In reality these short attention spans are connected to technology and philosophy by a dense network of facts in which they play one small but interesting part.

Everyone knows about children's short attention spans and, for the record, studies confirm them. Very young children have another related characteristic that's harder to study but just as interesting. If you listen to an intelligent two-and-a-half-year-old holding forth, you may notice that his conversation has a plastic quality: one topic turns abruptly into another, with no respect for narrative logic (Garbarino et al. 1989, 77, make observations along these lines). We might call this "stream of consciousness"-style conversation, but it strongly resembles another phenomenon as well. Dreams work this way. It's perfectly normal in the course of dreaming for one scene to transform itself abruptly and "illogically" into a different one. "The narrative organization of dreaming," Foulkes (1985, 35) circumspectly observes, "occasionally breaks down in a relatively spectacular way."

Now it's an interesting fact, less well known, that some ancient literature is marked by this same kind of plastic, illogically put-together quality. Take the Bible as an example. Most people are aware of the theories claiming that it consists of many separate narrative strands stitched together. Ask yourself: why would such a theory be plausible? Answer: *in part*, because of passages where there is no sustained logical thread. Where the narrative bobs and weaves and doesn't seem (*seem*) to make sense: like a young child, or a dream.

If you were a literary critic attempting to analyze a dream or the conversation of a two-year-old transcribed and presented to you as "literature," you'd notice all sorts of abrupt, implausible transitions, and many contradictions. You might easily decide that you were examining not the production of one author, but a bunch of separate accounts crudely patched together. In the case of the Bible there are other good reasons for guessing that there *are* multiple strands in play, and these good reasons have obscured a deeper point. Having observed a phenomenon and explained it we're tempted, by and large, to go away satisfied. But suppose there is *more than one* explanation?

What is it about dreams, childhood, and the ancient mind that makes thought run, sometimes, in funny ways?

Could it be something they share? These *states of being* have been compared often before, for example in the mind-obsessed poetry of the English Romantics, or in Freud's anthropology. There's a certain obvious vulnerability in all three states. We sometimes dream about childhood; in the discredited "recapitulation" theory of earlier decades, the individual in the course of development was thought to retrace the evolutionary history of the species (Gould 1977). But I have something different in mind. I refer to a more specific resemblance, in *styles of thinking*, in the method by which thought-trains are assembled.

Returning to dreams: their defining quality is that, although they are constructed of memories, they seem real. "Dreams are hallucinations" (Hall 1966, 9). And on reflection, thoughts *about* childhood and *in* childhood are both tinged, also, with hallucinatory overtones.

Some authorities claim that young children actually do hallucinate routinely (for example Freud [1958], or Jaynes [1976]—of whom more shortly). Perhaps, but I have different and more subtle phenomena in mind.

First, certain childhood memories, suddenly recollected, can take an adult out of the present and place him in a different time and place with near-hallucinatory force. Not everyone knows the experience first-hand, but for those who do, it is striking. William Wordsworth explains: "Musing on them"—on memories of his early childhood—"often do I seem two consciousnesses, conscious of myself and of some other being" (*Prelude* I). This is a popular literary theme. E. B. White (1942): "I seemed to be living a dual existence." The Russian novelist Esther Salaman (1970), in a moving and beautiful study of what she calls "involuntary memories" of early childhood: "a *then* becomes a *now*." These are not hallucinations, but their vividness is uncanny. They reach out towards the hallucinatory.

As Salaman describes it, some thought or perception leads, for no evident reason, to a sudden, vivid recollection of a childhood scene. If our low-focus briefcase thinker's contemplation of the Schwartz party had been followed by a sudden recollection, nearly hallucinatory in its intensity, of a mossy mountaintop home he had visited once at the age of six; if he had re-experienced the damp musty-smelling wooden-sided sandbox where he had passed an uneasy half hour alone—then he has experienced an involuntary memory of childhood.

Further: young children are often themselves observed to have vivid imaginations. (Again this is just obvious; but see, for example, Singer and Singer's 1990 discussion of imaginary playmates for one striking example.) And what does a "vivid imagination" mean? If I ask you to close your eyes and imagine lying on the beach, the better you succeed, the closer you've come to staging a small-scale auto-hallucination. If we say *you have a vivid imagination*, we mean that *what you imagine seems real to you*.

What is it about the mental states of dreaming and of early childhood that causes thought-trains to be built, sometimes, in funny ways, and *mere thoughts* to take on hallucinatory color? Is it something they share?

It's a striking fact that the same strange phenomenon, thought-processes tinged with the hallucinatory, is also associated with ancient man. The fact becomes clear when we react to ancient literature in the natural, unstifled way we would to a modern text. The psychologist Julian Jaynes read ???*The Iliad* this way, and was astonished (as any modern reader should be!) to discover that so many key decisions in the story are said to be dictated verbatim by the god on duty. We are accustomed to thinking of God or gods in sanitized, metaphoric terms. It's apt to completely pass us by when ancient man, speaking of the felt presence of the divine, *actually means it*! Jaynes concludes (1976) that ancient man was prone to routine auditory hallucinations—untenable, I think. Still, as judicious a critic as the great classicist E. R. Dodds observes that hallucinations were most likely "commoner in former times than they are today" (1951, 116). Another great classicist cautions that "we must not forget the power of hallucinations . . ." (Gilbert Murray 1955, 25); "primitive men seem to have dealt more freely than we generally do with apparitions and voices and daemons of every kind" (26).

I would like to dispense with expert testimony and revert to common sense wherever I can. Hallucinations to the side, it is impossible to listen carefully to these texts and not to conclude that, in peak form, ancient man drew on a wildly vivid imagination. Wordsworth comments: "Turn where so'er I may,/ by night or day,/ the things which I could see I now can see no more" (*Ode: Intimations of Immortality*: 7–9). He refers to the lost, light-bathed vividness of childhood, but could just as easily have been describing the lost vividness of antiquity—when "holy were the haunted forest boughs,/ Holy the air, the water and the fire," as John Keats describes it (*Ode to Psyche*: 38–39). This vividly imagined, near tangible sense of holiness in the air *feels like* one step short of hallucination.

Now scholars have argued over whether ancient cognitive life was in fact different from our own. Some have claimed (for example, Miller 1986) that there is no reason to suppose that it was. Jaynes' view of Homeric man seems related to that of Snell (1953), which is pretty convincingly dismissed by Williams (1993). But there are concrete and specific reasons for believing that ancient thought *was* different: certain ancient texts prove that it was, by dint of making no sense under any other assumption. I will attempt to show in Chapter 8 that ancient thought-trains were just built differently, at least on some occasions, from our own; *and* we will see that these differently constructed thought-trains are associated with a vividly imagined or even hallucinatory mental life.

What is it that the mental states of dream, child, and ancient man share?

And why is it that, after the dream has passed, we have so much difficulty remembering it? And that after early childhood has passed, we have so much difficulty remembering *it*? And what's striking is that the *sort* of difficulty we have often seems to be very much the same in both cases. We feel intuitively that our failure to remember is often what psychologists call a "retrieval failure": the stuff is in there, but we just can't find it. Some psychologists suggest that this indeed is so, in the case of dreams (Cohen 1979) and of "childhood amnesia" (Shachtel 1947/1982).

Freud claimed that these two forgettings are related—that repression is the root of both. It's an intriguing claim that has occasioned many studies over the years, but they don't appear to bear it out, or at least not in any obvious way—although it is admittedly a very hard theory to test (Cohen 1979). The two kinds of forgetting *are* related, I think, but not in this way—or not only in this way.

No analogy between an individual and a social process can be more than rough, but if the analogy is evocative we are certainly within our rights at least to notice it. History itself emerges out of the mists, several millennia after the discovery of writing. The earliest stages of literate history are blanked out—except for the occasional vivid recollection. An event from the distant prehistoric past like the Biblical Flood recurs in many national mythologies. It haunts the world's literature like the "flashbulb memories" that fix a charged moment (say a president's assassination) in national consciousness (Brown and Kulik 1982, 23–40). Salaman's involuntary childhood memories are an even closer analogy. We can understand the Flood as mankind's involuntary childhood memory. It is a traumatic memory, as such memories (Salaman notes) so often are.

Why is it that memories of dream, childhood, and the ancient past are so hard to reclaim?

Symbolism is basic to dreaming. Everyone is aware of occasions on which X occurred in a dream, but we know immediately that X really meant Y. A symbol might be purely arbitrary. More often, there's some connection between "symbol" and "symbolized." In more ways than one, dream-thought traffics in *associations*, in unexpected connections. It's remarkable that childhood thought does too. "A common characteristic of young preschool children's conversation is *chaining*—that is, free-associating" (Garbarino et al. 1989, 78). On reflection, anyone who has ever listened seriously to a young child will agree; but unexpectedly, and at odds with the previous best guesses of developmental psychologists, a series of studies have shown young children to be strikingly good at *metaphor* as well (for example Gardner and Winner 1979, and Billow 1988). Metaphor hinges on meaningful but nonobvious connections.

What is it exactly that dream and child share?

Let's shift gears. What are children *bad* at?

Logic and analysis are not childhood specialties. More generally, children tend to be poor at manipulating abstractions. This is obvious and again, for the record, studies confirm it (e.g., Sternberg 1984). But adults are also conspicuously incompetent at logic, analysis and abstraction—when they are sleepy. A psychiatry textbook notes that drowsiness is characterized by, among other things, a "tendency to concrete thinking." (Freedman et al. 1976.) Adults are *very* bad at logical thought when they are asleep. A certain amount of problem-solving can occur in a dream, but dream-thought is notably *not* logical and not analytical. Nor is it abstract: dream imagery may be a concrete reduction or embodiment of a dreamer's thoughts. (Thus for example the psychologist C. S. Hall, who made exhaustive laboratory studies of dreaming, 1966, 95.) Freud (1900/1965, 330) remarked that words are treated in dreams as if they were concrete things; *concrete* is a word that keeps recurring in the literature on dreams.

Logic, analysis and abstraction are nonspecialties of ancient man as well. The great archeologist William Foxwell Albright (1940, 1964) used the term "proto-logical" to distinguish the thought style of the oldest class of western literature from ordinary logical thinking.

There is an obvious antithesis, then, between the mental universe of antiquity, dream and child and the analytic rigor of "rational man." But it isn't by a long shot merely the timeworn, threadbare antithesis between "metaphoric thought" and "logical thought." There is a whole rich world of mental phenomena that accompanies the nonrational states of mind. It is a strange-seeming world, uncanny even, in which thoughts are vivid (verging on hallucinatory) and thought-streams can be oddly and illogically built, where unexpected connections emerge like the features of a moonlit landscape as you grow used to the dark, and memories are slippery: it's hard to recall just what has happened, and where you have been . . .

That there are two styles of thinking is an old observation. It dates back to Aristotle. In modern psychology, an "analytic" or "rational" or "convergent" style is contrasted with something called "divergent" or "productive" or "lateral" or "primary process" or "metaphoric" thought. Sometimes "left-brain thinking" is held up to "right brain" in a broadly similar way. None of these dichotomies is a good match to the antithesis I've been describing. But in any case, the dichotomy itself is not the point. Mine is a story of *continuity*: of one cognitive style unfolding smoothly into another. What the dichotomists miss is merely the crux of the matter: that these two styles are *connected*; that a spectrum joins them, a spectrum that runs in one continuous, subtly graded arc, from the intense violet of logical analysis all the way downward into the soft slow red of sleep. They fail to grasp that there *are* any colors but red and violet; most important, that red *is* violet!—but for a *single* adjustment. Merely change the frequency. Leave everything else the same.

Let's invent something called a person's mental *focus*. For now I won't say what it is—it doesn't matter—beyond asserting that it correlates with current position on the mental spectrum. One end of the spectrum corresponds to maximum mental focus, and the other end to minimum. As we twiddle the knob from the high "analytic" end to the low "metaphoric" side, we are gradually turning *mental focus* lower.

Many separate cognitive events accompany the move down-spectrum, ranging from a loss of control over the thought-stream to an increased propensity to have creative insights and to encounter vivid imaginings or even hallucinations, a relaxation of logic, a loss of "goal directedness" and *all* directedness, and the emergence of emotion as the main glue of thought. But it is essential to grasp that this is no mere jumble of processes that just happen (allegedly) to be correlated. *These are all consequences of one underlying event.* They are all consequences of the *relaxation* or *lowering* or *widening* of the crucial property I have called mental focus. Lowering mental focus causes all of these processes to occur.

This cognitive spectrum, which is merely lots of well-known observations connected in a new way, is also the central fact of human thought. And it is the prime mover of cognitive history: of the cognitive transitions occurring over a day, over a lifetime and over the historical emergence of rational man from prelogical antiquity. A broad range of other hitherto scattered facts will fit comfortably into this framework.

The existence of the cognitive spectrum is supported, at least indirectly, by a fair amount of data, which I will be marshaling throughout the book. And although the spectrum itself is novel, many other thinkers have laid out theories that are similar in part or sympathetic to the spirit of the whole. Nonetheless: the spectrum idea is radically at odds with today's mainstream thought science. The mainstream sees thought as reasoning, problem solving, analysis and mental modeling, with an occasional dash of common sense. When the cognitive psychologist Robert Sternberg (1982, 225) writes that "reasoning, problem solving, and intelligence are so closely interrelated that it is often difficult to tell them apart," he is trying to tell us something: that intelligent thought is directed at a goal, dedicated to the rational solution of a problem. Anyone who has ever looked out the window, let his mind wander and realized that indeed he is still, right now, manifesting his intelligence, knows that this is false. From my perspective, the mainstream's view of thought is a parody. Thinking is vastly richer than that. A thought theory that never comes to grips with intuition, hallucination, spirituality or dreaming cannot possibly be a serious account of cognition.

––––––––

Let's methodically descend the cognitive spectrum. What happens when, starting in a high-focus, alert, analytic frame of mind, we gradually turn focus lower?

Driving is an odd but useful starting point. It's possible to drive in a state of high focus, intent and alert. Beginning drivers have no choice, and everyone ticks into this style occasionally. But ordinarily, a practiced driver allows a great deal of focus to boil off: doesn't concentrate intently on driving; devotes to driving a "lower focus" mental effort. The result is that he finds himself thinking about other things as he drives. Dennett points out (1991) that we shouldn't imagine driving to be carried out "unconsciously" under these circumstances, that it's merely absorbing a lowered level of attention.

As focus falls, attention becomes more diffuse. No single point in the perceptual or mental landscape is sharply illuminated. Many points are less strongly lit. (But this is no "spotlight of consciousness" theory, of the sort criticized by Allport 1989, 631–682. His "spotlight" is a fixed-focus beam playing across memory. It will become clear, if it isn't already, that the model and intent here are completely different.)

When focus drains away to disperse over a wider mental landscape, a person has less attention to devote to driving, and more to something else. That "something else" can't *itself* be a high-focus activity: a certain amount of mental focus is "pinned down" by driving or whatever. As a person moves down-spectrum, focus gets dispersed—meaning what, exactly? Here's a first clue. This lowered-focus state is specifically associated with another crucial mental phenomenon, *creativity*. It is consistently singled out as *the* mental state that gives rise to creativity or inspiration.

Many writers have said so. For example, Roger Penrose. Creative thoughts are most likely to occur to him when he is thinking about a problem "perhaps vaguely," "consciously, but maybe at a low level just at the back of my mind. It might well be that I am engaged in some other rather relaxing activity; shaving would be a good example" (Penrose 1989, 419). Shaving, driving, whatever—this is strikingly similar to the (in our terms) "lowered focus" state that Dennett describes.

Creativity in turn is a phenomenon that centers, according to a fairly solid consensus, on *restructuring* (Holyoak 1990, 117–146): on finding unexpected *analogies* that allow a person to see old problems in a new light. If lowering your mental focus allows creativity to happen, then it must encourage the discovery of unexpected connections. Analogies, metaphors, unexpected connections start to emerge as we make our way down-spectrum.

Unexpected connections are also part of childhood cognition ("chaining," metaphor); and are central to dreaming.

One special facet of creativity is the next clue, to another related phenomenon that intensifies as we continue down-spectrum. We say that an inspiration "hits us," that it happens unsought. An inspiration seems to happen *to* us, not to be a willed consequence of our own mental acts. Many witnesses have said so—that inspirations "come suddenly, as we say, 'into a man's head' " Dodds (1951, 11).

Salaman (1970, 59) in a striking observation links her idea of *involuntary* memory directly to creativity: "An involuntary memory has this in common with the solution of an artistic, mathematical or any other problem: it is a swift and usually unexpected contribution of the unconscious mind. . . ." By *unconscious mind* she means that an unexpected link *just happens*, unsought (or, not consciously willed).

Of course, to the extent thoughts happen *to you*, your thought-stream is out of control. An inspiration or a creative thought is only a minor, momentary loss of control. "Fancy," after all, is "blended and modified by choice" according the great romantic poet Samuel Taylor Coleridge (in Edel 1982, 14). Creative thoughts hit you unexpectedly, but then you pick yourself up, dust yourself off and get on with it, regaining control over your thought-stream and putting your new insight to work. Psychoanalysts cultivate this medium level of focus—asking to be knocked over by an association or an insight, but primed to leap immediately to their feet again and retake control (see, e.g., Gay 1985, 42).

But as a person ventures further down-spectrum, his grip loosens and his train of thought runs away from him, and he comes closer to being swept away. A single creative fancy is a momentary loss of control; an involuntary memory is a step further, towards the outer limits of hallucination. Then there is such a thing as a "creative *state*" in which you are closer to a sustained loss of control—where a flood of ideas and not just one seizes your attention. Thus Dodds again, quoting E. M. Forster: "In the creative state a man is taken out of himself." (64). Creative states presumably do not happen to everybody. But suppose, for the sake of argument, that our briefcase thinker is a talented architect; suppose that, in the course of his ferry trip across Long Island Sound, idle contemplation of the ferry's wheelhouse leads him suddenly to conceive the concert hall he is designing in vertical rather than horizontal terms. So he finds a sheet of paper and sketches for an hour, more or less oblivious of his surroundings, as ideas tumble out and the entire design reorganizes itself. That's a creative state.

Taken out of himself: remember that we are still talking about mere sustained creativity. The poet Percy Bysshe Shelley makes us feel that a sustained *spiritual* state of mind might be even closer to a complete loss of control over your own thought-train:

The everlasting universe of things
Flows through the mind, and rolls its rapid waves,
Now dark, now glittering . . . (*Mont Blanc:* 1–3)

This is still *thought* that he is describing, but it seems to be happening by itself.

You cannot, of course, make yourself have an inspiration: every folk psychologist is aware of the fact. You cannot make yourself have an "involuntary memory" and ordinarily you cannot through an act of will induce a sustained creative or spiritual state. Such states just happen; "these things come suddenly 'into a man's head.' " To reach the bottom of the spectrum, just connect these facts to another: you cannot make yourself fall asleep . . .

And what happens *as* you fall asleep? As the subjects in an experimental sleep study drifted off, they "lost their control over the course of mentation" (Vogel 1991, 131). Dreaming is a near-total loss of control over your thought-stream: the entire thought-stream seemingly happens *to* you. "Volitional control doesn't seem to be operative in creating dreams" (Foulkes 1985, 22). You used to be driving the thing but somehow it has taken on life and is driving itself. Dreaming is the bottom of the spectrum.

The conventional philosopher's and computer scientist's view of thought as a keen, docile instrument is a mere reflection of our rational biases. But in dreaming our thoughts submerge us completely, and at low tide near the spectrum's bottom they still regularly oversweep us—these thoughts we do not control and that may verge on hallucinations, threatening to submerge us again. Only as we move up-spectrum does the tide withdraw and thought gradually transform itself into the keen, docile instrument we prefer. Any serious folk psychologist knows that the conventional cognitive science view of thought—that thought is merely "mental modelling," that it centers on analysis, abstraction, logic, reasoning and problem solving—is drastically incomplete. And is it true that software and computers provide *the* crucial metaphor in the struggle to understand thought, that "the concepts of computer science provide the crutches of imagination we need" in order to grasp how the brain realizes the mind, as the distinguished philosopher Daniel Dennett (1991) puts it? Hypotheses like these are the heart and soul of modern thought science. But competent folk psychologists understand thought to be an integrated whole, and specifically the type of activity that is as likely to wield you as you are to wield it. You can be in the grip of thought as surely as you can be gripped by love or animal craving or a very bad cold. Consider carefully before you assert that such a thing can be reduced to, or understood in terms of, software.

I don't mean *just* that thinking isn't merely reasoning or problem solving—that it is also, as the philosophers Jerry Fodor or Hubert Dreyfus might say, intuitive and holistic (Fodor and Lepore 1992). Unless you are a cognitive scientist, that much should be obvious. What I mean is that thought may generate *its own* agenda as it goes along, *completely abandoning* any "extrinsic" agenda ("solve this problem"); setting off entirely "on its own." When our low-focus briefcase thinker finds himself remembering a boat ride or a childhood morning or the concert hall he is designing, these thoughts come to him "by themselves," unsought. I will argue that such excursions are the heart and soul of intelligence.

A computer that never hallucinates cannot possibly aspire to artificial thought.

———

So we've traced our way down-spectrum from a release or draining-off of focus in the process of (for example) driving, to the observation that such lower-focus states are where *creativity* occurs, to the observation that the emergence of creativity means the emergence of unexpected connections—to the association of creativity with *involuntary memory* and the momentary loss of control over a thought-stream, to the onset of sleep as an unravelling of control and dreaming as its near-total absence. As we approached dreaming, unexpected connections emerged, and thought took on hallucinatory overtones. In dreaming, we reached the bottom.

If we run this process backwards we will have something strikingly like, in its base features, the process of a child maturing; or the rational mind emerging from prelogical antiquity. Imagine a "cognitive campsite." It's the place on the spectrum where a person is most at home. He makes excursions up and down, but returns there. The transitions of sleep, maturing and the emergence from antiquity are big, complicated stories reflecting countless influences, but they all share one underlying theme: the slow, steady trek of the cognitive campsite up or (for sleep) down the cognitive spectrum. And by the way, why is the sound of rain restful? *For the same reason that shaving is "inspirational"—*

Driving, shaving, whatever, are excuses to diffuse consciousness, *mental focus*, over a wider field. They pin down *some* mental focus but to the extent they are uninteresting (that is, unpleasurable) in the role of sole thought-focus, they encourage *some* mental focus to wander elsewhere. Searle quotes William James' formulation that "consciousness goes away from where it is not needed," but points out that "attention goes away from where it is not needed" is closer to the truth (1992, 139). Of course, as Searle concedes, it doesn't go away *entirely*. So long as a person is devoting a certain amount of attention to the wheel or the razor, the other ongoing mental activity *cannot* be a high-focus activity.

Low-focus mental activity sets the stage in turn for creativity, and at the extreme for sleep. No matter how physically exhausted a person may be, he cannot achieve normal sleep unless he is in a low-focus mental state. (I'll argue that insomnia is in many cases nothing more or less than unwanted high-focus thought.) The sound of rain or anything similar helps to lower mental focus, by pinning down *some part* of the thinker's attention, thus leaving less to be shared by any other mental activities. By insinuating itself into awareness, the sound of rain broadens and thus lowers focus. A louder or more "interesting" sound wouldn't have the same effect—just as hard driving or a dull blade doesn't lend itself to restful, productive musing: it steals the thinker's whole attention and *itself* becomes a target for high-focus thought. But allowing the sound of rain merely *to enter your awareness* drives focus wider, and in so doing forces thinking down-spectrum, towards sleep.

———————

So we have a notion of "focus," and twiddling the focus knob controls your location on the mental spectrum. It's time to expand the model one small step further.

Thought at high focus isn't merely narrow; it's penetrating. To associate "penetrating" with "narrow" seems natural, suggesting that, other things being equal, the same force spread over a smaller area will have a more concentrated effect. So: the high-focus thinker can spindle a stack of memories—glom them together into a temporary composite (a "memory sandwich") and examine *one* aspect of *all* of them. High-focus thought is capable of penetrating a whole stack of memories at once. When our high-focus briefcase thinker notes that the combination lock won't open, and it occurs to him that such locks may have had their combinations reset—that hypothesis results, probably, from many experiences with combination locks, not from the recollection of a particular incident. Or suppose the same morning he'd noticed it was snowing, and grabbed his scarf. He happens to know that if it is snowing, it must be cold. How does he know? On countless occasions reaching back to early childhood, he's observed that snowy days are cold. At some point the child stacked up many memories of snowy days, noticed that, for all their idiosyncrasies, *cold* figured in all of them—and has known ever since that snowy days are cold.

As the focus dial is nudged lower, attention spreads out and becomes not *narrow and penetrating* but *broad, inclusive* and "superficial"—*many aspects* of *one* memory hold the thinker's attention, not *one* aspect of *many*.

When a memory is recalled at low focus, it is *the whole memory* that comes to mind. Not merely the technique whereby the briefcase was successfully opened when it was last jammed (if opening a jammed briefcase is the task at hand), but the *whole memory* in which this briefcase-opening experience is embedded: the jet fuel and stale cigarette smell of the airport waiting lounge, the headache, the destination, the weather outside and anything else that memory succeeded in trapping on that occasion.

"Abstract" versus "concrete"—think what the two words imply, and what we should conclude on that basis about the mental states that dwell on each. An abstraction is defined by the *few* traits shared by *many* instances. What is *concrete* includes many traits of one instance. Think of bravery in the abstract versus a concrete instance. The concrete instance is full of particular, individual details that have nothing to do with the abstract concept—

Now connect these obvious facts to low-focus thought in general and to dreaming as its radical end point. We know that dream-thought tends to be concrete. We also know that it is "out of control" in several ways. It is hallucinatory, and it is capable of presenting to the dreamer thoughts and memories that he doesn't want to have—that he has rejected or (perhaps) repressed in waking life. "Impulses that are kept in check during waking life" emerge in dreams (Hall 1966, 14). The reality of concrete thinking may be associated with both aspects of lost mental control. Concrete thought has the richness of texture that is required if we are to be enfolded by an imagined or hallucinated world. By exactly the same token, concrete thought is *inclusive*. We will explore later the connection between this all-inclusiveness, this inability to focus and thus to edit, and the occasionally tactless mental landscape of dreams. The power to focus-on is also the power to turn-away-from.

But there is still one other facet of the loss of mental control at low focus: the way thoughts "hit you," occur "by themselves"; the way a thought-stream can run away from the thinker. I'll return to it.

Of course abstract thinking emerges at high focus, and low-focus thought is concrete. An abstraction is merely a bunch of related memories "held up to the light" and examined as a single bundle. The salient features of this memory bundle are exactly the features that *define the abstraction* (the abstraction *blue, dog, true, irony*) as opposed to any one individual blue thing, dog, truth, or ironic incident. Because high-focus thought is penetrating and picks out details, it's the state of mind in which shared details come to light.

And because abstraction is a high-focus phenomenon, so is language, insofar as language deals with the meaning of words. A child learns what "blue" means by forming an abstraction. *Blue* is simply what all things called "blue" have in common. "Children under the age of seven are more responsive and attuned to nonverbal language—gestures and actions—than they are to words. They interpret words by relying on their understanding of the concrete circumstances around them" (Garbarino et al. 1989, 68). The emergence of language in childhood is a complicated process, but it takes place to a steady underlying beat: children as they mature move their cognitive camping grounds gradually, inexorably up-spectrum—and gradually, inexorably, language becomes possible.

Memories *recalled at high focus* are the stuff of abstractions. A thinker pierces them *en masse* with his focussed attention and picks out the salient shared details. What about memories *formed* at high focus? Perceptions becomes memories—"turn imperceptibly into memories" (Dennett 1991, 136); it follows that, other things being equal, *memories formed at high focus are easily recalled*. A thinker pulls a memory back into awareness by grabbing some detail that stands out. At high focus, details do stand out. They become natural handles for pulling the scene back into awareness.

At low focus, the mind is occupied by the whole of *one* scene. Hence, thought tends to be concrete—that is, full of the particular, specific, idiosyncratic detail that sets a scene and creates an ambience. (In drowsiness, your thought grows "concrete." Children's thinking tends to the "concrete.") The breadth and inclusiveness of memories *recalled at low focus* give those recollections their potentially hallucinatory power to transport the thinker to another time and place. The breadth and inclusiveness of memories *formed at low focus* make them slippery. What emerges isn't detail but ambience. If a memory is formed, not of anything in particular but of everything in general, then, other things being equal, *it's hard to grasp such a memory*; hard to find any mental handhold. (The very quirk that makes memories slippery is the same quirk, of course, that makes thought vivid and potentially hallucinatory; and makes thinking not abstract but concrete.)

Childhood memories are hard to recall. Dreams are hard to recall. Many factors are at work in each case. In no instance do I wish to wave a magic wand over a complex phenomenon and announce that low-focus thought explains it all. But low-focus thought is an ingredient: it *sets the stage*. It creates the necessary condition. Childhood and dreaming are rich in low-focus thought—and that is a recipe for a vivid mental life, and amnesia afterwards. Young children themselves are bad at "deliberate recall," at reconstructing past events on demand, but they "often display remarkably accurate recognition memory" (Garbarino et al. 1989, 43)—when a *whole scene* is presented to them for examination, they can tell you whether or not they have encountered it before.

We've made progress, but are still a long way from a complete picture of the spectrum. The scheme as I've described it has a problem: as we move down spectrum, thought trains *ought* to unravel, simply come apart at the seams.

After all, the stuff that is conventionally held to be the prime glue of thought—logic, analysis, problem solving—fades as we move down spectrum and eventually vanishes. So what is it that holds thought together? Why doesn't your thought-train behave, as focus sinks, like a neatly stacked tower of blocks that goes up in a spaceship? As gravity slackens, the tower gradually becomes prone to dissolve into disconnected floating objects. But thought holds together. Some "mystery force" must kick in as logic fades. A force *different* from logic but a force nonetheless. What is that force?

To put the question another way: why should a thing like shaving induce a loss of control over your own thought-stream?

We have seen that activities like shaving, which may lower your mental focus, are associated with creativity. We know that creativity is felt by folk psychologists to be (as Dodds says) "not the work of the *ego*." What is it about a thing like shaving that might cause "a man to be taken out of himself"?

There is a basic mechanism that governs the assembly of thought-trains. It is a regular process, the cognitive equivalent of a pulse. On the basis of your "current thought" (say, "the briefcase is jammed"), you present a probe or cue to memory ("jammed briefcase"); memories emerge in response (involving, let's say, jammed briefcases, other jammed things, other kinds of briefcase); those memories are the basis of a *new* current thought ("usually if I do this, it opens").

This cycle is fundamental. It is mental breathing, or a cognitive heartbeat: a current thought giving rise to a probe, probe to memories, memories to a *new* current thought, new current thought to another probe . . . It's a simple observation, not so different at base from the old associationist doctrines of the British empiricists.

The "pulse" analogy is loose: the *cognitive* beat can be interrupted. The thinker calls time out to build mental models, and to explore and tweak them. During the periods in which he is examining these imagined models or scenes, the steady reaching back into memory for new material is suspended. But such halts are temporary. After a pause, the beat resumes.

We can recognize this simple notion of thought in the conventional view, if we simply stand the conventional view on its head. Most standard definitions are (granted) too complex to pin down, but insofar as the field has a simple, cogent view of what thought is, the view is probably that thought is "mental modelling" (Gilhooly 1988). That is, it's the process of somehow creating things in the brain that correspond to things in the outside world. Expectations about the outside world are formulated on the basis of such models. That is: if a wine glass is on a table, the thinker creates a "mental wine glass" in response; by examining the properties of this mental wine glass, he makes guesses about the actual wine glass— for example: if it falls, it will break. In this view, traffic with memory is the sideshow, not actually part of thought *proper* at all. Building mental models is the main act.

Wrong, though: this view is upside down. Playing with mental models is the interruption and *traffic with memory* is the steady, defining beat. *Thinking* is primarily, overwhelmingly *remembering*. This fact becomes clear as we move down-spectrum. Mental models are created in order to solve problems. But direct problem solving simply disappears as focus diminishes. *Thought* doesn't stop!—but mental model-making *does*. The pulse of thought grows steadier, more regular as we move down-spectrum.

Now, the central question: how does a probe latch on to a memory? If the probe-thought, the "bait," is *tomatoes* or *truth* or *stuck briefcases*, which memories will rise from the depths in response? Clearly, the manner in which probes latch memories is crucial in determining how thought-streams are put together.

It's obvious how the latching is accomplished at high focus. Thoughts are focussed on a few salient details, and recollections are fetched roughly on the basis of the extent to which they "match up" with the details the thinker cares about at the moment. If he cares about briefcases and stuck locks, he grabs memories that include either or both. The result is a thought-stream that is, roughly speaking, logical. A number of models have been developed to explain with mathematical precision how it all works (e.g., Hockley and Lewandowsky 1991)—what constitutes a "good match"—and they do so fairly well.

But as focus sinks, this simple latching mechanism breaks down. If "stuck briefcase" is the bait, the obvious candidates to be lured from the depths are ones that include a stuck briefcase. But if the bait is sprawling and diffuse—a *whole memory* with, potentially, a large and ill-defined, run-together collection of sights, sounds, colors, random circumstances—it's nearly impossible that *any other* memory will include all or even most of this stuff, in the sense that "stuck briefcase" can be neatly included in one or many other memories.

So *what* if some other memory happens to match a *few* features of the "whole memory probe"?—if the probe is a complex scene at the airport, and the memory it grabs in response also happens to involve the same uncomfortable pair of shoes that figured on that occasion, but is otherwise unrelated? Such purely accidental linking does happen, but can't possibly be the whole story. Whole memories can and *do* suggest other memories to which they bear no superficial resemblance at all. Metaphors arise when two seemingly unrelated thoughts become linked. ("Metaphor ignites a new arc of perceptive energy," George Steiner writes. "It relates hitherto unrelated areas of experience . . ." [1971, 68].) The "restructuring" to which creativity is attributed centers on exactly this sort of linking. How does it happen? *To answer this question is to understand how low-focus thought works*, to understand why low-focus thought-trains *cohere* and don't just fall apart.

The psychologist C. E. Osgood makes an interesting comment. Metaphor is driven, he claims, by the fact that "such diverse sensory experiences as a *white* circle (rather than black), a *straight* line (rather than crooked), a *rising* melody (rather than a falling one), a *sweet* taste (rather than a sour one), a *caressing* touch (rather than an irritating scratch) . . . can share a common affective meaning" (cited in Paivio 1979, 159).

Coleridge writes in a remarkable letter to the poet Robert Southey that

I hold, that association depends in a much greater degree on the recurrence of resembling states of Feeling, than on Trains of Ideas . . . I almost think, that Ideas *never* recall Ideas, as far as they are Ideas—any more than Leaves in a forest create each other's motion—The Breeze it is that runs through them; it is the Soul, the state of Feeling—(cited in Willey 1957/1973, 96)

Wordsworth writes, in *Tintern Abbey*, of *a serene and blessed mood* in which *the affections gently lead us on* . . .

Affections are the key. To find the gist of low-focus thought, look to the *emotions*.

———————

Virtually any serious survey of the topic will include a sentence such as, "The area of emotional experience and behavior is one of the most confused and ill-defined in psychology" (Izard, cited in Ekman 1977, 9). But we have to start somewhere. Lazarus and Smith cite the following from Drever's 1964 *Dictionary of Psychology*:

Emotion: differently described and explained by different psychologists, but all agree that it is a complex state of the organism, involving bodily changes of a widespread character—in breathing, pulse, gland secretion etc.—and, on the mental side, a state of excitement or perturbation . . . (610)

Let's accept this definition, but turn the volume down. An emotion is a mental state with physical correlates; it is a *felt* state of mind, where "felt" means that signals reach the brain that are interpreted as bodily sensations, however fleeting and subtle.

"Happy" and "sad" and "angry" and "scared" are emotions, but it's crucial that the list not stop there—that it also encompass what are sometimes called the "aesthetic" emotions. Happy, sad, and so on are the emotional equivalent of saturated primary colors. But there is a vast range of subtler intermediates.

It's hard to get a purchase on such mental states—what a person might feel on an unexpectedly warm spring morning, on an empty beach in winter, on driving past a childhood home, or hearing a clock tick loudly in the silence, or pounding a nail squarely into a wooden plank. Such occasions might evoke an emotional response.

But those emotions are a far cry from "happy" or "sad." They have two distinguishing characteristics. They are subtle. No grand passions need apply. They are *idiosyncratic*, blended to order for a particular occasion. They may contain recognizable traces of "primary emotion" (a touch of sadness, a trace of anxiety), but these are nuanced, complicated mixtures. *They have no names.*

Now, here is the key. An entire complex scene may be wrapped up in a *single emotion*. That one emotion can play the role of the narrow, relevant detail at high focus: it can peg this thought to another one that *shares the same emotional content*. But this pegging-together-by-shared-emotion, what I'll call the *affect link*, takes hold only *as focus sinks*.

Because for affect linking to happen, remembered feeling must be *felt*, not just dispassionately examined. Sometimes I merely *observe* that on such-and-such an occasion I felt happy. Other times, the recollection makes me *feel* happy—I *re-experience* the recollected emotion. (*I have owed to them*, says Wordsworth of certain happy recollections, *sensations sweet, felt in the blood, and felt along the heart* . . .) For the affect link to work, the thinker must "re-experience," *feel* his memories. Thus the cognitive psychologist Margaret Clark describes the "priming process" whereby a mood predisposes a subject to recollect memories of the same emotional color; the "feeling tone" associated with an experience may, she notes, be stored in memory along with the experience (Clark 1982, 266; also, e.g., Bower and Cohen 1982). Such studies tend to deal in fantastically unsubtle emotional gradations, and yet they are deeply suggestive.

The same process that entails a gradual loss of control over the thought-stream, a gradual loss of distance or separation between the thinker and his thought and a gradual rise in the hallucinatory presence of thoughts, naturally makes him increasingly prone to *feel* (and not merely dispassionately to examine) his remembered feelings. There is a reason why abstract thought on the one hand, and thought with emotional content (however subtle) on the other, seem intuitively to be antithetical. Emotional content is summoned by the concrete details as a whole. There are exceptions, particularly in the case of obvious and noisy emotions, but the more subtle and idiosyncratic the emotional response experienced at the time, the more likely that a detailed, concrete recollection of the original scene will be required in order to bring it back. We feel our thoughts as they become concrete, and the affect link emerges at low focus.

T. S. Eliot (1950/1976, 100) coined the famously odd phrase "objective correlative" to designate "a set of objects, a situation, a chain of events" that represents and summons forth a particular emotion in a literary text. The phrase remains to some degree obscure ("enigmatic"—Shusterman 1988), but it directs our attention to the link between concreteness and emotional content.

As focus sinks, we lose our neat, sharply bounded set of "points of interest" to serve as memory cues—and logic starts to dissolve. But another effect kicks in: we start to *feel our recollections*, and the affect link gradually exerts its power over our thought-streams. At first it causes isolated mental events: a single creative insight, an imagined metaphor, an involuntary memory, interrupting but not destroying the logical train. But as focus sinks further, *of course* the thinker has the sensation of a thought-stream gradually running out of control, being impelled not by him but by something else. These two facts are related: (1) an inspiration "just hits you"; (2) you cannot choose your emotions. Emotions choose themselves. As we continue down-spectrum, the affect link becomes a tidal force that makes thought start to *flow*. Listen to Shelley again on his mental state at the foot of Mont Blanc:

> The everlasting universe of things
> Flows through the mind, and rolls its rapid waves,
> Now dark, now glittering . . .

Wrapped in the envelope of its characteristic emotion, one thought may conjure its successor from the opposite corner of the mind.

The role of emotion in thought, then, is exactly to glue low-focus thought-streams together. At low focus, one thought is connected to the next by an emotion the two of them share, as one coach is coupled to the next by steel latches. There are no trains without couplers. There is no low-focus thought without emotion.

(High-focus thought can be "emotional" too—in the sense that it can be accompanied by emotion. A productive stint of high-focus thinking might, for example, induce satisfaction; even elation. But those emotions don't drive or shape the thought-stream. They are mere side-effects.)

And why, then, might a thing like shaving or driving induce you to lose control over your own thought-stream? Why might it cause a state of mind in which a person is "taken out of himself?" Because as focus widens, you come to feel your thoughts. The feelings you re-experience aren't things you chose, nor did you choose to recollect them. More important, those recollected feelings may hurtle you suddenly to a far-off corner of the cognitive universe, by connecting you to other recollections of the same emotional color; and that dizzy flight through cognitive spacetime is wholly outside your control. It happens because of the "laws of the mind," because of the way affect linking and recollection work, and because of certain emotional responses in your own past. The mental experience I have called the affect link is the type and progenitor of all *sane* "out of control" mental experiences, all divine inspirations and implantations. But does such a claim diminish the idea of inspiration? I don't believe so; because at the same time we tentatively propose a psychological account of a key mystery of the cognitive universe, we affirm that this phenomenon *is* truth-revealing! I will pursue the point further below.

Eventually, at the bottom, you are asleep. The neurobiologist and psychoanalyst Morton Reiser (Reiser 1990, 46: my emphasis) searches for the connection between the imagery of dreams and the concrete memories they symbolize. "Dream images and the memory traces they represent may be associatively linked *by a capacity to evoke the same emotions*".

We can now develop a somewhat clearer view of the spectrum as a continuum. The end points are defined, metaphorically, by an intense, focussed-down-to-a-pinprick, highly penetrating "thought-beam" at the high end and a soft, diffuse, nonpenetrating beam at the low. What happens in the middle? As focus declines, the beam retains its narrow focus but loses its intensity—its capacity to penetrate; only then does it gradually "spread out." (Clearly, the focussed-beam metaphor can take us only so far . . .) Thus, nothing is more characteristic of sloppy thinking, I believe, than the tendency to reason from a single prominent example rather than experience as a whole. This is what we expect to encounter partway down the spectrum, where the "beam" is still narrowly focussed but no longer penetrating. (Sloppy thinkers, who can't be bothered to push focus to "maximum" even when reasoning is required, are especially prone to draw conclusions from stereotype examples—conclusions that seem immune to experience, however extensive.) As we push focus lower, the "beam" spreads out; it lacks the precision required by reasoning, but isn't sufficiently all-encompassing to support affect linking—so, thoughts tend to be hooked together on the basis of a shared incidental detail. Our briefcase thinker contemplates a person, then a dress that person wore, then a store where the dress was acquired, and so on. One more step down, and affect linking sets in.

A low-focus train of thought is profoundly different from the conventional high-focus variety.

"Train of thought" is a term used and understood by specialists and nonspecialists alike, and it suggests that conscious thought is a kind of hooked-together sequence. A single thought—one car in the train—is a mental scene that we formulate or recall more or less as a whole. It may involve pictures, sounds, words, any kind of remembered or constructed representation.

Granted, we can't always understand our mental life in such terms, as a train of separate elements. Some thoughts are clear and distinct, but others are fleeting fragments. And at times I may be aware of *no* thought, only of a nonspecific emotion (one that lacks intentional content, in technical terms: free-floating anxiety, fear, elation); or maybe I've got nothing whatsoever inside my head (or nothing I can discern). And yet much of the time, the question "What are you thinking right now?" does have an answer. You are able to say, if pressed, *I am now thinking Z. Before that, I was thinking Y. Before that, X.* There is an ongoing philosophical dispute about how seriously we can take such accounts—whether they actually mean that your brain passed through a "thinking about X"-state and then a Y-state and then a Z-state. I believe this is exactly what they mean, but for our purposes it doesn't matter. Our goal is to arrive merely at a clear view of the "mind's own view of mind," in the philosopher Andy Clark's (1988) useful phrase. The mind notices thought-sequences happening. It watches thought-trains chugging by. And our question is: just how are those trains put together?

We know how tones are assembled into tunes. We know how words are assembled into sentences. We know how logical propositions are assembled into proofs. But how are thoughts assembled into thinking?

A low-focus train of thought obeys rules just as faithfully as the familiar high-focus version, but they are different and unfamiliar rules: rules under which one thought is linked by shared emotional content and not by logic to the next. In structure, a high-focus thought-train is logical (at least informally) and runs in a certain direction, from premises to conclusions. A low-focus thought-train is not logical and tolerates contradictions (has no *concept* of contradiction)—and it is just as coherent backwards as forwards. It has no direction; no premises, no goals, no conclusions. (In Chapter 8, for example, I will discuss an ancient text—thus, a piece of ancient thought—that is organized not as a linear, logical narrative but as a sort of solar system, where emotional gravity anchors a collection of stories in place.)

In substance, a high-focus thought-train tells you what it is about. One of the hardest things for the high-focus mind to grasp about low-focus thought-streams is that they *don't* tell you what they are about, and this *not telling* is crucial to their character. Low-focus trains aren't random; they are thematic; but their themes are emotional themes. Consider our briefcase thinker and a short two-element thought-train: first the Schwartz dinner, then a ferry ride. This thought-train might well have a pronounced theme—"high spirits with suppressed anxiety"; but the theme is latent and plays no role in the manifest content of the thinker's recollections. The elements of such a thought-train are bound by shared emotion, but if we *express* those thoughts rather than merely having them, there are no grounds for assuming that the theme—the emotion that underpins the train and gives it coherence—will appear at all in the version that has been reduced to language. But why would we reduce a thought-train to language? Because we're speaking our thoughts, or writing them down, or making literature—which will naturally reflect our native style of thinking . . .

The "absent theme" quality of low-focus thought-trains, as much as their illogic and undirectedness, makes them powerfully strange to the high-focus mind. Such a thought-train is a series of variations without a theme—a *chaconne* without a bass—a concerto performed with an absent soloist, where each listener is expected to *infer* the solo part and to hear it only in his own mind. A listener who blunders into such a performance unawares will find it formless and weird. But in fact it is not. It's every bit as coherent as a high-focus thought-train. We merely need to understand the rules and know how to apply them, and be prepared to understand what we perceive in the unfamiliar light of a nearly forgotten style of thinking.

Now certain fascinating passages of ancient literature display to the modern mind, to the onlooker who blunders in unawares, *exactly* this sort of formless, bizarre character. Ancient texts were routinely produced at lower settings of the focus dial than we are used to. Dreams have something of the same character. There are in fact, as I will attempt to demonstrate further on, intimate connections between the structure of dreams and of some ancient literature. And the discourse of young children can have this character too.

A thought-train that works just as well backwards as forwards, that is oblivious to contradiction and conspicuously omits the heart of the story, is a strange, alien creature to the modern mind. (When, for example, Jerry Fodor [1985, 18] refers to "trains of thought" as "largely truth preserving," he says as much implicitly.) But if we can't understand such creatures, we have no hope of understanding thought.

So here we are, at the bottom. I've described the spectrum as a descent from high-focus to low, but we could just as easily see it the other way round. Imagine that our starting point is affect-rich, free-flowing, low-focus thought. As we inch upwards, gradually raising or tightening our focus and asserting control over our own thought-streams, logic emerges. But at the same time, thinking starts unmistakably to grow numb. We are less and less able to *feel* our recollections; we merely witness them. We inch farther up-spectrum and the screen shrinks; thought loses its vividness. As focus tightens further, logic and affect contend for a stretch, but in the end we are left to the cold comfort of logic alone to peg together a powerful and penetrating—and numb and pale—thought-stream and drive it forward. At journey's close there we are, triumphant in the bright light of reason. But to a prophetic ancient, this transformation would have seemed catastrophic. To a young child, the revelation of its own cognitive future would be bleak or maybe shattering. From our own position at the spectrum's pinnacle, we assume that we are on top of the world, and presumably we are. But an exceptionally insightful modern adult may still, looking back, have an *inkling*, no more—Wordsworth calls it an *intimation*—that things were once profoundly different in his own cognitive past—

> *Turn where so'er I may,*
> *by night or day,*
> *the things which I could see I now can see no more.*

If we follow the spectrum model to its logical end, we will gain insight into the cognitive meaning of spirituality. We will hear a new voice in the complex harmonies of cognitive development and language acquisition. We will learn something useful about the transition from waking to sleep.

We will achieve at least some sort of grasp of the famously inscrutable, all-important cognitive process of analogy.

We will develop a key to help us decipher some of the strangest passages of ancient literature. We will be able to suggest why the rabbis of the Talmudic period (Leiman 1976) came to believe not merely that there were no prophets around at the moment, but that *prophecy itself* was dead; and why Wordsworth describes his childhood self as a "mighty prophet" who no longer exists.

Of course, loads of open questions will still be open when we are done. The spectrum model is intentionally limited in what it seeks to accomplish, and it's fair to understand those limits from the start. The spectrum idea plays the role of a "coordination framework," a term I've borrowed from computing. A coordination framework is (to draw on a technical example) the strip of plastic that turns a mere bunch of cans into a sixpack. The spectrum ignores completely many crucial aspects of cognition. It can't aspire to be the plumbing, wiring, or paint job of the Cognitive Colonial; it's merely the wooden frame.

But however sketchy and incomplete, this model *will* allow us to emerge with, for the first time, a coherent picture of the shape of thought.

––––––––––

The cognitive spectrum as I will describe it puts emotion right at the heart of thought. This fact has large consequences for artificial intelligence and, I believe, for the philosophy of mind. Emotion is not a matter of brains alone; it cannot exist without bodies. Emotions are inextricably tied up with bodily states. The bodily state is part of the emotion, feeds it and helps define it. This means that, ultimately, you don't think just with your brain; you think with your brain and body *both*. And this "cognitive unity" of brain and body means that *the* basic tenet of modern thought science, that *mind* is to *brain* as *program* is to *computer*, is wrong and should be junked.

Coming from an establishment computer scientist, this whole argument is apostasy. Influential critics of artificial intelligence such as Searle, Dreyfus and Penrose snipe from a safe distance and are uninvolved in computer research. (Although their contributions are important! Searle especially is the Great Satan to much of the cognitive and computer science communities, and evidently he returns the compliment, but in fact his probing questions make him one of the field's greatest benefactors.) On the other hand, I myself am in the business of building artificial intelligence programs. My aim isn't merely to bulldoze cognitive science and wash my hands of the whole mess; rather, to point the computer-based study of mind in a new and in some ways fundamentally different direction—and then, to get on with the fascinating business of building fake minds.

––––––––––

As I noted at the start, Jerry Fodor in his *Modularity of Mind* presents an intriguing argument leading him to the belief that the core of thought, what he calls the "central processes" of mind, are just "bad candidates for scientific study" (1983, 127).

He concludes that we are simply fated *not to understand* these central processes. It never occurs to him that there is any other kind of study.

Fodor is onto something important, but I believe he hasn't quite got it right. In this book I propose to study the mind as if it were art. And what emerges is, I claim, of real and pragmatic value, potentially testable, potentially important to the next generation of software. Granted, the key phrase, the active ingredient—to study the mind as if it were art—isn't intrinsically meaningful. But I hope that, by the end of the book, its meaning will have become clear; and at that point I will return to it.

Chapter Two

State of the Art

What does thought science say about thinking? The field is far-flung and involves many subdisciplines; it speaks with no single authoritative voice. But several beliefs are so widely held that they deserve special notice. Among these are, first, that thought centers mainly on reasoning and problem solving; second, that the computer is the supreme source of ideas, models and metaphors for cognitive science. Several other topics—emotion, "alternate" thought styles, and the cognitive past—are of no great concern to thought science proper, but important to us; and so we need to establish what the mainstream has to say. My goal here isn't to explain the substance of current theories—I'll do that in later chapters; rather, to convey something of the field's atmosphere and its state of mind.

After surveying the state of the art, I will take up the question of what the spectrum model has to do with computers. The answer is, in brief: a lot.

The nature of thought

How does thinking work?

That sounds suspiciously like a lazy softball of a question, but it's not. It's hard, simple and concrete. It's a question like, "How does walking work?" In essence, you put one foot in front of the other and then repeat. Beyond that—when you look at the details—it gets surprisingly complicated. But the gist is obvious. How does breathing work? How does eating, talking, mating work? In every case, a detailed physiological explanation is complex, but the *basic idea*, the essence of the process—you draw air into your body, let it soak in and then push it back out—is perfectly clear. *Not because breathing is simple!* A thing doesn't have to be *simple* in order for us to be able to grasp the essence and convey the gist. A thing merely has to be *understood*. Now, how does thinking work? What's the gist?

If you ask this question of a specialist, he will have filled five blackboards before you know it. "Thinking is an omnibus term describing a wide range of high-level cognitive processes . . . conceptualizing, symbolizing, schematizing, analyzing, abstracting and forming concepts about the world with which man must make his adjustment" (Shouksmith 1973, 17). The field has proliferated theories in an attempt to make sense of it all; the philosopher Jerry Fodor (1985, 4) notes that experts are "attempting to understand thinking in terms of a baroque proliferation of scripts, plans, frames, schemata, special-purpose heuristics, expert systems, and other species of domain-specific intellectual automatisms—jumped-up habits, to put it in a nutshell." The problem with all this, says Fodor, is that it misses "what is most characteristic, and most puzzling, about the higher cognitive mind: its nonencapsulation, its creativity, its holism, and its passion for the analogical." In intellectual terms, this Disintegration Approach doesn't merely miss the forest for the trees. It denies the very existence of the forest.

So you listen patiently as your expert fills his five blackboards, and then you repeat: But what's the *gist*? He'll shrug and tell you "In the final analysis, there isn't any."

Wrong, claims this book. There *is* a gist.

The basic biases

Then, there's the question of the field's underlying bias about the nature of thought. Thought is usually confused with reasoning. Here is a standard, widely cited definition of intelligence:

> Intelligence is the aggregate or global capacity of the individual to act purposefully, to think rationally, and to deal effectively with his environment. (Wechsler 1958)

The import of the phrase *to think rationally* is clear. Rationality (that is, logical cogency) is the touchstone of good thinking. Thinking and intelligence and reasoning and problem solving are consistently glommed together into an undifferentiated mass. I have already mentioned Robert Sternberg's (1982, 225) comment that "reasoning, problem solving, and intelligence are so closely interrelated that it is often difficult to tell them apart." The psychologist K. J. Gilhooly (1988, 3) notes the "strong emphasis on problem solving" in the literature on thought.

In *Mind over Machine* (1986), Dreyfus and Dreyfus oppose this trend and perform a valuable service by insisting on the centrality to intelligent behavior of what they call intuition—"the understanding that effortlessly occurs upon seeing similarities with previous experiences" (28). To my mind they don't get very far in explaining how intuition works or how it meshes with the rest of cognition. The book is more successful at putting across a compelling negative message about artificial intelligence and cognitive science than at showing us what to do now, how to proceed. Penrose's *Emperor's New Mind* is similar in this regard; it's a fascinating book, and I will discuss it in later chapters.

"Alternate" thought-styles

Of course, the field does acknowledge the existence of "nonrational" thought styles. They crop up in the literature in many guises, generally filed under "None of the Above." From the literature on mental training, for example:

> Beyond the training research that aims at relatively well defined intellectual ability and skill constructs, there are myriad studies concerned with the promotion of one or another kind of complex—and often not well defined—thinking skill. Descriptions of these skills have employed terms such as *productive, divergent, inventive, metaphoric* or *creative* thinking. The research on such constructs has not progressed substantially compared with work on other general abilities . . . (Snow and Yalow 1982, 544)

No substantial progress is a fair description of the "alternate thought style" efforts to date.

The psychologist Nathan Kogan's (1980) dichotomy between divergent and convergent thinking comes closest to the contrast between low- and high-focus thought. Divergent thinking resembles low-focus thinking in some ways; of course, characteristically for modern psychology, it is defined not by what it *is* or how it *works* but rather by how you *test it*. The most important test has to do with "ideational fluency," which "refers to the sheer number of ideas elicited by a stimulus . . . (e.g., 'Tell me all the ways that a cork can be used')" (Kogan 1980, 247–282).

Convergent thinking is defined as *problem solving* or sometimes as *logical thought*. Test results for convergent thinking tally well with test results for intelligence. Tests for divergent thinking do not: you can be a good divergent thinker but not too smart (as intelligence tests define "smart"), and vice versa. This in itself should make us a bit suspicious of current intelligence tests. Divergent thinking tests *do* seem to tally to some extent with *creativity*—to the limited extent (*very* limited) to which one can pretend to measure creativity.

At any rate, we have two separate, independent clumps of tests, one having to do with convergent thought, problem solving, "intelligence," what I'm calling *high-focus* thinking; the other having to do with divergent thought and creativity. "The most robust finding in the creativity domain is the statistical separation of divergent- and convergent-thinking measures across a wide space of age groups . . ." (Kogan 1980, 247–282).

In other words, being good at one doesn't necessarily make you good at the other. (Of course, it doesn't exclude that possibility either. A certified-genius thinker is likely to be outstanding at both.)

Bottom up?

Many of thought science's most vigorous researchers don't care about this sort of question at all; they are attacking the mind problem bottom up, by studying the physiology of the brain. Brain science is a fascinating topic, but it's quite different in subject and methods from cognitive science. Broadly speaking, the two approaches complement each other. George Johnson (1991, 223) puts the point well. One group of researchers cares about "watching how the symbols bubble up from below as a by-product of the neural interactions." Another group cares about "concentrating on the symbols themselves. There seems like plenty of room for compromise." Agreed. In this book, we deal strictly with the top-down approach.

For all their top-down interests, cognitive scientists often feel, nonetheless, an overwhelming urge to drag in neurophysiological facts that seem to support their point of view. Such urges ought to be resisted. They call to mind the fourth-grader who, in his enthusiasm for all the great new stuff he's just learned about atoms, proceeds to expound theories about every small granular phenomenon in his life in atomic terms, up to and including the crunchiness of Grape Nuts. The fact remains that, however seductive the resemblances, however powerful the explanatory force of the argument, however great it feels to be talking about real wet, smelly science and not just this *cognitive* stuff, the phenomenology of atoms is separated by many orders of magnitude from the phenomenology of Grape Nuts. While the separation between neurons and thoughts isn't quite that wide, it's wide enough.

Neurons are fascinating and fun, but they don't absolve us from the responsibility of understanding thought on its own terms.

The intellectual hegemony of the computer

Thought scientists tend to be obsessed with computers.

Computers are their chief source of mind metaphors, and their models for human thought. The consensus view of cognition has tracked the evolution of computer hardware, evolving from "serial processing" to "parallel processing" as computer technology has made the same transition. The computer is regarded as as a sort of simplified person on which one can experiment. And it is a treasure trove of illuminating images: "Broad verbal analogies between man and computer provide an orientation for thinking about human thought processes" (Gilhooly 1988, 11), as a cognitive psychologist explains it. A memory researcher recounts the historical moment at which "students of memory began thinking and speaking the language of information processing" (Tulving, 1983, 23). A founding father of artificial intelligence speculates that perhaps "computers were made (unintentionally) in the image of man" (Simon 1982, cited in Clark 1988).

The reverse proposition is more like it: human cognition has been cut down to computer-like size. The computer is the Procrustean bed of modern thought science. Aspects of human thought that don't fit are (unintentionally) lopped off. Thought science has been bent out of shape by the force field of computation, a topic I will pursue in Chapter 6.

Emotion

One unsurprising result of this fact is the tendency to downplay or wholly to ignore the role of emotion in cognition.

There are exceptions. In one of the first examinations of the issue from the cognitive science perspective, Herbert Simon (1967) notes that researchers have "generally been silent on the interaction of cognition with affect." Fifteen years later, little has changed: "cognitive science has lived for several decades," Simon writes in 1982 (342), "essentially without affect, attending to its narrower task of explaining 'cool thinking.' " The psychologist R. P. Abelson (1963) had earlier referred to thoughts accompanied by emotions as "hot cognitions" . . .

But affect can be *very* cool! By affect or emotion, we don't mean only the gaudy, hot-pink passions. We mean the subtlest inklings as well. The hardest-to-put-your-finger-on, faintest whispersome nuances. The tendency to mistake "the emotions" for "the most vivid, most readily named, *peak, maximum, saturated, pedal-to-the-metal* emotions" is endemic in psychology.

The best and farthest-ranging discussion of computers and emotion is probably Marvin Minsky's in the *The Society of Mind* (1986). "Our culture wrongly teaches us that thoughts and feelings lie in almost separate worlds. In fact, they're always intertwined." An important point; this statement recalls earlier ones by (for example) the psychologist R. B. Zajonc (1980, 154): ". . . in nearly all cases, . . . feeling is not free of thought, nor is thought free of feeling." The philosopher Douglas Hofstadter (1981) says something similar.

Minsky continues: "We'll propose to regard emotions not as separate from thoughts in general, but as varieties or types of thought" (Minsky 1986, 163). Which recalls an earlier claim by the psychologist Howard Leventhal (1982, 122) that "emotion itself is a form of cognition." Now it seems to me that these claims are wrong.[1] You don't actively think two thoughts simultaneously, but you actively *think* about the coming weekend and actively *feel* happy simultaneously. (Feeling happy may be the whole *point* of thinking about the weekend, in the sense that it may be the whole point of having a few more beers.) And your ability to think and to feel *simultaneously* is crucial to cognition, because it is crucial to thought at low focus. Granted, you may have a degenerate "thought" (if you want to call it that) consisting *only* of fear about *nothing in particular* (an emotion without intentional content; thus, e.g., Searle 1983); but that's an atypical kind of thought. I don't believe you would want to build a theory on it.

However we assess Minsky's claims about emotion, or Simon's, their work is remarkable for grappling with the topic. The more usual thought-science approach to emotion is to ignore it altogether. "It must be said that AI researchers and cognitive scientists have generally tended to avoid the subject of emotion," Mitch Waldrop remarks in *Man-made Minds* (1987, 131) which is an unusually thoughtful survey of artificial intelligence. A magisterial synthesis of AI by one of its founders, the late Alan Newell, is called *Unified Theories of Cognition* (1990). (Having read the book, I still know of no such unified theories.) Newell presents a list of "areas to be covered by a unified theory." It is an ordered wish-list; he acknowledges not having reached the elements towards the bottom. "Motivation, emotion . . ." is fifth on the list of six, one up from "Imagining, dreaming, daydreaming . . ." bringing up the rear. That's a fair summary of the field's priorities.

---

[1] In case you were wondering, all of my claims are right. (It's good to have *that* settled.)

The cognitive past

Finally, a topic that is wholly irrelevant so far as most thought scientists are concerned, but one that does attract the notice of the occasional philosopher.

Prophecy used to be real as mud to mankind. Of course there were skeptics as well as visionaries in antiquity. But it's clear that, on the whole, informed opinion was at one time prepared to accept prophets and visionaries as ordinary parts of the workaday cognitive landscape. *What happened?* We merely got smarter? Wised up? That is exactly how the philosopher Daniel Dennett (1991) explains it. "The 'magic' of earlier visions was, for the most part, a cover-up for frank failures of imagination." This refreshingly brisk condemnation resembles the classic developmental psychologist's view of the alleged "magic" of childhood.

The philosopher Stephen Stich (1983, 229) kindly reminds us of how stupid our forebears were, those "ancient shepherds and cameldrivers"—the whole lot: "However wonderful and imaginative folk theorising and speculation has been, it has turned out to be screamingly false in every domain in which we now have a reasonably sophisticated science."

Granted. All the same, prophecy is dead. Stich is not prepared to regard this as an interesting fact. I believe he is wrong.

Summing up

A notably thoughtful psychologist synopsizes the state of the art: "Thought, which we know how to use but do not understand, poses as formidable an enigma as the origin of the universe" (Kagan 1989, 179).

The computer and the spectrum

Cognitive artificial intelligence is the pursuit of computer programs that are capable of reproducing some aspect of human cognition. The ultimate goal is to build full-blown fake minds out of software. "Why would anyone want to do *that*?" is an excellent question to which I'll return at the close of the chapter. For now, I'll note only that by accomplishing the fake-mind feat, one might learn a great deal about human cognition and wind up with a distinctly useful gadget.

"Cognitive artificial intelligence" is an area that should be distinguished, first, from "applied artificial intelligence." The applied variety isn't concerned with how humans do what they do; it merely wants machines to be capable of doing the same, using whatever methods, human or inhuman, fall to hand. Software that has emerged from this research effort might be capable of diagnosing disease, playing championship chess or figuring out how to synthesize organic compounds. Applied artificial intelligence has been a robust and successful field. But it hasn't taught us much about how *humans* think; hasn't attempted to.

In cognitive artificial intelligence, research to date has focussed mainly on reasoning and problem solving—unsurprising, given the biases of the field. Considerable effort has been spent on topics like language understanding and commonsense reasoning as well.

The arguments laid out in this book suggest that much of this research is misguided. The first step in a computer model of mind ought to be a computer model of the cognitive spectrum. If we don't know how to build such a model, we have no idea how a truly convincing fake mind would actually work.

One part of the spectrum model has to do with an issue of immediate practical and not just theoretical concern. It has always been clear that a computer model of human creativity is a vital part of the artificial intelligence agenda. Achieving human-like creativity does *not* reduce to the specious goal of building a computer that can write Mozart symphonies, or whatever—humans (with exceptions too rare to be worth mentioning) can't write Mozart symphonies, or carry off any other stupendous feats of creativity, but that hardly consigns them to the cognitive trash heap. The goal in practice is to understand the sort of garden-variety ingenuity and insight that ordinary humans rely on constantly. If we don't, we can't possibly claim to understand the basics of human cognition, nor can we ever hope to field a convincing "thinking computer."

From the standpoint of the cognitive spectrum, the field's attempts so far to model creativity on the computer (and there have been quite a few) are uniformly unconvincing. Creativity can only emerge, I believe, as a byproduct of *affect linking in low-focus thought*, and no existing computer program has ever grappled with low-focus thought—

With one partial exception. In Chapter 6, I'll describe our own software research effort—the computer program developed in my research group at Yale. It is a very small, halting and tentative step in the spectrum's direction. Still, it can do a number of interesting tricks that other programs can't, and it suggests that the spectrum *is* a useful motivating model in building computer software.

Our research software does *not* tackle yet (but will tackle soon: I'll explain how) what stands out as the hardest and most thought-provoking issue in computerizing the spectrum. To simulate the spectrum, a program must be capable of affect linking. This means that it must have some notion of affect. What's required isn't quite "a computer that has feelings"; merely a computer that *acts* for all intents and purposes *as if* it did. A decent actor can assume the attributes of happiness, even if he isn't happy; roughly speaking, that's the sort of thing a computer will need to accomplish. This is not as hard a chore as actually *having* feelings, but it's hard enough, and it's far beyond today's state of the art. I will discuss in Chapter 6 how we propose to sneak up on this goal.

In the meantime, the sleight of hand in the last paragraph should not pass unnoticed. I claimed that computerizing the spectrum requires merely that computers *act as if* they have feelings, and actors accomplish this trick all the time, so how hard could it be? We'll just have computers do the same. But this is a questionable analogy. It's true that an actor can behave as if he is happy, even if at the moment he isn't; but could he behave as if he were happy if he hadn't been happy *ever*? When people simulate emotion, they use their own real emotions as raw material. Computers, presumably, can't do that.

There's a hard problem looming: not a problem that defeats progress in a practical sense, but one that gets us to wondering whether ultimate success might be *in the nature of things* impossible . . .

Recall that, according to the spectrum model, emotions are fundamental to thought. This is a key point and is worth underlining: emotions are not a form of thought, not an additional way to think, not a special cognitive bonus, but are *fundamental* to thought. If we subtract emotion, the only part of the cognitive spectrum remaining is the radical high end—and to identify this narrow high-focus band with thought in general is absurd. Emotions are fundamental to thought; but the body, inconveniently enough, is fundamental to emotions. After a bit of reflection it becomes inescapable that you don't think *just with your brain*; you think with your body too—this holds in the sense, roughly speaking, that a violin uses its strings to produce sound; but take away the sounding board—the instrument's bridge and its body—and the sound you wind up with is a thin parody of the real thing.

(My claim about the body's essential role recalls the philosopher Hubert Dreyfus's (1972) arguments about "situated understanding." Dreyfus concludes that the body plays a central role in human intelligence. He makes an important case, but I intend to make a different and more general one. The key to Dreyfus's argument lies in his description of "the standard AI line," which he rejects, as the claim that "knowing-how must be explained in terms of knowing *that*. Thus all intelligent *doing* is assumed to involve *thinking*" [Dreyfus and Dreyfus 1986, 97]. Now intelligent *doing*, so far as Dreyfus is concerned—for example swimming, or pouring a bottle of beer—actually *must involve* the body. But I will claim that intelligent *thinking per se* is *itself* impossible without the body.)

Unfortunately, this innocent little proposition—that you think not just with your brain but with your body—the "cognitive unity of brain and body," as I'll call it—destroys the whole basis of modern thought science. As I'll explain in Chapter 6, it means, when we look at it carefully, that the proposition, "mind is to brain as software is to computer," is just false. Which *does not* mean that cognitive artificial intelligence is futile, or not worth doing. Nor does it mean that computers won't be able to simulate the reality of an emotional life; they will. (In fact, I think they will come to be very good at it.) They will never have bodies, but they will act as if they did. It *does* mean that the whole edifice of cognitive artificial intelligence needs to be uprooted and trucked across town (as if it were a fine old building whose foundation has rotted), to a different and sounder footing, and pointed in a new direction.

Finally, this argument has implications for one of the key vexed questions in the philosophy of mind. If a computer should one day tap you politely on the shoulder, clear its throat and remark "fancy that; I'm thinking!"—should you believe it? What trick would a computer have to perform in order to convince you that it is thinking? Is there *any* such trick? And once we have figured out under what circumstances a computer can claim to be thinking, does that help us decide when it can claim to be conscious? Does it help us understand what consciousness *is*? Those questions are addressed in Chapter 7.

There are many connections, in short, between the spectrum model and computing. I am about to continue onwards to discuss the spectrum and these relationships. But before I do, one last little unresolved question about cognitive artificial intelligence—

What are we doing this for??

I've claimed that one of the chief reasons the spectrum is important and worth knowing about is that it can guide cognitive artificial intelligence. If you don't understand the spectrum, you have no hope of building a realistic fake mind. But why would anybody *want* to build a realistic fake mind? Is this really a good idea? Or is it pointless?—or even dangerous?

That's an important question, but in one sense also irrelevant. The urge to build fake minds stands at the nexus of two of the most powerful tendencies in the history of civilization. These two are so powerful that it's pointless even to contemplate *not* pursuing this kind of research. It will be pursued, to the end.

People have always had the urge to build machines. And *people have always had the urge to create people*, by any means at their disposal— for example, by art. Ordinarily these urges operate in unconnected intellectual areas, but with artificial intelligence they come together. The drive to make a machine-person is the direct offspring of both. It is the grand culminating *tour de force* of the history of technology *and* the history of art, simultaneously. Will we attempt this feat? It is predestined that we will.

Chapter Three

Cognitive Pulse, and the Reality of Focus

My goal in this chapter is to fill out the spectrum story, and then to use some well-known facts to drive home the reality of the spectrum and the idea of mental focus. I've already introduced the spectrum in the context of sleep, childhood development, and cognitive evolution. Here I'll touch briefly on another aspect of the story, the role of focus in personality.

The pulse

My strategy is to posit only what is essential to the argument. We might spin endless pages on the spectrum mechanism and how it works. But let's not. I prefer to describe the bare minimum necessary to carry the argument forward. Where details are left out, those are sacrifices in the interests of moving along with a minimum of baggage.

So: a current thought gives rise to a probe, the probe to memories, memories to a new current thought, the current thought to a probe, the probe to memories . . .

You call time out, I've claimed, to build mental models and to explore and tweak them. During the periods in which you are examining these imagined models or scenes, your steady reaching back into memory for new material is suspended.

Let's add a bit more detail. The mechanism's basic cycle takes the following form.

The cycle starts with a probe. The probe attracts memories in response. The probe may be focussed ("apple") or unfocussed ("buying apples at the roadside stand on Route 14 on a sunny Sunday afternoon . . .") or intermediate, depending on your current mental state.

> *Comment:* I don't mean that a probe need be embodied in the *word* "apple" or the *phrase* "buying apples at . . ." The probe can be anything a thought or a memory can be. *Probe, thought* and *memory* are three instances of exactly the same entity— three roles for the same player.
>
> The field (as I've noted) is well aware of this kind of match-on-features remembering. What's missing in the literature is a notion of the pulse as I have described it and, of course, of the spectrum.

At high focus you "disengage" from memory after the responses have emerged. You "inspect" the responses. If there are many responses (a probe may call many recollections to mind), you tend at high focus to examine all the responses in a single bundle.

> *Comment:* When you grab hold of a bunch of memories and examine the whole stack, in the fashion of (very roughly) holding a sheaf of transparent images to the light and staring through the whole pile at once, *similarities* in those stacked-up memories *reinforce each other.* Aspects that are shared by many of those memories stand out clearly when you examine the stack. *Those* aspects are the interesting bits that attract your attention. Aspects that aren't widely shared fade quietly into the background.
>
> Psychologists are aware that "the mind may, in fact, superimpose representations into composite memories . . ." (Metcalfe, cited in Hockley and Lewandowsky 1991, 420). In most current memory theories, the *circumstances* under which this occurs aren't clear. But in any case, the psychologist Janet Met-

calfe makes this particular observation in a fascinating context. She is describing the late nineteenth-century fad for "composite photographs." Superimposing the photographic images of many individuals—"twelve mathematicians," "sixteen naturalists"—was said to produce the image of a prototypical mathematician. Aspects that were shared by many images stood out clearly in the composite. Aspects that weren't widely shared faded away. The mind's abstractions at high focus are certainly not superpositions of remembered images. But composite photographs suggest the *sort* of thing the mind can accomplish, although not by the literal manipulation of images, when it is building memory bundles at high focus. Thus, you can draw a house—your idea of a plain typical *house* captures the common features and edits out the peculiarities of a large number of examples. Likewise you can draw a dog, or describe an amusement park or a trip to the gas station. You have experienced many instances within each of these categories; you are able to stack up the individual memories, notice the common features and disregard the others.

At high focus, "prominent" or "interesting" aspects of the response memories capture your attention.

Comment: This *focussing* process, this selection of interesting aspects of the responses, is the same kind of process that is entailed in the inspection or manipulation of any mental image. You can imagine a purple cow, and you can inspect or manipulate the image—imagine the cow rotating slowly, hopping up and down on its snout, wearing green sneakers; in the same fashion, you can focus on certain aspects of a set of response memories.

Wittgenstein (1953, 32) refers to a "concept" or abstraction as a "family resemblance." He asks what a concept like *game* could mean, given that there doesn't seem to be even one attribute that every game shares. What he finds instead is "a complicated network of similarities overlapping and crisscrossing". This conception of "concept" fits in well with the overlay mechanism I've defined. When we form an overlay, a set of features emerges clearly, but in order for this to happen it is *not* necessary that each feature be represented within each element of the overlay. The overlay model accounts well for an interesting fact that emerges from Wittgenstein's observation: we may have a clear idea of some concept without being able to point to even *one* paradigm example. "The strength of the thread does not reside in the fact that some one fibre runs through its whole length, but in the overlapping of many fibres" (32). The character of the overlay by the same token emerges from the superposition, not from the features of a "typical individual."

Eventually, you choose a new probe. In many cases, it's simply one of the details you've picked out from among your response thoughts. Then, with new probe in hand you (so to speak) *re-engage*: clutch back in. New response memories emerge.

Comment: During these disengaged periods you accomplish your problem-solving, fitting partial solutions together, inspecting the emerging conceptual structure. If the problem before you is "open this stuck briefcase," you construct a strategy (say, fiddling systematically with the lock, which may have been reset to a new combination) in the form of a mental image or structure of some kind. It might be an imagined picture, or a mere mental sketch involving, perhaps, no imagined *visual* imagery at all.

The nature of the mental structure doesn't matter; but if you are thinking about a problem, you are building a mental structure of *some* sort. If the problem is to "understand this page of text," you build some kind of mental structure that captures your notion of the text's meaning. As you read more phrases, you tack more pieces onto the mental structure, or revise it. You build these structures during the periodic interstices between your probes to memory, while "the clutch is disengaged" from the memory engine that drives thought. At high focus, you disengage regularly.

As focus declines, your disengagements become briefer, your selection of details becomes fuzzier, exactly *less focussed*; your ministrations to any evolving mental structures become more cursory.

At minimum focus, a probe might (in principle) call many memories to mind, just as at high focus. But at the bottom of the spectrum, you don't sandwich memories together and pick out interesting highlights. You *enter into* a single memory . . .

Comment: How do probes attract responses? The principle—like attracts like—is always the same. (I will explore it further in Chapter 4.) But as focus declines, the "likes" that attract are no longer "like features" but "like emotional content."

Let's make the story more concrete by focussing on two examples, perception and reading, and following them down-spectrum. Then I will glance at one less-familiar phenomenon, hypnosis.

Perception

You have a thought stream, and a perception stream—the "perception stream" being merely the series of "scenes" you perceive. The two streams are intimately related.

Perceptions influence your thought stream—you perceive a noise behind you, then think: I wonder what that is? Thoughts influence your perception stream—you think *I wonder what that is?*—then look behind you and gather some fresh perceptions. Your mental focus governs your relationship to your thoughts. It also governs your relationship to your perceptions.

Here are two well-known facts; let's place them in context, integrate them into a big picture . . .

Some people, some of the time, perceive the world in a way that fastens on detail—that clips interesting details out of a scene, in roughly the fashion of clipping-out interesting stories from a newspaper. Such observers wonder and ask questions about details. In the course of perceiving, they may be physically active: they may notice something, and move closer to inspect.

Some people, some of the time, perceive in a "diffuse" way, simply watching the world go by. They are more likely to notice mood and ambiance than to fasten analytically on particular details. They are more likely, too, to be physically passive than to go hunting about the landscape inspecting points of interest.

Most people will recognize these two styles immediately. Everyone experiences both, at least in some measure.

After all, a character like Sherlock Holmes ("Beyond the obvious facts that he has at some time done some manual labor, that he takes snuff, that he is a Freemason, that he has been in China, and that he has done a considerable amount of writing lately, I can deduce nothing . . .") is plausible insofar as readers are willing to concede that some people *do*, sometimes, perceive in a style that fastens actively and aggressively on salient details.

But when Keats imagines, in the greatest lyric poem in the language, that *tender is the night*! (*Ode to a Nightingale*)—when he sums up the rich and complex ambiance of a particular moment, we understand that this style of perceiving is the very opposite of all that is Holmes-like. It is not active or aggressive; it is passive. (Perhaps he might "Fade far away, dissolve . . ." says Keats; "I do not know what flowers are at my feet, nor what soft incense hangs upon the boughs . . ."). It is not focussed or selective; it is all-embracing. (The poem's central stanza begins *Darkling I listen*, without saying *to what*; but that *listen*, poised as it is at the crux, seems to embrace not just the nightingale or the flies, but the whole night and the poet's whole mind.) The thinker does not control but is rather controlled, in fact transported, by his train of thought, and his thoughts take on the characteristic hallucinatory overtones of vivid poetic imagining. ("Already with thee! Tender is the night . . .") Details are important not because of their logical implications but because of their emotional fragrance, their contribution to the whole mood. And that mood is heavy with exhaustion. ("A drowsy numbness pains my senses . . ."; ". . . take into the air my quiet breath"; ". . . do I wake or sleep?")

We know that these two styles of perceiving exist. What remains is only to point out that one is a high-focus style and the other is low-focus. The features of these two styles and their relationships make perfect sense in the context of the spectrum model just as I have described it.

Wordsworth gives us another beautiful description of low-focus perception:

. . . with an eye made quiet by the power
Of harmony, and the deep power of joy,
We see into the life of things. (*Tintern Abbey*: 46–48)

What's important isn't merely the seeing itself, but the psychological context of the seeing: this passive all-embracing perception is associated with a kind of stillness verging on sleep—". . . we are laid asleep in body, and become a living soul . . ." (44–45); more striking yet, this is exactly the state in which affect linking occurs, in which "the affections gently lead us on" (42).

Turn focus up high: the thinker tends to fasten penetrating attention on details, and mentally to investigate their implications. Turn focus lower: he comes at length not to penetrate details analytically, but to experience the whole scene passively. At high focus, the thinker controls his thought stream and his perceptions: sees something interesting; proceeds to investigate. Low focus is accompanied by an unravelling of control and the onset of an all-inclusive, all-seeing passivity.

Curve fitting

When you emerge from the laboratory with a bunch of data points, you may well want to mark them on graph paper. Then the question often becomes: on what curve do these points lie? Of what continuous trend or phenomenon are they part? How do we connect them, see the big picture, predict the presence of other measurements as yet unknown?

The cognitive spectrum is a good fit to these two "perceptual" data points. The data have been known all along; our task is to infer the underlying pattern. And that's what we will continue to attempt.

Enter personality

Virtually everyone will have experienced vaguely Holmes-like and vaguely Keats-like moods, in which perception happens in distinctly high-focus or low-focus ways. But not everyone *is* Holmes or Keats; these characters clearly favor particular cognitive styles.

Consider the following account of high-focus perception, from the autobiography of the great physicist Richard Feynman (1985, 94). Feynman is a graduate student, sitting in his dorm room and contemplating his window sill. "One day some ants came out on the windowsill and wandered around a little bit." Most observers would have taken this development in stride. They'd be unlikely to be roused to action. Feynman is different. "I wondered, how do they know where to go? Can they tell each other where food is, like bees can? Do they have any sense of geometry?" An impromptu experiment follows, which evidently takes all afternoon.

High focus is a *state of mind*. It isn't brought about by the *a priori* existence of something problematic (in the world or in your mind) upon which to focus; it is a *prior disposition* to snip details out of the bigger picture, and to focus penetrating attention on them.

This roving, restless inclination to snip out details and to fasten or focus on them is the signature of a high-focus personality. It is characteristic of the fictional Holmes and the real Feynman. There is something not quite normal about the behavior Feynman describes. It is recognizably *related* to "ordinary" behavior—occasionally we all focus on specific details in a big picture, and then probe further. But Feynman evidently needs less of an excuse to focus more narrowly (not merely on the ants, but on particular questions about their behavior) and to probe further. This is a high-focus personality in action.

And there is something out of the ordinary about Shelley's mood, for example, at the foot of Mont Blanc:

The everlasting universe of things
Flows through the mind . . .

The experience is recognizably like "ordinary" experiences, but is unusual in its sweep—which is characteristic of a low-focus personality.

I'll use the term *mental gait* to refer to your typical, comfortable, average level of focus. It isn't a fixed attribute that is wired into your brain. Everyone is capable of a wide range of focus settings. But your mental gait *is* the most important determinant of your cognitive personality. Thinkers with a relatively high-focus gait approach the world on radically different terms from lower-focus thinkers. Mental gait has nothing to do with intelligence—although intelligence tests are biased towards the high-focus end of the spectrum. (Psychometricians don't know what low-focus thought *is*, so how are they supposed to measure it? I tend to believe that it *might* be measurable in principle. Measuring a person's skill at low-focus thought would depend on assessing his "emotional acuity"—a term I define in Chapter 5.) The fact remains that whatever your mental gait, you can be smart or dumb, depending on the mechanism that your focus dial controls. (A radio tuned to 800 kilohertz can produce good sound or bad, depending on how good a radio it is.) Nonetheless, there are profound similarities in approach among all thinkers with roughly similar cognitive gaits, despite the vast range of individual variation at any focus setting. We'll see more examples below.

Reading

Again, the data are well known; we need merely to infer the underlying pattern.

Understanding a sequence of written words requires a fairly high level of focus. Sentences, phrases, individual words in the text will bring many response memories to mind, but you must *focus* on those responses and select exactly the *meaning* of the phrase. If the phrase is, "he tossed up an apple and smacked it with the bat as if it were a baseball," you need to understand the referants of the words involved. You need to extract from your memory the fact that the word "apple" is associated with a certain kind of object with certain properties and then, having "focussed" on just the *meaning* of "apple," you need to stop there—if you pause to contemplate at greater length some *particular* apple memory you happen to possess, if you linger over some particular scene (the bag of apples you bought at the supermarket two weeks ago), your focus is declining and you are losing touch with the text.

At high focus, you read with comprehension, engaging the memory motor and disengaging with disciplined regularity, allowing each phrase to serve as a probe that brings responses to mind, picking out, *focussing on* the meanings of the phrases without being distracted by extraneous stuff, fitting the newly selected bit of meaning into a growing mental construct that represents your understanding of the passage, then re-engaging memory—new phrase, new probe, new responses . . .

As focus declines, your selection becomes more cursory. Your disengagements from memory become shorter, and accordingly your attention to the growing mental structure becomes lax. You might not understand the import of phrases exactly. You might forget the precise context. The time you spend on ancillary recollections increases. As focus declines you tend merely to skim the text; as it declines further, skimming becomes more superficial, more and more of the thought occasioned by the text merely uses the text as a starting point for a thought stream in which a parade of whole memories occupies your mind, before you dutifully (wearily?) disengage (it takes energy to press the clutch), do another probe, superficially, fuzzily, messily select the meaning out of the responses . . . At lowest focus, you are paying no attention to the text at all. "And so I brooded all the following morn . . . mine eye fixed with mock study on my swimming book" (Coleridge, *Frost at Midnight*: 36–38).

Your "best reading" (like your "best driving") happens at high focus, when you are intent on what you're doing. Other things being equal, we'd expect children who are good readers to be ones who show a decently developed capacity for high-focus thought. There's a clue that this is so in the fact that children who are good readers are also good at focussing attention (Forrest-Presley and Waller 1984, 65–108).

But there is a role for lower-focus reading too. A phrase of poetry may have no literal sense at all, but have meaning and power nonetheless. When Yeats writes of gravediggers that

> they but thrust their buried men
> back in the human mind again, (*Under Ben Bulben*: II)

the high-focus approach to understanding the couplet simply fails. There *is* no literal meaning. Of course, the reader needs to maintain a fairly high degree of focus long enough to understand the plain sense of the words. But to a low-focus reader, this high-focus state is a temporary stretch; he quickly, "automatically" relaxes into a lower-focus state as soon as the plain sense has been established.

To a purely high-focus reader—a reader whose focus stubbornly *remains* high—the lines make no sense, or they are outlandish. To understand them it's not sufficient to dig their literal meaning out of memory; *affect linking* must happen. It's not merely that we need to augment a rational, high-focus reading with an emotional low-focus one. We need to *replace* the high-focus reading. Keats's friend Benjamin Haydon reports his reciting the newly written *Ode to a Nightingale* in a "low, tremulous undertone, which affected me extremely" (Scudder 1899, 144). Notice the verb: of course, poetry is supposed to *affect* us—meaning, to engender an affective or emotional reaction; which can only happen at low focus.

We know of course that some people don't care for poetry. Personality asserts itself again: some students easily absorb material presented in lectures. Others come to understand mainly by studying written material. These two data points fit handily, again, into the spectrum just as we have described it. Absorbing material by way of "auding" (a psychologist's term for listening with comprehension) requires a more intent and sustained concentration than reading does. In reading, the written text takes much of the burden off the mind to remember what has been going on, leaving it freer to depart on excursions (e.g., Crowder and Wagner 1992). Higher-focus personalities are comfortable camping out for sustained periods at the higher ends of the spectrum. Lower-focus personalities aren't.

In sum: some people notice and investigate wandering ants, read precisely, follow lectures comfortably—and don't get it (or experience no visceral reaction, which amounts to the same thing) when Yeats writes of returning buried men to the mind. Other people don't clip details out of their perceptions, do allow their minds to wander as they read, prefer reading logically dense material to "auding" it—and are moved by Yeats. Or this could be *one* person at two different times, in two different moods—but each mood, in any case, is a coherent bundle of traits.

Both bundles fit perfectly with the much bigger story of the spectrum in general. After all, to pick merely one example, being a scientist in the Feynman vein is a good deal like having insomnia. These are both *high-focus* states. Anyone who has ever wanted to fall asleep but been too "keyed up" to bring it off has experienced a state of free-floating high focus: a restless inclination to fasten on details. Of insomnia John Updike writes

> . . . The air conditioner hummed;
> I turned it off. The plumbing
> in the next apartment sang;
> I moved away, and found a town
> whose factories shuddered as they worked
> all night . . . (in Oates 1982, 67)

Clipping out details—fastening on them with a penetrating mental focus—sets the scientist and the insomniac apart from lower-focus types. The scientist *can't help but notice* ants; the insomniac *can't help but notice* the air conditioner's hum. This *notice* is a high-focus noticing, of course, profoundly different from a peaceful, peripheral awareness of falling rain (or the steering wheel or the book or the razor). Scientist and insomniac huddle together at the high end.

Hypnosis?

Let's consider one final interesting state that is relevant both to low-focus thinking and to the relationship between the spectrum and personality. We'll briefly consider both the nature of the hypnotic state and the sort of person who is susceptible to hypnosis.

The hypnotic state is a complex and elusive thing to characterize. But in his classic study, Hilgard (1965) presents a list of seven phenomena with which it is associated. What's interesting is that this cluster of features resembles, *in some ways*, the cluster that identifies low-focus thought.

The list includes "availability of visual memories from the past, and heightened ability for fantasy-production" (8). It includes "tolerance for persistent reality distortion"—the "trance logic" of hypnotic states recalls in some ways the illogic of dreaming. It includes "increased suggestibility," which Hilgard elsewhere relates to "the general passivity of the subject" (11); also related to *passivity* is the listed feature "subsidence of the planning function"—"the hypnotized subject loses initiative and lacks the desire to make and carry out plans on his own." (6). It includes "amnesia for what transpired within the hypnotic state" (8–10).

None of these features invariably accompanies a hypnotic state, but collectively they are characteristic.

Of special interest is the second item on Hilgard's list, *redistribution of attention*. Some authorities believe that sustained concentration is a prerequisite to becoming hypnotized. Indeed they have explained on just this basis the fact that children under age eight are relatively insusceptible to hypnosis (for whatever reason, data indicate that ages eight to fourteen seem to be the period of maximum susceptibility, with susceptibility falling off steadily after that). Children under eight are presumed to be incapable of sufficiently intense concentration to make them good candidates. Now of course, the association of the hypnotic state with intense, focussed or sustained concentration would undercut our budding contention that hypnosis is related to low-focus states—

But Hilgard writes that "it does not follow that hypnosis is characterized by an unusual concentration of attention; it may be, in fact, that *attention under hypnosis is generally diffuse*" (7: my emphasis). He goes on to account for a number of phenomena from this point of view. The insusceptibility of young children may relate to their insufficient grasp of language (you must understand what the hypnotist is saying to you), or to any of a number of other factors.

In sum, hypnosis is a complex and incompletely understood state. Yet it's striking that, in Hilgard's list of seven attributes, six have already occurred somehow or other in our description of low-focus thought. (The seventh in Hilgard's list is willingness to act out suggested roles.) So, the *"low-focus" clump of features do indeed occur together*. Passivity and vivid recollections, diffuse attention and amnesia afterwards *do* occur as part of one mental state. We have only to associate the same clump with many other related cognitive states, and to place it securely in context on the cognitive spectrum.

A last datum from the Hilgard book is striking as we attempt to grasp the personality implications of the spectrum. "The reader who becomes absorbed in novels, adventure stories, mysteries, science fiction, and related types of literature [why not poetry?] is likely to have his imagination stirred and his emotions aroused . . ." Such absorption-prone readers "tend to be highly hypnotizable" (352–353).

The reality of focus

A number of psychological observations underline the reality of mental focus.

Consider the following generic anecdote related by Dennett (1991). It's a familiar experience: you become aware of a bell tolling, say, and then you find that you are able to make an internal, mental count of how many strokes have tolled so far, despite the fact that you were *unaware* of the initial strokes while they were happening.

The story underlines the fact that focus is real—that you are capable of attending to certain parts of a percept or memory, and disregarding other parts. The anecdote illustrates that it is *not* true (not in this case, anyway) that your sensory apparatus is somehow narrowed down so as to allow merely the interesting bits of reality to slip through. Rather a *whole scene* of some sort, *including* the tolling bell and presumably (if it included the bell!) lots of other sights, sounds and sensations as well, entered your memory; and then (or, simultaneously—it doesn't matter), you *focussed* on a certain part of the scene; and in so doing, disregarded the rest. But the scene in its entirety, including the tolling bell, is still there when you are induced to go back and check. (Of course, this level of detail dissipates quickly. Short-term auditory memory in particular doesn't seem to last longer than around 10 seconds. But much detail remains . . .)

Between the two facts that (*a*) an entire scene, including the tolling bell, entered your memory, and (*b*) you were initially unaware of one part of the scene, namely the tolling bell—some sort of *focus* operation must intervene.

By the same token, a recollection summoned out of memory may be "a whole scene" with much detail *beyond* what you select as your particular focus. An entire percept, tolling bell and all, enters your memory, though you choose to focus only on a part of it; a whole memory returns, though you may choose only a narrow focus. At lower or more relaxed focus, *there is far more to recollect*, to experience, than what emerges at high focus. (Of course, hypnotized, some people are capable of recollections that elude them when they are awake.)

You have far more experience stored in your memory than you will ever see at high focus.

A related example: consider the "cocktail party effect" (Keele 1973). The gist is that you are able to follow one conversational thread while remaining aware of many others. If you overhear your name (or some other evocative word) crop up in a conversation on which you aren't concentrating, you still notice. Now it can't be that every other word of this peripheral conversation was turned away by border guards outside your ear; the whole conversation *got in*, somehow or other; it's just that your mental focus was largely elsewhere. But the minimal levels of mental attention devoted to the peripheral conversation were sufficient to grab your attention when something really interesting (like your name) cropped up. By the same token, an unusual event as you are driving or shaving would grab your attention and redirect it.

One final example. The "Pötzl phenomenon" was first described in 1917, then discounted; but recently, some researchers have resurrected it in slightly different form (see Cohen 1979, 222). Experimental subjects are shown pictures; aspects of the picture they don't notice at the time may nonetheless emerge into consciousness later—particularly during dreams.

Again, the observer's focus is elsewhere but he *perceives* more than he knows. Focus is real. And it can hardly be surprising if dream-thought is the main occasion for ignored, unacknowledged, or simply unnoticed perceptions to surface. If dream-thought is low-focus thought, then it is fundamentally *inclusive*. It lacks power to turn away.

I will return to dream-thought and pursue these threads below.

Conclusions

I have outlined the spectrum and attempted to convince you of the reality of "focus," discussed the special viewpoint of the spectrum on some issues of personality, and (earlier) on the cognitive transitions of sleep, childhood and the emergence of the modern mind.

Next I will flesh out the spectrum idea, by examining the nature of thought at the high- and then the low-focus ends. The high-focus chapter centers on abstraction and logic, and the chapter following it centers on creativity, spirituality and the main cognitive transitions.

In the three chapters after those, I will consider the implications of the spectrum for computing and artificial intelligence, for certain questions in the philosophy of mind, and for literary criticism—particularly, for the study of ancient texts.

Chapter Four

High

Sport marches forward. The four-minute mile used to be phenomenal. No longer. Centuries ago, sustained high-focus thought was presumably a rare and specialized accomplishment. Today, any high-school student has mastered it. The elevation of sustained high-focus thought from rare to commonplace is modern man's great cognitive achievement. Sustained high-focus thought makes possible logic, analysis, rationality—science, mathematics, engineering and all rigorous, cogent scholarship; and these are the achievements that define the modern mind.

The spectrum shows us that these achievements have a darker (or at least ambiguous) side. It shows us that high-focus thought, just in virtue of *being* high-focus, must be numb. It is literally unfeeling. Just because it is unfeeling, it excludes creativity and intuition and spirituality. We must dip lower into the spectrum in order to locate these cognitive commodities. As centuries pass and sustained high-focus thought becomes (as it must) more of a settled habit, will thinkers find themselves dipping into the lower regions less and less frequently? Sustained high-focus thought is, after all, adaptive. Rigorous analytic thinking yields reliable benefits to the thinker that are far more tangible and useful than the vague and elusive prizes that low-focus thinking offers. Faced with a tricky business decision, or a broken-down car, or a stuck briefcase, or two alternative paths of uncertain relative value, the thinker who responds with cool analysis is more likely to succeed (in modern terms anyway) than the one who wanders off into undisciplined musing.

High-focus thought has its limitations, but its huge power is obvious and we must consider how it works. Most writers discuss the topic descriptively. They tell us what logical thinking is like. My intention is to talk *constructively*. If logical thought is the goal, what sort of mind mechanisms are required in order to accomplish it? We will discover that remarkably few mechanisms are needed, and they are strikingly simple. Most important, these mechanisms fit neatly at one end of the continuum that constitutes the central fact of mental life.

The mechanism

Suppose you had the capacity to do this: to grab hold of a bunch of memories and examine the whole stack, in the fashion (very roughly) of holding a sheaf of transparent images to the light. In examining that memory sandwich, *similarities* among separate elements would reinforce each other. Aspects shared by many memories would stand out; you would focus on those. Aspects that weren't widely shared would fade quietly into the background. Thus (as I described in the previous chapter) if focus is high and the memory probe is "amusement park," similarities among your various amusement park memories would emerge to form your impression of a typical, *just plain* amusement park (sunny, noisy, roller coaster—whatever). Details belonging only to some particular amusement-park episode (your Aunt Agnes, hurricane Gloria, lost your car keys) would recede and disappear.

If you had that capacity, what would it buy you? It would buy you the ability to form and manipulate abstractions. It would allow you to learn the meaning of words. It would enable you to think logically.

My goal in this chapter is to tie these three cognitive feats—

abstractions, word meanings, logic—into a single package. The cognitive spectrum, specifically its high-focus end, will be the ribbon that holds this package together. The aim is, again, *not* to claim that three distinct and complex cognitive phenomena amount in reality to the same simple one; rather to point out that a simple, underlying phenomenon *creates the necessary conditions* for all three. That it provides the basic tools, and sets the stage.

Abstractions

What is truth, irony, beauty, purple? You can't define these terms by pointing to an example. They do not lend themselves to, as philosophers say, "ostensive" definition. You can't get the meaning of the word *blue* across merely by pointing to, say, a blue crayon and announcing, "This is blue." The obvious question then becomes, "*What's* blue?" Does "blue" mean crayon, Crayola crayon, tubular object, wax, paperwrapped thing, or what? (Thus, for example, Quine 1969, 29ff.)

But how *do* we come to understand such words?

Clearly we must posit a mechanism in which memories can be examined *en masse*, in such a way that the points they share emerge. (The "memories" I mean are the kind psychologists usually call *episodic*: recollections of specific occurrences in the past. See Tulving 1983.) When you overlay lots of memories, their points of agreement reinforce each other and stand out clearly. Less "reinforced" points—points of relative disagreement—stand out less clearly. Points of complete disagreement blur out: don't emerge at all. Jorge Luis Borges' "Funes the Memorious" (Borges 1964), whose pathologically acute memory retained "the shapes of the clouds in the south at dawn on the 30th April 1882," was also, "let us not forget, almost incapable of general, platonic ideas." Incompletely but provocatively, the Funes narrator tells us that "to think is to forget a difference, to generalize, to abstract . . ."

A young child has no intrinsic reason to think of horses, fish and chickens as examples of the same general category. But if we tell the child, "An animal is, for example, a horse or a fish or a chicken," it's essential that the child be able to summon horse, fish and chicken memories, overlay them, and consider the common features that emerge. Those common features may be hard *or impossible* to capture in words, but whatever they are, they form the basis of the child's understanding of the concept *animal*.

A concept like *blue* makes an even clearer instance. In principle one might explain *animal* by referring to other abstractions, if the child happens to understand them—you might announce that an animal is, roughly speaking, something that is alive and is capable of moving on its own. But there is no way even in principle to define *blue* without recourse to memory overlays. *Blue* simply *is* whatever common feature emerges when many *blue* memories—memories of objects with which the word "blue" is associated—are overlaid. There is no other way to define it.

Does this mean that we need to perform a high-focus overlay operation, to puzzle out the meaning of *blue* on the basis of the raw data, every time we hear the word? Of course not. Your memory can remember things about *itself* as well as things about the outside world. It can recall the results of its own previous machinations. It can remember the sensation of blueness that emerged in the memory overlay formed in response to the word "blue." It can store a two-element memory, consisting of the word blue and the blueness sensation that emerged as a common feature in the overlay. And in the future, you can grab this memory directly when you hear the word "blue."

And what does *color* mean? Again, the only way to convey such an elusive concept is to say that *color* designates precisely those features that emerge when your memories of *blue*, *green*, and so on are overlaid. There is no way to *explain* what "color" means; rather you *perceive* its meaning as a result of an overlay operation.

In sum: you are capable of grasping abstract concepts because your cognitive spectrum has a "high-focus" end. As I'll discuss further on, memories that are similar tend to stick together by themselves: we might say that they attract each other. But a child's memories of assorted blue things aren't likely to be similar at all. Blueberries and a clear sky don't share a great deal; only blueness. At high levels of focus, you are capable of forcing *dissimilar* memories to cohere, and of picking out their points of similarity. Such memories don't attract. They don't "want" to stick together. But at high focus, they are forced to.

A world of exclusively low-focus thought would be a world without abstractions. Not an incoherent world, however: emotions would take the place of abstractions. I'd have no *concept of* but would presumably have a *feeling for* "truth." True things would sound some characteristic emotional tone. Rather than responding to a perceived truth by stamping it with a formal label—"this thing is true"—the thinker would experience a *feeling* of some sort—let's say, a certain vague tingling at the base of the spine. He would accordingly classify true things not as instances of the abstract category called Truth, but as "things that give me that lower spine-tingling sensation." True things get lumped together in either case . . .

Memories have structure

The analogy between memories and translucent images is loose, but it does have one important valid implication. Memories have structure, and similarities among memories are reinforced in a way that respects the structure of each memory.

When you overlay many memories, you take their structures into account. You recognize that a peaked roof on top of four walls is a house, and that four walls on top of a peaked roof is not a house. You are able to abstract not merely a list of features but a common structure out of many house memories, and you associate the word "house" with the common structure.

"Structure" doesn't mean visual structure only. You recognize that dialing a number and then talking into a handset makes a phone conversation, whereas talking first and then dialing doesn't. Structure can be temporal.

Of course, your episodic memories are not *much* like translucent images on film. They may include images, but also sounds or smells or feelings, and so on. They do not come in neat, clipped-off rectangles. And I haven't said what precisely constitutes a "point of agreement," although the topic of similarity among memories and what it depends on has been studied in detail—for example by Tversky (1978).

Language

One aspect of language is grasping the meaning of words. I have already discussed high-focus thought as the mechanism that allows you to form abstract concepts, and thus to understand the words that refer to them. (My claim that learning the meaning of words is a special case of concept learning recalls a similar claim by Jerry Fodor in *The Language of Thought* [1975]—see also Sterelny [1991] for a good discussion of this aspect of the Fodor argument. I don't draw the conclusions Fodor does, but my basic claim is supported by his.)

Another aspect is *syntax*, grasping the structure of language. Learning syntax is thought to depend not on general intelligence, but to a large extent on inborn specialized capacities—on "an innate, species-specific module that is distinct from general intelligence" (Pinker 1991, 202). It's hard to explain how children could master the intricacies of grammar without an innate cognitive compass pointing them in the right direction, predisposing them to view certain phrases as natural and others as unnatural.

Of course, when a child learns how to eat breakfast cereal with a spoon, the structure of the arm predisposes a certain way to go about it. Certain movements are natural and others are unnatural. You might say that the child's inborn eating-cereal-with-a-spoon capacity merely awaits actualization. But the story doesn't end there; the child needs general intelligence to learn which possibility is the right possibility. It's logical to guess, by the same token, that general high-focus thought provides at least *part* of the cognitive machinery needed in mastering syntax. Your ability to overlay dissimilar memories and extract their common features, in a way that respects the *structure* of those memories, accounts for your capacity to recognize a house or a typical phone conversation. A sentence is a structure too.

Reasoning

Reasoning centers on the drawing of inferences. "Logically correct inference"—the sort of inference that is guaranteed to be true, if your premises are true—is called *deduction*. Deduction centers in turn on the application of syllogisms, rules of the form, "If this is true, that follows." (For a discussion, see, for example, Charniak and McDermott 1985, 14ff.) There's a lot more to the complex process we call "reasoning" than merely formulating and applying syllogisms. But the manipulation of these rules is the heart of logic, the *basis* of reasoning. If we can understand how the process works, we won't understand the whole story, but we will have learned something significant.

The mechanisms of high-focus thought provide an adequate basis for just such an understanding. You know that *if it's snowing out, then it must be cold*. You know that the reverse is not true. Not only do you know rules, you know how to apply them. If you look outside and see that it's snowing, then you conclude—although *conclude* is too formal a word, better say that you simply *know*— that it's cold. If you're informed that it's cold out, you draw no conclusions about snow. How do you perform these mental tricks? How do you learn and apply syllogisms?

Exactly the same cognitive mechanism can explain both phenomena. You can formulate syllogisms *and* apply them by examining memory overlays. Let's say the probe is "snow." Lots of snow-related memories come to mind, and at high focus you sandwich them together and examine the overlay. Of the shared features that emerge, one is *cold*. Memories that include "snow," that is, are likely to include the detail "it's cold" as well. This simple high-focus mechanism has accounted for the formulation *and* application of the rule at a stroke. The probe (or "premise") "snow" causes you to make the deduction "it's cold"—*not* by means of formal logic, but as a consequence of ordinary high-focus thought. On the other hand, if "cold" is the probe, the memories that include "cold" do *not* tend to agree on "it's snowing." Snow will be present in some of those memories and absent in many others. Hence, "snow" makes you conclude "cold"; "cold" does not make you conclude "snow."

In this simple formulation, *logic* and *language* are one. They are driven by the same cognitive engine. You know what *blue* means in exactly the same way you know that *if it's snowing, then it's cold out*. The probe *blue* brings blue-related memories to mind, and blueness is a characteristic they share. The probe *snow* brings snow-related memories to mind, and coldness is a characteristic they share. Grasping word meanings and thinking deductively are two names for the same phenomenon. That phenomenon is high-focus thought.

(Of course there is far more to reasoning, as I've noted, than the formulation and application of isolated syllogisms. To chain syllogisms together, one conclusion is the probe that summons forth the next rule. If "it's cold" is the conclusion, then "cold" can summon the next rule—perhaps, if it's cold, I should put on a coat; if I need a coat, I should visit the front hall closet, and so on. There remains much more to reasoning and problem-solving than this simple chaining, but I won't pursue the topic further; a serious consideration of problem-solving would take us too far off the topic. I believe that a fair amount of problem-solving will fit into the high-focus framework—but for present purposes, I will leave that as an undefended assertion.)

Physics, mathematics and personality

Re-enter personality: why should it be that people who are strong analytical thinkers (good at math, for example) are so often good "empirical investigators" too—also good at science? And *vice versa*? We are so used to the fact (at least we are in academia, where we inevitably encounter scientists who are good at mathematics and mathematicians with an interest in science) that we are apt to miss its strangeness. We are apt to consider this state of affairs "natural" just because it's commonplace. But what exactly *is* natural about it?

Your typical Joe Blow physicist who loves to grub around in the dirt, build fancy lab set-ups, play with machines and contemplate nature is also apt to be at least a decent mathematician, capable of operating in the radically different intellectual surroundings of abstract logical assertions and purely mental machinations. And mathematicians are often observed to have at least some interest in nature as well, and often some ability at science. The fact is surprising, because science and mathematics are very different activities at base, not a lot more similar, at least superficially, than dentistry and hippopotamus training. Of course, doing physics in practice requires doing a good deal of mathematics. By the same token, writing novels requires a good deal of typing. But the *character* of physics and mathematics is radically different. Natural science is relentless, hands-on detective work. Mathematics is a game of invention in a world of pure abstraction. If a fair proportion of dentists also happened to have a flair for the hippopotami, we'd wonder why this should be so.

The spectrum provides a ready explanation. Empirical science is, at base, a high-focus approach to the world. Mathematics is a high-focus approach to your own thoughts. Approaching the world at high focus means that you fasten onto details and probe deeper. Approaching your thoughts at high focus means that you fasten onto details and probe deeper—and in the mental realm, "fasten onto details" implies that you are capable of penetrating deep overlays, picking out the shared details and tossing out the rest—operating, in other words, in the realm of abstractions. A high-focus personality, other things being equal, will approach *both* the world *and* its own thought stream in a high-focus fashion. The narrow penetrating thought-beam that (metaphorically speaking) skewers a stack of recollections, picking out shared elements and defining an abstraction, is the same narrow penetrating thought-beam that picks out a small crowd of strolling ants . . .

Natural stickiness

I claimed earlier that similar memories tend to stick together. The more similar, the greater the "mutual attraction." Where memory is concerned, the fundamental rule is: *Like attracts like*.

We can see the principle at work in every act of remembering. If *apple* is your memory probe, why do apple-related and not dill-pickle-related memories come to mind? Because there is a degree of likeness between the probe *apple* and the apple-related responses. Obviously they have something in common. This likeness principle tends to be obscured when we think of remembering in terms of "associations." If in your experience a flash of yellow light is invariably followed by the arrival of a mushroom pizza, then a yellow light will bring pizza to mind, despite the lack of likeness between the two thoughts. But of course at one point, early in your training, the yellow light reminded you not of *pizza* but of a particular set of episodes in which the light and the pizza both figured. This particular "likeness reminding" is the root cause of your subsequent tendency to be reminded by a yellow light of the pizza directly.

The natural stickiness of similar memories is on display in the most common type of *forgetting* as well. Consider the "confusion forgetting" that happens when several memories get tangled together, and you are unable to say whether you bumped into Cousin Irmgard on your first or your second trip to the Lake in the summer of '79. "Experiments have shown that most memory failures or memory distortions result from the activation of related or overlapping information that becomes mixed with or substitutes for the original information" (Potter 1990, 18). But two memories may get mixed up to the extent that they are *like* each other in some way. The more like, the more apt to be confused. And what does this "confusion" consist of, exactly? The two memories seem to have become blended and bound together in such a way that their attributes can't be distinguished. Like memories attract. If they are like enough, they attract inseparably.

(Talking about one memory attracting another, or a bunch of them sticking together, suggests that memories are afloat in some kind of viscous mind-ether and, of course, nothing of the sort is remotely possible. The stickiness idea doesn't require that memories be physically mobile inside the brain, or actually capable of sticking together; it merely suggests that this is a good way of understanding memory. Any computer can *behave as if* "attraction" existed between the data items it stores internally, if you program it to do so. The brain is presumably no less resourceful.)

The stickiness principle—like memories attract—holds at *any* focus level. It is independent of focus. As usual, we will posit a continuum. The more similar two memories, the more tightly they bind.

The Semantic-episodic continuum

An "episodic" memory records some particular episode in your own life-story. A "semantic" memory recalls not an episode but a timeless piece of information. Episodic memories deal in "personal happenings and doings," semantic memories in "knowledge of the world that is independent of a person's identity and past" (Tulving 1982, 9).

Are these two memory types really *separate*, or merely endpoints of a continuum? Endel Tulving is the psychologist who first identified the distinction. He notes that "a number of theorists who are willing to adopt the episodic/semantic distinction in general terms nevertheless are not quite willing to accept the idea that the two systems are in some sense separate, and prefer to think of them as constituting a continuum" (Tulving 1982, 67). Tulving rejects this claim. He thinks of the two memory systems in terms of an automobile's engine and brakes, or of flexor and extensor muscles—as two entirely separate operations.

But this claim flies in the face of a ubiquitous experience: the gradual and continuous transition of knowledge from episodic to semantic.

Thus at present, my ability to distinguish Thomas the Tank Engine from his charming steam-engine colleagues rests on semantic memories. I can describe Thomas, James, Gordon, and so on without reference to any particular occasion or "historical moment." But at some point a few years ago, I'd seen the children's TV show exactly once, and my knowledge of Thomas, such as it was, was strictly episodic. It was tied up with the one occasion on which I'd made his acquaintance. Between the two extremes, a gradual transition occurred. Indeed, by the overlay principle, such a transition *must* occur. As I accumulate memories of essentially similar episodes, the depth of sandwich that responds to the probe *Thomas* grows. Unshared details become gradually more obscure, and shared features emerge more emphatically. A semantic memory is just a bunch of episodic memories overlaid. This point is worth making to help establish the robustness of the mechanism I have described. Stickiness between memories explains remembering, but too much stickiness causes memories to adhere and brings about forgetting. The elements of a shallow stack of memories are "episodic"; a deeper stack, constructed under exactly the same principles, produces semantic memory.

The psychologist Marigold Linton undertook a remarkable experiment in which she systematically studied her own memory over a six-year period. In a section called "transformation from episodic to semantic memory," she confirms this intuition:

> Increased experience with any particular event class increases semantic (or general) knowledge about the event and its context. Increased experience with similar events, however, makes specific episodic knowledge increasingly confusible, and ultimately episodes cannot be distinguished . . . (Linton 1982, 79)

In other words, as you accumulate similar memories, you tend to confuse them. This confusion is manifest in two ways. On the one hand, you can no longer distinguish separate episodes. "Episodic" memory is failing. On the other hand, you are able to make confident assertions about a phenomenon in general, without reference to a particular example. "Semantic" memory is emerging. (Potter 1990 also notes the similarity between *generalizing* and confusion-forgetting.)

Conclusions

High-focus thought centers on two related mental acts: *honing in*, and *suppressing individual idiosyncrasies in favor of common features*. Honing in, on some aspect of your thoughts or of the world before you, has the side-effect of causing you to disregard context and ambiance. Sandwiching memories together in such a way that only the common features emerge suppresses, in the same sense, the accidents of detail and tone that set individuals apart. High-focus thinking is abstract and numb. But it is rational, powerful, and leaves the thinker firmly in control.

Making high-focus thought the norm, setting it at the center of our cognitive universe, is the supreme and defining achievement of the modern mind.

Chapter Five

Low

What happens when you fall asleep? "With each successive. . . . stage there was a steady decline in control over the course of mental activity and an awareness of the immediate environment and a steady rise in the frequency of hallucinatory experience" (Vogel 1991, 126). Why? What cognitive mechanism is at work?

The curious thing about this statement is what happens when we invert it. *With each successive stage there was a steady rise in control over the course of mental activity and an awareness of the immediate environment and a steady decline in the frequency of hallucinatory experience.*

Whatever process we are *now* describing is the same process as falling asleep—only backwards. What process is it?

I'll return to this question.

Minimum focus

As I have discussed, at minimum focus you are working *in breadth*: with *whole memories*. Your response to a probe is a whole memory. Your probes are whole memories. Whole memories are the currency of your thought.

Suppose I ask you a question requiring a reasoned response—
say, "Are books heavier than videotapes?" Suppose your focus is
minimum—let's say you're on the point of falling asleep, which is
typically a low-focus state of affairs—but you do hear the question
and use "books" as an initial memory probe. You wind up thinking
not "books in general weigh . . ." but rather about some particular
book-related memory as a whole. Say, an occasion on which you
bought a paperback with a shiny black-and-purple cover at the airport in Hartford on a fall day when you were travelling to San Francisco to have a meeting with José Schwartz and his red-headed
assistant, and your feet hurt because your new shoes were too tight.
In other words, *all aspects of one memory*, rather than *one aspect of
all*. At dead-minimum focus, you will never answer my question,
never "disengage" from your memories. Unless I succeed in catch-
ing your attention again, you'll wander onward from there. This
book experience will be the probe that brings some other whole
memory to mind, and so on.

How does minimum-focus thinking work? At low focus, any old
thing can hook two thoughts together. The response called forth by
that particular whole book memory may be a recollection involving
another incident at the same airport, another book of the same
color or by the same author, some incident related to your reading
the book.

But the link can be accomplished in another way too—a deci-
sively important other way. A whole-memory probe may engender a
response thought *that shares the same emotional content*. That is, just
as "batteries may bring "voltmeters" to mind (because they both
"have to do with electricity"), and *buying the paperback at the airport*
may bring *missing the connection in Chicago* to mind (because they
both happened on the same trip), so *buying the book at the airport*
might alternatively bring *standing at the train station in Jamaica on a
spring day in 1989* to mind: *if*, for whatever reason, *buying the book*
and *standing at the station* are two memories with the same emotional content.

The *character of the memory as a whole* is subtly captured by the
feeling it evokes, by its *emotional content*. But this "emotional
code" to which a memory is reduced isn't necessarily unique: more
than one memory may evoke the same or almost the same code.

This is the basis of affect linking. Two memories that seem completely different might nonetheless evoke the same emotion. At low focus, memories that underlie two adjacent thoughts in a train might be completely different in every detail *except that*, for whatever reason—maybe, for a deep and evocative reason—they made you feel the same way when you originally experienced them. They might be photographs of two utterly different scenes, with the same cryptic note scrawled in both their margins.

First, I will take up some consequences of low-focus thought; the landscape down here is radically different from what it was at the high-focus end. Then I will consider the "big three" cognitive transitions, and their relationships to the spectrum.

Creativity (or, determining the longitude)

The affect link allows us to associate two memories that seemingly share nothing. And yet, affect linking means that they *do* share something: in some cases, a deep and subtle something.

Fastening two seemingly different but deeply related thoughts together is one of the greatest and most important tricks of cognition. The ability to think metaphorically or in analogies—to recognize that one entity is *in some way* like a superficially very different other—is a supremely valuable accomplishment. Affect linking is a way of connecting two memories that may be wholly different on the surface and even in substance. Yet those two connected memories clearly do share *something*—for whatever reason, they engender the same emotion—and that *something* may be a clue to a new metaphor, analogy, model, paradigm.

How does "creativity" work? Where does "insight" come from?

Creativity: how does it happen?

A plausible and widely cited explanation dates back to the Gestalt psychology of the 1930s and '40s, particularly to a classic 1945 monograph by Duncker. This explanation relates insight to "restructuring." Rather than beating your head against the wall of a difficult problem that doesn't yield to ordinary, methodical approaches, you discover a different way to *see* the problem; you

conceive of the problem in new and different terms; you "restruc-
ture" the problem. Restructuring clearly has to do with *finding
analogies*. If the solution to a hard problem eludes you, inspiration
takes the form of an analogy that allows you to see the problem in a
new light. Put another way, "The creative thinker comes up with
useful combinations of ideas that are already in the thinker's reper-
toire but which have not been previously brought together"
(Gilhooly 1988, 186). Or, as Shelley wrote in 1821, "Reason
respects the differences, and imagination the similitudes of things"
(Shelley 1821/1966, 416.) Cognitive psychologists have investigat-
ed the analogy-discovery process in detail. (For example Gick and
Holyoak 1980, and Holyoak 1990. See also Hofstadter's 1985 discussion of analogy finding.)

The "restructuring" process is usually illustrated with "Tales
from the Great Scientists." The description of the molecular structure of benzene by the nineteenth-century German chemist
Friedrich Kekulé, who envisioned a ring of snakes each biting the
tail of the next, is a particular favorite.

This "restructuring" process is important enough to deserve concrete illustration. Instead of citing the standard anecdotes, I'll draw
on a story of zero scientific importance, but closer to home: my
own first technical paper. As we take up the story, an eager young
graduate student in computer science is looking for a way to pre-
vent the messages in a computer network from getting stuck—
from becoming "grid-locked" by other messages and unable to
proceed. He's sitting in the library idly contemplating pigeons con-
gregated on the asphalt far below when—he has it! For some reason, he has "restructured" the problem in terms of Grand Central
Terminal in Manhattan. Grand Central has concourses on two levels. In a manner of speaking, walkers on the upper level can never
become frozen in place so long as it remains possible to move
downstairs, and the same holds for downstairs walkers so long as
they can move upstairs. The solution to my problem centered on
dividing the computer network into two "levels," and keeping the
staircases free.

The idea isn't easy to explain realistically, and the details are fairly complicated. But they all became clear when the analogy
appeared and "restructuring" occurred. Writing the technique

down and proving that it was correct were mere formalities after that (Gelernter 1981). In all its key respects—a "restructuring" out of the blue, leading to a sudden, clear glimpse of the whole solution—this anecdote is typical of countless others in the literature.

Such phenomena aren't specific to science, of course. They are everyday occurrences and they are part of everybody's cognitive repertory. They manifest themselves in observations as commonplace as "you remind me of my brother," in ordinary metaphors (so long as they are being used not merely as clichés but with some cognizance of what they mean) like "you demolished his argument." If I notice a resemblance between you and my brother, there's some cognitive leverage in that: I haven't penetrated the mystery of benzene, but I have put myself in a position to explain your actions and to make predictions about your behavior. Trotting out a phrase like, "You demolished his argument," doesn't exactly constitute a creative *tour de force*, but the meaning I wish to convey gains force and clarity from the metaphor. An argument isn't literally a structure that can be demolished, but seeing it in those terms yields a species of garden-variety insight.

Restructuring and analogy-finding are crucial to creativity. But they remain mysterious. How do they come about? How do we accomplish these enormously useful tricks?

Some theories

The published literature on creativity is enormous, but the number of distinct explanations is much smaller. Here are some of them.

The psychologist Keith Holyoak has published influential papers on the role of analogies in achieving insight. But, "How can a useful analogy be found?" His view is rather bleak. "It is often difficult . . ." (1990, 138). He reports that, in essence, it's up to the features that collectively characterize a hard problem to summon the appropriate analogy out of memory. And it follows that, the greater the direct similarity between the problem and the insight-yielding analogy—the more features they share—the more likely that you will in fact discover the analogy. Thus you are more likely to hit on (say) an analogy between a hippopotamus and a rhinoceros than one between a hippopotamus and a Land Rover.

In Holyoak's view, problems attract analogies in the same way that one trip-to-the-lake memory attracts another. The more obvious the analogy, the more likely you are to discover it. Fine: but it is precisely the *less* obvious analogies that interest us if we care about insight and creativity. "The more mutually remote the elements of the new combination, the more creative the solution" (Mednick 1962). How do these "mutually remote elements" come together? "With difficulty" is *not* quite a satisfying answer.

Another widespread view exists in multiple versions that amount to the same or similar accounts at base. The gist is that finding analogies in particular (and insight or inspiration in general) comes down to thinking up lots of possibilities and rejecting the bad ones.

One version of this argument originates with computer scientist Herbert Simon (1969); Dennett (1978) and many others have accepted or expanded on it. Another version is associated with the notion of "ideational fluency" that has emerged in psychological testing. The term refers to an ability to generate *large numbers* of associated thoughts when you are presented with a cue. It seems likely, writes psychologist Nathan Kogan (1980, 653) that "the route to originality and flexibility is through fluency."

This generate-and-test approach, with its methodical, beating-the-bushes flavor, doesn't explain exactly the aspect of insight that is most in need of explanation, its *out-of-the-blueness*.

Roger Penrose holds this generate-and-test view of creativity too, although (as usual) he gives it an idiosyncratic twist. In seeking to answer the question "what constitutes genuine *originality*?" he replies that "there are two factors involved, namely a 'putting-up' and a 'shooting-down' process." (Penrose 1989, 422). (Simon referred to the first stage as "generation" and the second as "testing.") But in his creativity-as-skeet-shooting view, the "putting-up process"—the stage of thought in which you generate lots of possibilities for eventual acceptance or rejection—is largely unconscious. He imagines that "there must be a powerfully impressive selection process that allows the conscious mind to be disturbed only by ideas that 'have a chance' " (422). Eventually he advances an explanation in terms of a quantum-mechanical view of the brain; I'll return to it in the next chapter. The explanation is intriguing, but it's hard to regard it as either compelling or well integrated with the other cognitive phenomena that clearly relate to creativity.

The philosopher Andy Clark (1989, 124) advances a different, rather peculiar but interesting view. Clark is defending a theory of mind, the "connectionist" view, that (he admits) has particular difficulties in accounting for the discovery of new analogies, of "*unanticipated* similarities." The explanation he advances is that these similarities are discovered because of cognitive glitches that allow pieces of separate but similar memories to be accidentally mixed up. As I understand him, when the nose of a Land Rover accidentally gets hitched to the tail of a hippopotamus, a brand new analogy is born, roughly speaking.

There is nothing unlikely about the glitch in itself. It is a near relative of the strong mutual stickiness with consequent confusion-forgetting that I described in the last chapter. But this glitch is the *wrong* glitch for our purposes. Clark's explanation, like Holyoak's, works best in exactly the easiest cases: those in which the original problem and the analogy are closest. Where an analogy is truly interesting and "creative" because it is truly unexpected—because the problem and the analogy are seemingly very *un*similar—Clark's explanation seems far-fetched. It assumes that these very different memories just happen to be stored right on top of each other, in such a way that they can be accidentally confused. And it seems psychologically far-fetched as well: discovery of a good insight or analogy is distinctly *not* accompanied by a sensation of *confusion between* the problem and its analog, as in the confusion you feel in trying to distinguish two visits to the same lake. It is rather accompanied, reports suggest, by an *ah ha* feeling of discovery and recognition.

I could go on. Creativity is a fascinating phenomenon and it has been studied endlessly. Much of this work has a training flavor: inculcating creativity, in children or adults, has always seemed like a good idea, if you could only figure out how. Many psychologist-educators have addressed the problem. No master key has been discovered. Which is hardly surprising: creativity has always impressed its students as one of the most individual and idiosyncratic ingredients of a cognitive personality. In the end, it's still hard to dispute Jerry Fodor's (1983, 107) judgement on the state of the art, which I cited earlier. "It is striking that, while everybody thinks analogical reasoning is an important ingredient in all sorts of cognitive achievements that we prize, nobody knows anything about how it works." Not even, Fodor adds, in a "dim, in-the-glass-darkly sort of way."

The problem of creativity and analogy in thought science is in sum (as I mentioned at the start) something like the problem of longitude, which bedevilled seamanship in the seventeenth and eighteenth centuries. It's fairly easy (so they say—don't take my word for it) to find your latitude by measuring the distance above the horizon of some astral body of known habits. Longitude is much harder. Until a solution was finally developed in the form of accurate, portable clocks, determining your position at sea was accordingly a half-solved problem, and half-solved was little better than not solved at all. Today, the logical or analytic component of human thought is understood, at least to some extent. But analogy is not. Until we glimpse a solution, thinking can't possibly be more than—at most—half-understood.

Facts about creativity

The explanations I've cited are unsatisfying because they fail to grapple with three key facts.

First, the core achievement of restructuring and creativity is the linking of ideas that are *seemingly unrelated*. The originality we impute to an insight centers just on the seeming *dissimilarity* between the problem and the analogy. Of course, similarity between the two must exist on some level, otherwise no analogy would exist. But that similarity must be deep, hidden, obscure, indirect—not a mundane matter of two ideas attracting each other because they share obvious similarities.

Second, inspiration comes as a bolt out of the blue. It occurs as a moment of sudden awareness. It is not something to which you work up gradually, on which you advance step by step. Third, a related point: hard work does not pay. You do not achieve inspiration by concentrating hard, by *putting your mind to it*. Inspiration occurs *not* when you are concentrating on the problem to be solved, but exactly when you are *not* concentrating.

Both of the latter points are supported in the creativity literature. An interesting study by Metcalfe and Weibe (1987) supports the proposition that insight occurs suddenly. Subjects who
were given ordinary algebra problems tended to report sensations of approaching the solution steadily, "getting warmer" until
a solution was reached. When they were given a problem whose
solution required insight, not the mere application of known
rules, they tended *not* to report any sensation of "getting
warmer." Solutions hit them suddenly, unprepared by any feeling
of a gradual approach. (See Holyoak 1990.) Dodds (1951, 11)
puts it this way:

> The recognition, the insight, the memory, the brilliant or perverse
> idea, have this in common, that they come sudently "into a man's
> head." Often he is conscious of no observation or reasoning which
> has led up to them.

And Wordsworth thanks "Nature" for making it possible to be
inspired unexpectedly by a fresh truth—for "that happy stillness of
the mind which fits him to receive it *when unsought*" (*Prelude* XIII
9–10: my emphasis.)

Penrose (1989) supplies a particularly useful discussion of the
related "unconcentration" point. He cites for example a case in
which the great mathematician Poincaré conceives the key to a
hard problem not while thinking about the problem, or about
mathematics at all, but in the process of casually boarding a bus.
"This complicated and profound idea apparently came to Poincaré
in a flash, while his conscious thoughts seemed to be quite elsewhere . . ." (Penrose 1989, 419). He gives personal examples too. I
have cited his report that insights are most likely to occur to him
when he is thinking about a problem "perhaps vaguely," "consciously, but maybe at a low level just at the back of my mind." He
might be shaving (Penrose 1989, 419). In short, Penrose, the distinguished and highly creative physicist, doesn't achieve inspiration
by concentrating. He achieves it when he is *relaxing*, when he is
precisely *un*concentrating.

In sum, any satisfying explanation of inspiration must account
for its characteristic three-part signature. *Unexpected connections,
sudden awareness*, in a state of *un*concentration.

Creativity and the affect link

Affect linking has exactly this signature.

It brings together (couples in your thought-train) memories whose only connection is the particular emotion with which each is associated. Hence *unexpected connections*. The space between these two (potentially) wildly different memories is spanned not step by step but in one leap, by a single affect link: hence not gradual approach but *sudden awareness*. Affect linking occurs at low focus, and low focus occurs exactly when you are relaxing, when you are *not* concentrating. Hence *un*concentration.

Emotions are (funny) abstractions . . .

In the mechanism I've described, an emotion serves as a kind of "abstraction" of a thought or memory, in the sense that the many aspects or details of a mental scene are captured or summarized in a single emotion. But an emotion is a "summary" or "abstraction" of a special kind—I will call it a "content-transcending" abstraction. The *vocabulary of the abstraction* is completely separate from the *vocabulary of the thing being abstracted*.

We might say that "a green sphere above a brown cylinder" is in some sense an abstraction of a tree. But the sphere and the cylinder are simplified instances of forms that are present in the tree itself. The "vocabulary" of the abstraction—certain forms in space—is the same as the "vocabulary" of the thing being abstracted, of a tree itself.

An "executive summary" or a volume of Cliff Notes uses the same language and probably some of the same phrases as the document it's abstracting. But if you turned to the executive summary and discovered a few bars of music or an abstract watercolor, you'd have come upon a *content-transcending* abstraction.

Now if we say that a particular emotion is a summary or abstraction of a particular thought or mental scene, the elements of the emotion are *not* merely *excerpted from* the scene. An emotion that might (for example) be roughly described as "a happy but nervous anticipation" could be a sort of summary of a particular moment of your life (or of many moments). But if the physical scene at issue happens to be "standing at the mailbox on a spring day preparing to open a letter from X," the emotion isn't merely a simplified or abstracted version of that physical scene, in the sense that a sphere on a cylinder is a simplified version of a tree. The emotion represents your reaction to the scene as you experienced it at the time; and the "vocabulary" of this reaction—your emotional palette—is wholly separate from the vocabulary of the physical reality to which you were reacting.

Well, so what?

So it is *exactly* this property of emotions that makes affect linking work, and makes the affect link so powerful. A hippopotamus doesn't resemble a Land Rover. A computer network doesn't resemble Grand Central Station. But emotion is a content-*transcending* abstraction. It's conceivable that viewing a hippopotamus in some sense makes you *feel* the same way as viewing a Land Rover; that listening to an argument being refuted in some sense makes you feel the same way as watching your son kick over a building-block house. An emotion is a kind of summary or abstraction, but one that transcends content. Hence, emotions can link memories whose contents are completely different.

(It's true of course that hippopotami and Land Rovers do share certain traits. There could be no analogy if they did not. They are both chunky, heavy-seeming, lumbering. How do we know that shared emotion and not these shared attributes is responsible for the analogy? Because the shared attributes simply don't explain enough. A hippopotamus shares exactly the same features with a DC-3 as it does with a Land Rover—chunky, heavy-seeming, lumbering. Why is Land Rover-Hippo a better analogy than DC-3-hippo? Because it simply *feels* better. How do we know, for that matter, that hippopotamus-hippodrome isn't a good analogy? Hippopotamus and Hippodrome are imposing, heavy-seeming objects that begin with the same two syllables and are rare in North America. But clearly we can't build an analogy on shared features alone. A shared *feeling* must come first.)

A creative insight is notably associated with an *ah ha* feeling of discovery. That sensation is concocted, I believe, out of two separate emotional ingredients. First, surprise. You didn't anticipate being hurtled at this moment into another region of cognitive spacetime, and the farther you have travelled—the more superficially *unrelated* the analogy-thought (where you just landed) to the problem-thought (where you started)—the more surprised you are. The fact that the creative insight happened at all is, in many ways, just a lucky accident. The problem-thought happened to occur to you when your focus was just right to support "creative leaps." It was fairly low, but not *so* low that you merely rambled onward to the next thought in a low-focus stream without allowing your attention to be fixed by what just happened—by the leap just taken. The other emotional ingredient that goes into a good hearty *ah ha* is a sense of certainty. That sense reflects, I believe, your certain, implicit, "automatic" knowledge that the distant place you've landed *must be related* to your cognitive starting point, because you *know*—you can *feel*—that its emotional content, the "emotional code" associated with your landing site, is *just the same* as the emotional content of your starting point.

The fortuitous affect link, that quick leap through cognitive space-time, is not *sufficient* of course to make creativity happen. You must scamper back up the spectrum and apply some analysis to the analogy that has just happened. If you don't, no creativity occurs. The affect link isn't sufficient but I claim that it is *necessary* to creativity.

Low-focus overlays

Memory overlays were central to high-focus thought. It is now time to confess that they can occur at low focus too—but with a radically different character. A low-focus overlay is less a deep stack penetrated by a shaft of focussed attention than two delicate sheets of gold-leaf stuck together. Low-focus overlays occur when a small number of thoughts or memories (usually two) that are linked by affect blend together. In a high-focus overlay, individual details are suppressed. In the low-focus variety they emerge clearly. The details and idiosyncracies of the overlaid memories are simply blended. What emerges isn't a "general principle," but a new and idiosyncratic image.

A creative insight may hinge on a synthetic image that combines the attributes of several recollections—Kekulé's ring of snakes, for example. The effect crops up in dreams all the time. A character in a dream will clearly be a composite of two separate people, blending the attributes of each. I will return to this effect later in the chapter and in Chapter 8.

What makes you creative?

Now you might object at this point, "you've merely substituted one hard problem for another. You have provided a mechanism that accounts for creativity, but now we have to account for the fact that a hippopotamus and a Land Rover each engendered the same emotion in our hypothetical observer. How does *that* work?"

The objection is valid—indeed I haven't accounted for the fact that Land Rover and hippo might engender the same emotion; and I don't plan to. Nonetheless, we *have* taken a major step towards understanding creativity. We have reduced a large and general problem (what mechanism accounts for it?) to a well-focussed and narrower one (how does a perception induce an emotion?). And we've made concrete assertions about creativity: that it hinges on *the emotional response to perceptions at the time they are experienced*, on *the ability to store and then to recollect emotions*, and on the ability or the predilection to *use low-focus thought*—to think in such a way that affect linking has a chance to work.

Obviously, some people are more creative than others. In my account, that observation translates into the claim that some people are better at low-focus thought than others; which translates into the base claim that some people are better at affect linking than others.

It's entirely plausible that this should be so. A "talent" for affect linking centers on a subtle and nuanced emotional response to the world around you.

Thus, some people have relatively more acute vision or hearing or sense of smell than others. Likewise for many other properties—coordination, sense of direction, whatever. We might speak of "emotional acuity" in the same way. Possessing a high degree of emotional acuity doesn't mean that you take an "emotional" (in the sense of histrionic or overwrought) view of the world. Rather (1) that you are able to register subtle or nuanced emotions—to experience subtle emotional reactions—where less acute people would have no emotional reaction at all; and (2) that you are able to distinguish many elements in a subtle emotional palette, where a less acute person would distinguish the emotional equivalent of red, green, blue.

The affect linking mechanism suggests that exactly this kind of sensitivity lies at the root of creativity.

It also suggests that the freightload of "creativity-enhancing" techniques that have been advanced over the years, most centering on some species of fluency—getting you to produce more "associations" to a given stimulus—is wildly off the mark.

Where does emotional acuity come from? My guess is that it has the same mixed basis as other sorts of talent. An inborn proclivity is the starting point; upbringing determines the extent to which potential is realized.

(In a 1990 paper, by the way, Salovey and Mayer define something they call "emotional intelligence" [89]. It's an evocative phrase, but their idea of "emotional intelligence" centers on "the ability to monitor one's own and others' feelings and emotions." As such it is largely unrelated to the "emotional acuity" under discussion here, which centers not on "appraising emotions accurately" (193) but on having them in the first place.)

Finally, the explanation of creativity I've advanced here reflects on a thought-provoking comment by Robert Nozick. "Perhaps for a product to be creative it must not only differ from what came before but also stand in no specific obvious relation to its predecessors. (Being derivable from what came before through mechanical application of a clear rule counts as being obviously related)" (Nozick 1989, 36). Intuitively, Nozick's speculation seems to be clearly correct—seems to jibe with the plain sense of the word "creative." And it would seem to follow from the parenthesized clarification that a computer is barred in principle from being creative. After all, whatever a computer produces can only result from the "mechanical application of a clear rule" or rules. Mechanically applying clear rules is the computer's one and only capability. Yet I have outlined at least the basis of what I would describe as a "clear rule" for achieving creativity, a rule that centers of course on affect linking. In the next chapter, I will discuss the computerization of this rule. Does Nozick's comment mean that my claims are wrong?

No. The affect link *is* a "clear rule," but it is a rule that comes (so to speak) with an empty gas tank; it doesn't *do* anything except in combination with some thinker's own particular way of responding emotionally to the world around him. Affect linking in practice is limited and defined by the manner in which emotions are associated with memories, and I have supplied no "clear rule" for how *that* happens. It just does, as the result of a particular human being's physical makeup and his stock of experience. In the next chapter I will outline a way for computers to simulate emotional reactions. But the method I have in mind amounts at base to having the computer study a particular person or persons, then aping those particular emotional reactions as accurately as possible.

So we can have our clear rule for creativity and eat it too . . .

In sum . . .

To put it another way: "To me the meanest flower that blows," writes Wordsworth, "can give/ Thoughts that do often lie too deep for tears." (*Ode: Intimations of Immortality*: 202–203.)

Spirituality

This ought to be a topic like "creativity." Just as certain people are generally agreed to be creative, others are said to be "spiritual." Any general account of human thought should account for both phenomena—should include mechanisms that cover both. We ought to be able to survey the literature, set out cognitive psychology's current best guesses as to what "spirituality" really consists of and why some people have it and others don't. But we can't.

The reason is simple. Creativity is useful and spirituality (according to most psychologists at any rate) just isn't. Cognitive psychology sees no practical value in spirituality, no reason to inculcate it, no reason to build computers that can imitate it—and we can't quarrel with any of these judgments. They are all fair and reasonable. A spiritual computer is not an item for which buyers seem to be clamoring. And if our supply of spiritual *people* were greater, would the world be any better off? Who knows? Maybe not.

Where we ought to take issue is with the *conclusion* that cognitive psychologists have drawn from these propositions: that spirituality can safely be excluded from a comprehensive view of thought. But that is absurd. If our goal is to understand how humans work, spirituality is part of how they work. Case closed. We need to grapple with this phenomenon.

There aren't many comprehensive accounts of spirituality in the research literature on cognitive psychology, but luckily there are other experts to whom we can turn for clear and evocative descriptions of what this mental state is all about.

What is the signature of a "spiritual" state? Shelley's description, quoted earlier:

> The everlasting universe of things
> Flows through the mind, and rolls its rapid waves,
> Now dark, now glittering . . .

(Starting the discussion with Shelley serves to underline that spirituality needn't be associated with conventional religiosity. Shelley was an outspoken atheist.) When the greatest poet since Wordsworth speaks of "the fluidic world" in association with spiritual experiences, or of "plunging . . . into the abyss of my own mind" (Yeats 1973, 128, 100), his words recall Shelley's. Interestingly, Yeats himself draws attention to Shelley's passage from *Mont Blanc* and to other related ones, in his discussion of Shelley's propensity to conceive thought as liquid and flowing (1968, 84).

To the Romantics in general, in fact, "the movement of poetry was conceived as a flow" (McFarland 1987, 242). Since classical Greece, the poetic and the spiritual have been felt to be associated—the finest poems, Democritus believes, are composed "with inspiration and a holy breath" (Dodds 1951, 81). McFarland continues:

> Good poetry, as Wordsworth defined it, was "the spontaneous overflow of powerful feelings." "Shelley," wrote Mary Shelley, ". . . was thrown on his own resources, and on the inspiration of his own soul; and wrote because his mind overflowed." "The poem entitled *Mont Blanc*," confirmed Shelley himself, was "an undisciplined overflowing of the soul." Romanticism, said Kierkegaard in synopsis, "implies overflowing all boundaries." (242)

The great literary critic and novelist George Steiner (1989, 181) writes that "all of us have experienced twilit, penumbral moods of diffuse attention and unresistant receptivity on the one hand, and of tensed, heightened focus on the other." Steiner's observation recalls the *religious* state of mind defined as that "rise of consciousness in which the mind listens to itself before it is fully awake," by the philosopher Louis Dupré (1972)—paraphrasing the early nineteenth-century philosopher and theologian Friedrich Schleiermacher, memorably and curiously.

Everything we hear from these authorities makes it sound as if spiritual states are associated with the experience of a wide-ranging flow of thoughts—Shelley speaks of a *flow*, Yeats says *fluidic*, Steiner speaks of *diffuse attention*. The essence of the phenomenon might be a sense of *connectedness*—among the creatures, objects, and events of the outside world, and between this outside world and the inner world of the thinker; the spiritual state of mind is preeminently the sensation that "all life is linked . . ." (Bokser 1981, 1). I say *sensation* on purpose. No-one has to convince you that the sky is blue—you perceive that it is; and the mind in a spiritual state perceives a kind of all-encompassing connectedness, the "undefined sense of connectedness" that Romain Rolland, among many others, "took to be at the heart of religious sentiments" (Gay 1987, 17; see also Jones 1963, 477). Rolland described the feeling to Freud—"a feeling as of something limitless, unbounded—as it were, 'oceanic,' " is the way Freud (1930/1961, 11) renders it. Freud himself has no truck with this feeling, and his ordinarily unfailing acuity is utterly defeated by it.

But what is this state, in cognitive terms? How does it come about?

As usual, an important part of the problem is to grasp what is strange here, what begs for an explanation. At one moment, Shelley (let's say) is methodically checking the addition on his lunch bill at a cozy bistro in downtown Chamonix. An hour later, he is experiencing a universal flowing through his mind. What caused this flow to happen? What *motivates* it?—drives it forward, or pulls it along? After all, it isn't as if there is any problem to be solved, any analytic task that could engender a step-by-step sequence of thoughts. To approach the question from a different angle, here is the sort of answer we would *like* to discover: Robert Lowell, in one of his most beautiful thoughts, describes Racine, *the man of craft,/ drawn through his maze of iron composition/ by the incomparable wandering voice of Phèdre* . . . (*Dolphin*: 2–4.) (What a magnificent line!) And what draws the man of spirit onwards? What draws Shelley? What force makes his contemplations flow?

The flow Shelley describes is obviously not a mere random succession of unrelated thoughts. There must be some kind of relationship among them. A thought experiment: if we put Shelley in front of a screen, make him promise to contemplate whatever image we project, and then show him a random sequence of color slides, is he likely to experience the resulting mixed-up thought stream as in any way "spiritual"? Granted we can't know for sure. But it seems . . . unlikely.

We have, in short, a phenomenon with the following signature. Something motivates a long train of thought; the thoughts are very wide-ranging (the whole *universe of things* flows though Shelley's mind), and yet a *sensation of unity* ("all life is linked") results . . .

And the solution is immediate, *sustained low-focus thought*: a thought-stream that is pulled image-by-image out of memory, with the affect link binding the stream together. On this account, Shelley must first have relaxed and allowed his mental mood to "unfocus"; then some percept must have evoked some emotion, and the thought-stream is under way. The ability to sustain this mental mood, to keep a low-focus thought-stream going, is exactly the ability to experience a "spiritual" state of mind. The emotions that couple these thoughts together no doubt vary subtly as the train proceeds. A thought that is evoked by some emotion is also capable of giving rise (if we look at it from a slightly different angle) to a subtly different one, and this subtly different one summons a new thought, and so on. A sensitivity to the nuanced emotional iridescence of recollections is the engine that powers sustained low-focus thought. And the experience of a sustained low-focus thought-train just *is* that "all life is linked," because one emotion—or a closely related, subtly evolving succession of emotions—ties the whole train together.

Low-focus thought produces exactly the sense of unexpected *connectedness* between seemingly unrelated thoughts or memories. It produces a sense of "flow," of "unresistant receptivity," because at low focus, the thought-stream is literally out of control: control presupposes at least some degree of *choosing*, that is, of focus. The sensation that "all life is linked" arises ultimately out of affect linking. The language Steiner uses is strikingly in accord with the claim that it is exactly *low-focus* thought that he is describing. Without any plan of putting forward his own mind model, without describing anything like the cognitive spectrum or the affect link, he hits exactly on differences of *focus* as the metaphor to convey the essence.

Creativity centers on a single match-up, giving you the sense of having discovered something and maybe startling you back up to higher focus. Spirituality involves a sustained and more passive run of low-focus thought. But the same talent—*emotional acuity*—underlies both phenomena.

The cognitive spectrum leads us to see connections that are simply *there*, whether we buy the model or not. It is a catalyst, and once we see these connections we can, if we wish, dispense with the model and take away a sharper view of the mind's own view of itself. (I don't recommend this course of action, but it's on the table.) Positing the spectrum leads me to claim that "creativity" and "spirituality" are related phenomena. And on reflection, they clearly *are*. After all, creativity does have to do with seeing connections. And spirituality is, at base, a sensation of the connectedness of things. The relationship is plain.

In any case, we have arrived at a rather strange point. I am developing a "mechanism of mind," which implies obviously a *mechanistic view* of mind—and making the whole thing run on a computer is always a possibility in principle once you have described a mechanism; yet, here we are in the middle of spirituality. What are we doing here? Here is the unvarnished claim: spirituality is just *one setting of the dial*, given the mechanism I have described. But of course, as I have conceded, not all mental apparatuses, not all instances of the cognitive spectrum, are the same. Dialing down to low focus produces spirituality only in the presence of a certain kind of emotional acuity. Be that as it may, the place where we have arrived is a strange world to modern thought science.

Finally: what is *spiritual* about spirituality? What gives this state its special status, so often associated with religiosity?

The special status of the "spiritual"

The first step is always to succeed in becoming surprised—to notice that there is something funny going on; and in this case, clearly there is. Here is the puzzling question. If a mystic, poet, or prophet sits in Wordsworthian repose on a hillside over a river and loses himself in a sustained low-focus reverie—in a thought-stream animated by the affect link, "gently led on" by his emotions—we have seen clearly why he might experience a sensation of the underlying connectedness of things. But what does that have to do with *God*? Why does a perceived tie among all worldly things lead so many thinkers to thoughts of a (by definition) *other*-worldly Being? Why does Rolland (in Freud's account) insist that the "oceanic" feeling he and other spiritual-minded people experience "is the source of religious energy which is siezed upon by the various Churches and religious systems" (Freud 1930/1961, 11)? Why does Coleridge report, after a period of contemplation in which his being is "blended in one thought," that "when I rose, I found myself in prayer" (*To William Wordsworth*: 109; 112)? What's to pray about? What brings this sort of thing on?

This is not a question about theology! It is the sort of cognitive question that any serious account of human thought must confront.

You might answer that anyone decently versed in religious doctrine is aware of the claim, common to many religious views, that God created everything, and that (in some variants) he imbues or animates or is immanent in everything. And you might claim accordingly that the sensation of connectedness reminds the thinker of a particular doctrine learnt in Sunday school. But this explanation misses the point. In the literature of religious spirituality and mysticism, the "sensation of connectedness" gives rise to *sensations* of the presence or immanence of something identified as

"God." The powerful ties between this particular cognitive state and the idea of God derive from the state's propensity to produce a particular *sensation*, not merely to remind the thinker of an article of dogma; to produce, in Wordsworth's poetry, "a sense sublime of something far more deeply interfused . . ." (*Tintern Abbey*: 95–96.) Why should this sensation be one possible outcome of sustained low-focus thought?

Recall my earlier claim that an emotion is a *content-transcending abstraction* of a thought. The same claim might be rephrased: an emotion can be a *meaning*-transcending abstraction, where the "meaning" of a memory is simply its contents. The meaning of memory *A* might be "listening to Schwartz refute Piffel's argument," of memory *B* "watching my son demolish a five-foot-high tower of blocks." If these two scenes gave rise to the same emotion—the same nameless, subtle, probably fleeting feeling—then emotion transcends meaning.

We can say, then, that *the experience of sustained low-focus thought* produces *the sensation of transcending meaning*. Just as riding a roller coaster gives you the sensation of weightlessness (let's say), of gravity transcended, sustained low-focus thought gives you the sensation of meaning transcended: you move from thought to thought, sensing that each thought is related to the previous one—and yet their *meanings* are not related. Hence the sensation of meaning *transcended*, of moving forward in a plane separate from the plane of explicit meaning; the sense of (you might say) *defying* meaning, as an amusement-park ride might give you the sensation of defying gravity. Meaning impels ordinary thought trains, but not low-focus ones.

Now, the mature religious imagination gives a name to "the sensation of transcending meaning." That name is "the experience of God," or "the sensation of the presence of God." The name might or might not make sense to you; whether it does or not is irrelevant. The fact remains that *this name* is associated with *that sensation*, and sustained low-focus thought produces *that sensation*, and hence, if you are sufficiently familiar with religious tradition, the term "God" naturally enters the picture. (The "experience of God" is a different topic, of course, from the attributes of God—from the way one conceives God in substance. When a religion gets down to serious moral and cultic business, it must say what God is like, not merely what "the experience of God" *feels* like. The *experience* has nothing to do with what one imagines God's "personality" to be. On the other hand, you can be a learned theologian and never have experienced "the sensation of God's presence" that is so important a part of mystical traditions across a wide spectrum of religious communities.)

In short, sustained low-focus thought produces the sensation of *underlying unity*, and the name "spiritual" is associated with exactly that sensation, and hence we can account for *spiritual* states of mind by positing the mechanism of *low-focus thought*. Further, sustained low-focus thought produces the sensation of *transcending meaning*, and the name "experience of God" is associated with exactly *that* sensation, and hence we can account for "experience of God" states of mind by positing the mechanism of *low-focus thought*.

I will close with a short excursus. My assertion that "experience of God" is a name for "the sensation of meaning transcended" might be mystifying. Here is an explanation, for those who care. This is off the topic, but it's brief.

The "God hypothesis" as it has emerged in the mature religious imagination is the hypothesis that there is some transcendent entity. It follows that whatever you might assert about such an entity is wrong, or at best incomplete: *ex hypothesi* the thing being described is immune to human comprehension; you *can't possibly* grasp the whole story. "Any attempt to give it a definite, positive content in ordinary language is bound to fail because ordinary language can deal only with ordinary life, while the transcendent is precisely what stands out of the ordinary." (Dupré 1972, 16.) Except that, of course, I'm not saying merely that you can't *adequately describe* this "God idea" in language; rather that, by definition, you can't even *conceive* it. (This claim is in a sense the exact inverse of the famous old "ontological argument" for the existence of God . . .) Kant says this, in William James's (1902, 55) paraphrase: "We have the strange phenomenon, as Kant assures us, of a mind believing with all its strength in the real presence of a set of things of no one of which it can form any notion whatsoever." James himself regards this Kantian pronouncement as "particularly uncouth." Uncouth or not, it is exactly right. It jibes with some of the most interesting facts on record about the nature of "religious" experience. Thus, Gershom Scholem (the century's greatest student of mysticism) comments on a curious tendency in Jewish mysticism to associate the experience of God with an experience of *nothingness* (Scholem 1961, 5).

Hence, the name "experience of God" is associated with the experience of being "beyond meaning." To escape from the limits of whatever humans can conceive, to enter some kind of state in which the mind dwells on no concept whatever—that is the essence of what is historically identified as the religious experience. Music has always been associated with religious experience. Music, particularly pure melody or a chant with meaningless syllables or unnoticed words, produces the sensation of transcending meaning by inducing a sensation of *many* meanings. Music induces a series of emotions and each emotion in the series may induce in turn, via affect link, a kaleidoscope of recollections. Low-focus thought accomplishes the same thing directly.

Sustained low-focus thought is the music of cognition.

Out of control

"Our greatest blessings come to us by way of madness," writes Plato in the *Phaedrus*—"provided the madness is given us by divine gift." (See Dodds 1951, 64.) Folk psychologists have always been fascinated by phenomena that seemingly "take us out of ourselves." Such phenomena are associated with creativity, but also in their more vivid and sustained forms with spirituality and divinity, with Rolland's "oceanic" feeling, Nietzsche's "complete oneness with the essence of the universe" (Nietzsche 1872/1956, 25). Wordsworth's "sense sublime of something far more deeply interfused," and Coleridge's "sense of wonder." I have cited Dodds' comment about inspirations and creative insights hitting a person suddenly, out of the blue; "but in that case," Dodds (1951, 11) inquires respecting the insights of Mister Newly Inspired, ". . . how can he call them 'his'? A moment ago they were not in his mind; now they are there. Something has put them there, and that something is other than himself". Inevitably, theological speculations follow. Modern accounts leave out the religion, but on the whole they are no less mysterious. If we bypass the "analytic" faculties and invoke "the emotional, involved, holistic right brain" (Dreyfus and Dreyfus 1986, 65), are we any farther along? I have now accounted for exactly this sort of intrusion or inspiration in terms of a clear, well-defined and fairly simple cognitive mechanism, the affect link at low focus.

And yet. The spiritual mind-state is denigrated in modern intellectual life. Freud's approach is still representative: he "professed an interest in analyzing that feeling but he did not really respect it" (Gay 1987, 17). Is my insistence on accounting for the spiritual within an integrated mind-model one more piece (and a particularly brazen one) of superior psychologizing? One more patronizing attempt to explain religious and spiritual phenomena out of existence? I think not. Because I can assert—the spectrum model allows me to assert—that the spiritual state of minds is in fact *truth revealing*. It produces not merely a certain something-or-other feeling but *fresh knowledge*, although not necessarily of a sort that can be communicated. The "connectedness" of which spiritualists speak is exactly the same stuff out of which discoveries of the structure of benzene are made. It is real connectedness. Not every affect link reveals a fact of scientific value, or of any practical value, but every affect link reveals a truth. That truth is that your emotional faculty, ultimately (as I will discuss) just your body, succeeded in extracting the same essence out of two separate types of raw material. So those two types of material are somehow related. As surely as a Geiger counter is a mechanism for detecting radioactivity, the mind in a spiritual state is a mechanism for detecting real but hidden connections. Or should I say, for divining them . . . ?

Sleep, childhood, antiquity

The passages that lead from awakeness to sleep, from childhood to adulthood, and from prehistoric, precultural man to a full-fledged modern specimen represent the Big Three cognitive transitions.

It has long been understood that there are connections of some sort among the conditions of sleep, childhood, and antiquity.

Freud believed that the three are related in a variety of ways. Dreams are (in his famous term) the royal road to the unconscious, and the unconscious is full of repressed childhood memories. Repression accounts for the forgetting both of early childhood memories and of dreams. In his later cultural books, particularly *Totem and Taboo*, Freud puts forward a reconstruction of early human history based on what he takes to be the key psychological events of early childhood. In a more general way, the equation between early childhood and early human history is fundamental throughout his system: the metaphor of psychoanalysis as archeology, as a systematic uncovering of strata layed down in the distant past and since buried and hidden, recurs in his writing (thus, for example, Gay 1978, 39, or Schorske 1991). When he writes characteristically that "the dream life proceeds altogether from the relics of the prehistoric period (age one to three)" (in Jones 1963, 232) he links dreaming and childhood, and by his use of "prehistoric" involves antiquity as well. But Freud's interest is in the *content* of dream-thought as deriving from early childhood, and the psychological experiences of ancient man as resembling the experiences of infancy. I am interested only in styles of thinking, not at all with what thoughts are about.

In an early phase of his career, Jean Piaget was interested in the connections between early childhood cognition and ancient philosophical systems (see Elkind 1968, vii). Carl Jung had broadly similar interests.

"Ontogeny recapitulates phylogeny" has fallen by the wayside. But a hypothesized link between the dreaming and the ancient mind continues to be commonplace: "Perhaps . . . our brains are submitted during dreaming to some coding during which archaic (or genotypic), primarily inherited programming serves to reorganize a kind of base circuitry responsible for the inner core of so-called personality or character" (Jouvet, cited in Cohen 1979). One of the earlier statements of this view and certainly one the most interesting is Friedrich Nietzsche's. He writes that

> the utter clarity of all dream-ideas, which presupposes an unconditional belief in their reality, reminds us once again of the state of earlier mankind in which hallucinations were extraordinarily frequent, and sometimes seized whole communities, whole nations simultaneously. Thus, in our sleep and dreams, we go through the work of earlier mankind once more. (Nietzsche 1880/1984, 20)

Let's summarize some of the interrelations that plainly do exist.

Sleep, childhood, and antiquity all seem to be predominantly "unreasonable"—not hospitable to sustained rational, analytical thought.

Memory struggles rather mysteriously with early childhood and with sleep. It's notably hard to remember your earliest childhood— those "days disowned by memory," as Wordsworth calls them (*Prelude* I:614–615); and it is hard to remember your dreams. But the contents of a dream, less often of an early childhood scene, can return in a flash when the provocation is right.

The development of childhood and of mankind both revolve, of course, around the emergence of language.

And a final interesting point: the onset of sleep is accompanied by a dissolution of the sense of self. The passage from infancy into childhood entails just the opposite. The development of modern man may have involved the same thing again, the creation of a sense of self. An ever more acute self-consciousness seems to accompany the emergence of the modern mind.

Let's consider in more detail the phenomenology of these big three transitions, and try to develop some sense of each one's signature.

The Big Three and their signatures

Consider childhood development. There is a negative and a positive side to this story—evidence bearing on what children can't do, and on what they can.

The Piaget consensus about development in childhood no longer exists. Piaget had a grand organizing framework that followed children through a series of developmental stages; each stage applied virtually across the board, to the child's entire cognitive apparatus. Today, most developmental psychologists emphasize the many separate processes that are part of development, that a child might simultaneously be sophisticated in some ways and naive in others, that conclusions respecting what a child is capable of may reflect all sorts of extraneous factors, and so on.

But certain givens about childhood development *do* emerge, even in today's refined and complicated understanding. The ones that are most important are also the most obvious. On the whole, young children aren't good at abstractions. The ability to think in abstract terms develops gradually as they mature.

On the other hand, a number of studies have discovered that children seem to be amazingly good at producing metaphors. Psychologists Howard Gardner and Ellen Winner report in one fascinating study that

> the highest number of appropriate metaphors was secured from the preschool children, who even exceeded college students; moreover, these three- and four-year-olds fashioned significantly more appropriate metaphors than did children aged seven or eleven. . . . Quite possibly, the most intriguing phenomenon encountered so far in [a different study of early metaphor] is the capacity of at least some young children to perform this game at an astonishingly high level. (Gardner and Winner 1979, 131, 132–133)

Gardner and Winner call their findings the "child as poet" theory. (See also Gardner's 1982 discussion of "the child as artist.")

In another study, Winner, Rosenstiel, and Gardner (1976/1988) draw attention to the "apparent paradox" of these findings. A child's ability to deal in abstractions takes a long time to develop; yet metaphor would seem to require that one deal with language in a rather abstract way. It's also curious that, as children develop, "spontaneous production" of metaphors "occurs first, followed by comprehension and then by the ability to explain the rationale of a metaphor" (313). In other words, children are capable of producing metaphors before they know what they're doing.

Consider a process whose signature is at least in part *a diminishing capacity for metaphor* accompanied by *an increased capacity for abstract thought* . . .

Now: what does it mean to fall asleep?

The delicate processes of "sleep onset mentation" have been described, but no very clear *mechanism* emerges: are these just random cognitive happenings? "With each successive . . . stage there was a steady decline in control over the course of mental activity and an awareness of the immediate environment and a steady rise in the frequency of hallucinatory experience" (Vogel 1991, 126). Why? What cognitive mechanism is at work?

Another observation about sleep onset: I can't find it in the liter-ature (which is not to say it isn't there), and so I will have to describe it and hope the reader will just happen to recognize it. It is possible to awake or be awakened in the middle of a dream, and to have the clear impression that you could resume sleeping, if you chose, simply by dint of *resuming the train of thought that you were experiencing in the dream*. In other words, you have a choice: you can plunge right back to sleep, by picking up your thought train where it left off; or you can choose *not* to resume that thought train (which might have been unpleasant), and accordingly *not* to resume sleeping—at least not immediately. The sensation is dis-tinctly that you would be "pulled back under" into sleep by resum-ing the interrupted train. The unavoidable conclusion is that, in this case at any rate, it is *your thought-train* that determines your *state of consciousness* (that is, whether you are asleep or awake). Ordinarily we assume, of course, that it is just the other way around: that your state of consciousness determines the quality of your thought-train.

Let's glance finally at the transition from the ancient to the mod-ern mind. A good place to start is with psychologist Julian Jaynes' *Origin of Consciousness in the Breakdown of the Bicameral Mind*. It's an unconvincing book but a fascinating one.

The best thing about it is not Jaynes's conclusion but his starting point. He is vividly aware that, in the archeological and literary remains of the ancient world as they have come down to us, there is something that cries out for explanation. He makes the crucial observation that ancient man must not merely have lived but have *thought* differently than we do. "The earliest writing of men in a language that we can really comprehend, when looked at objective-ly, reveals a very different mentality from our own" (Jaynes 1976, 82). His argument rests on the palpable *reality* of the gods to ancient man. Divinity has, throughout the ancient world, an imme-diate, tangible presence that is (at least) uncommon today. "Truly this is astonishing!" (Astonishment is Jayne's best achievement, by no means a minor one.) "We have known of the Delphic Oracle so long from school texts that we coat it over with a shrugging usual-ness that we should not . . ." (322).

The explanation Jaynes offers is fascinating but ultimately

untenable. Ancient man, he believes, went through a long period in which he was literally unconscious; in which one side of the brain perceived the other side as addressing it in the form of a disembodied voice, as an auditory hallucination. The mental processes we would experience as subjective reflection didn't exist; that role was filled by a seemingly external voice issuing commands. This voice was identified as a god's voice. The "bicameral" period drew to a close when, after centuries of society's official discouragement of the sort of "possessed" behavior it produced, brain development reorganized itself and the seemingly external voice subsided into the "voice of inner reflection" we know today. The transition is said to have occurred at different times in different societies, but in many cases the end of the second or the start of the first millennium B.C. is about the right period. The whole proposition seems farfetched, to say the least. Be it noted, though, that Jaynes presents an intriguing argument and makes some striking observations.

The argument fails, ultimately, to convince because it presupposes a radical discontinuity where no actual discontinuity exists. Jaynes makes the crucial observation that we must not dismiss the vivid *reality* of the gods to ancient man. And then he commits the same error himself, in discounting the vivid reality of God or gods in more recent centuries to fully conscious, non-"bicameral" thinkers down to our own day. (According to Miller (1986, 156), Jaynes wrongly asserts that "there has been a single breaking point, a great divide if you like, in the psychological history of the human race . . ." I agree: it is a wrong assertion.)

In all events, Jaynes does present a crucial piece of data. The immediate awareness of (what was taken to be) divinity was far more common in the ancient world than it is today. This awareness may indeed have been qualitatively different from what we know today—more immediate and vivid and tangible. I've noted assertions by several scholars that hallucinations were more common in former times than today. But there's no reason to conclude that *brains* were any different then; we needn't believe either in the Jaynes thesis or in "ontogeny recapitulates phylogeny." We aren't excused from noticing and seeking to explain the phenomena that induce Jaynes' theory—but a purely mental explanation, in terms of evolving cognitive styles or habits, will serve the purpose. Thus

T. S. Eliot (1932, 204), discussing the medieval sensibility of Dante: his is "a *visual* imagination. . . . It is visual in the sense that he lived in an age in which men still saw visions. It was a psychological habit, the trick of which we have forgotten." (Eliot's note reminds us that the transition from ancient thought styles to modern lasted many centuries and wasn't complete until the brink of modern times—if indeed it *is* complete.)

William Foxwell Albright, who ranks among the century's greatest archeologists and scholars, makes a different point about the cognitive distinctiveness of the past. He presents a sequence of "three principal stages in the development of human thinking," which he calls proto-logical, empirico-logical and logical. Historically, the Hebrew Bible (which originates mainly between the late second and late first millennium B.C.) is written in the empirico-logical stage—although it preserves a few proto-logical vestiges. Logic *per se* originates with the classical Greeks.

(Albright's scheme recalls Piaget, although Albright doesn't cite him. Jaynes' book for its part might have cited Albright.)

In the "proto-logical" period we encounter poetry that literally makes no sense. It is self-contradictory. Thus Albright (1964, 95) comments on Canaanite poetry in Ugaritic (a language that is close to Biblical Hebrew) dating from the centuries immediately before Moses: "We find much self-contradictory description. In fact, frequently in the same line one half-line contradicts the other. For instance, the first half-line says that a god 'drank wine from a cup of gold,' the next half-line that he 'drank it from a flagon of silver. . . .' " This sort of illogic is a separate phenomenon, of course, from the hallucinatory thinking I discussed earlier. "Illogical" thinking doesn't prove the existence of hallucination or vice versa. But as I discussed earlier, hallucination and illogic are both characteristic of low-focus thought.

The signature of this transition from the ancient past is, in short: from *hallucinations* (to use Nietzsche's term, and Jaynes'), or more likely an imagined but hugely vivid, tangible sense of the reality of the gods—the state Keats recalls in *holy were the haunted forest boughs, holy the air, the water, and the fire*; a state characterized for all this blazing excess of something-or-other by a striking *lack* of logical thought (as Albright notes)—from this strange state, to the "normal," modern mind. What sort of transition have I described?

Where have we seen these signatures?

It's hard to resist the conclusion that in terms of cognitive phenomenology, we are seeing three variations on one theme. There are striking similarities between the three transitions we have been discussing. (This assertion is completely unrelated to the old "recapitulation" argument: it makes no claims about any biological changes, only cultural ones, over the millennia during which the modern mind emerged.)

How so? At one end of each transition there lies a distinctly abnormal cognitive state. The character of the state is never completely clear in any of our cases, but clearest perhaps in the case of sleep. Dreaming involves outright hallucination. It entails a sharply diminished capacity for reasoning. Infancy and young childhood do *not* involve hallucination, presumably. (Although Freud believed that in fact they do; that in childhood, "whatever was thought of (wished for) was simply presented in a hallucinatory manner" [Freud 1958, 219; for a discussion see Gay 1985, 130]). Infancy and childhood certainly do, however, entail sharp limits on the capacity for logic and reasoning—or more generally and accurately, on the ability to manage abstractions.

What is the link between the hallucinations of sleep and the non-hallucinatory cognitive states of infancy and young childhood? The ambiguous characterizations of the ancient past we've cited make a kind of bridge. It's conceivable that ancient man regularly experienced "genuine" hallucinations. More likely, he drew on a vivid imagination. An imagination that is "vivid" is one that tends, as I have noted, towards the hallucinatory.

Of course, a vivid imagination is a childhood specialty. To the child Wordsworth, after all, "the earth and every common sight" is "apparelled in celestial light, the glory and the freshness of a dream."

What is the cognitive signature of a vivid imagination? For one, the things you observe tend to remind you of other things: you see connections or resemblances. (A vivid imagination and a strong ability to find metaphors can hardly be unrelated.) For another, a vivid imagination entails "entering into" versus merely observing critically from the outside. The "vividness" of a vivid imagination refers exactly to the hallucinatory quality of the delivered product.

And now the "far ends" of our Big Three cognitive transitions are coming together unmistakably as, of course, three different manifestations of low-focus thought. When my focus is low, I notice resemblances. When my focus is low, *whole memories* and not merely snipped-out details are available to me; and I expect to lose control over the course of my thinking. Everything I have said about the phenomenology of sleep and sleep onset, of early childhood and of the ancient mind, make these cognitive states sound like prevailingly *low-focus* states. Not that they are states in which high focus is impossible. Rather, that relatively low focus is habitual. The process of climbing out of childhood or antiquity involves a gradual nudging upward of the "average focus" dial. Falling asleep requires a gradual nudging lower. *Gradual* of course modifies a radically different time scale in the three cases, but the basic process would be the same.

As the dial is pushed higher, a person's ability to manage abstractions gains. And (as I claimed in Chapter 1) his memory emerges. Perceptions become memories. Your stream of perceptions runs into the pool of your memory. When you deal with a stream of perceptions at high focus, the details you notice will be good candidates for the cues that pull those memories back into awareness. As focus declines, you tend less and less to resolve particular details in the passing scene. But when you notice *nothing in particular*, rather *everything in general*, then *everything in general* becomes your only plausible memory cue. And this suggests in turn that memories laid down in a low-focus state of mind will be *less accessible* than those arising in higher-focus states. In the limit, memories that arise at low focus may be accessible *only* by means of affect linking. There may not *be* a single detail sufficiently separated from the scene as a whole to be memorable as such, to be capable of reminding you of the remembered scene; the emotion you felt at the time, which "summarizes" the entire scene, may be the only cue capable of bringing that recollection back. Only by recreating or re-experiencing the original emotion might you be able to find any purchase on the original memory.

Now of course, it is by no means even remotely plausible that these three cognitive transitions are *the same*. They differ radically in many ways. At the same time they share something, subtle but critical.

I'll close by addressing two rather specific implications of this claim, and another very general one. The first has to do with sleep onset. It asserts that, in normal people under normal conditions, a gradual lowering of mental focus is the immediate cause of sleep. This lowering of focus is promoted by fatigue, but fatigue *per se* can't cause sleep without lowering your mental focus first. Metaphorically, the lowering of focus drags consciousness down beneath some threshold, and the physiological sleep state sets in.

This assertion is supported by an interesting and curious piece of sleep data: dreaming starts *before* sleep does! "The most unexpected finding in the initial laboratory study of SO [sleep onset] . . . later replicated in three other studies . . . was the presence of substantial dreaming during SO" (Vogel 1991, 127). This "sleep onset" period specifically covers a succession of stages described as awake but drowsy, drifting off to sleep, and light sleep. The dreams occurred not only during light sleep but during the drowsy and drifting-off periods as well.

In other words, physiological consequences simply tag along in the wake of mental ones. A particular *cognitive* state—the state in which dreams are possible—precedes the associated *physiological* state of sleep.

My second claim is that dreaming is a species of minimum-focus thought. The contention is again not that dreaming is *merely* low-focus thought, but that low-focus thinking creates the necessary conditions, *sets the stage*, for dream thought.

The special character of dream-thought has been explained in many ways. Dreaming has been described as essentially random (for example by Dennett 1991, in an especially ingenious way). It has been described as a kind of updating and cross-referencing of memory files. It has been described, in connection with Pötzl's observations, as an attempt to catch up on cognitive material to which the dreamer paid insufficient attention during the day. It has been described in a phrase that remains, for all the damage the argument has sustained over time, one of the most charged and evocative in intellectual history—as the fulfillment of a wish (Freud 1900/1965). And there are many other explanations as well.

Studies have established that most dreams are mundane (see, for example, Foulkes 1985). But it also sometimes occurs that "impulses that are kept in check during waking life" are expressed in dreams (Hall 1966, 14), and that "dreams cut through the pretensions and deceits of waking life" (13). Sometimes, matters that we perceive but (for whatever reason) ignore during the day emerge in dreaming (Cohen 1979, 223); wishes that we suppress may emerge in dreams (Freud 1900/1965); fears may emerge in nightmares. Clearly, ignored or suppressed matters *do* emerge. But it's hard to believe that revealing such things is somehow the *point* of dreaming, because so much of dreaming is perfectly mundane.

Yet if we hypothesize that dreaming is a form of low-focus thought, then it *must have* exactly these paradoxical properties—at times rooting out secrets, but most other times revelling in the perfectly ordinary. *At minimum focus, you make no choices.* The power to focus-on is also the power to turn-away-from. When you are powerless to focus, you are powerless to exclude. Thus ordinarily you merely re-experience, in your dreams, whole memories from the recent past. But if memories recently created or recalled happen to have included elements that you chose at the time to ignore . . . those memories may return in dreaming, when you no longer have the power to avert your gaze. You see the whole memory, not just sanitized (or "censored") bits.

Dream-thought may be obscure. Something may occur that you know perfectly well *stands for or really means* something else. This is perfectly in keeping with the nature of low-focus thought, which deals in unexpected connections and hitches superficially different, emotionally related memories right beside each other.

Dreams may include strange images. Classically they may incorporate, for example, composites in which the features of two separate people are intermixed. Thus for example Foulkes (1985) on the "imaginal fusing of the physical properties of two different persons in one dream character" (24), and of course Freud (1900/1965). These are the low-focus overlays I described earlier:

two separate images hitched together by effect, by shared emotional content. (I cited earlier Reiser's description of shared affect in dream formation.) It's no accident that symbolism (juxtaposition of two elements, one replacing the other) and compound imagery (juxtaposition of two elements, one superimposed on the other) both happen in the same cognitive neighborhood. I'd claim that the compound imagery of dreams is a manifestation of exactly the same phenomenon that links two seemingly distant thoughts in a new analogy or a smooth-rolling spiritual thought train.

Whatever dreaming is, it has a cognitive component that can be abstracted from physical sleep. A series of studies have shown that dream-like thought occurs routinely to *waking* thinkers. Agreement on this point goes back at least to Ludwig Börne (in Jones 1963, 160), who described in 1823 how "you will be amazed at what novel and startling thoughts have welled up in you," if you record your thoughts uncritically for a few days. Klinger and Cox report a comprehensive study of thought streams in which 29 long-suffering subjects were beeped at random daytime moments and asked to record their thoughts. When the votes were tallied, it turned out that "25 percent of the thoughts reported were described as containing at least traces of dream-like mentation . . ." (Klinger and Cox, 1988, 124). These were all *conscious, waking* thoughts. "Pensive awhile she dreams awake," says Keats (*The Eve of St. Agnes*: 232); or Wordsworth—"gently was I charmed into a waking dream" (*Prelude XIII*: 343-344), and so on. Such studies suggest, as Weinstein, Schwartz, and Arkin (1991, 196) provocatively observe, that "perhaps dreams are better conceptualized as the end point on a continuum." Fine, and the obvious question is, "Continuum of *what*?" A plausible answer is immediate: dreams are the bottom of the thought spectrum.

Dream-thought is all-inclusive, and rich in unexpected connections. Dream-thought isn't logically constructed and abstract, but emotionally constructed and concrete; it is outside your control; it is not merely vivid but hallucinatory. And that's exactly how thought at the spectrum's bottom *should* be. It all fits. All of a piece.

The last implication is a very general one. People and civilizations used to be thought to "develop," to "progress." Nowadays many observers are uncertain about these terms; maybe all stages of the game are equally good; maybe there is no such thing as "progress" in any neutral sense. In fact, though, the original notions or progress or development were strictly *correct*; they merely omitted exactly half the story. The other half is *anti*development. As your mental focus sharpens, you become adept at new thought techniques. You grow accustomed to forming and manipulating abstractions, to picking out and probing interesting details, and this becomes your habitual cognitive approach. In consequence you reach logically valid conclusions and make interesting discoveries. But simultaneously you have grown *unaccustomed* to experiencing the world in low-focus terms: the terms under which visions lurk around every corner and the world is full of strange, deep, unexpected connections.

The human cognitive faculty becomes, in this view, a tent defined by a single round of cloth. As the individual or the civilization develops, the cloth doesn't get bigger—the tent pole merely rises higher. Knowledge ascends to encompass new realms, and at the same time the perimeter is dragged inwards, and experiences that were once inside no longer are.

Human knowledge deepens and narrows, continuously and inevitably, and on this view the pronouncements that attack "the 'magic' of earlier visions" are profoundly wrong. They deepen our understanding not because they are good diagnoses but because they are interesting symptoms. Outfitted as they are with modern minds and habits of thought, our own thinkers and philosophers are simply *unable to see* what ancient man saw.

What made Shakespeare end *King Lear*, history's most cogent piece of literature after the Bible, by observing *"we that are young will never see as much"*? Whatever, it is immeasurably satisfying.

Chapter Six

The Spectrum on a Computer?

Claim: I can demonstrate to you that there is (at the moment) no such thing as a "thinking machine" just on the basis of common language, with no reference to computer science at all.

We hear the term "thinking machine" or "thinking computer" from time to time, and it glows with high-tech panache. In fact there is a computer company in Massachusetts that has named itself "Thinking Machines" exactly to emphasize its cutting-edge-ness. But I'd conjecture that, if thinking machines really existed, the term "thinking machine" would itself be obsolete. At best, it would have a quaintly archaic ring—

After all, a real thinking machine would be useful and valuable to a nearly inconceivable degree. Imagine a dozen things you care about, and imagine setting "employees" to work thinking about them non-stop twenty-four hours a day, employees who enjoy immediate access to gigantic databases (information in huge quantities is pumped directly into their brains), never make sloppy mistakes and never get bored. You'd have full-time accounting, medical, legal, financial, and so forth staffs looking after your interests round the clock.

A machine that useful wouldn't even *be* a machine; wouldn't be a mere computer; it would be something else. By the same token, a horseless carriage proved to be so much more useful and valuable than any other kind that it really wasn't a carriage at all, when you got right down to it.

When and if such machines emerge, the term "thinking machine" or "thinking computer" will pack about as much technological pizzazz as "flying machine," "talking machine" and so on.

A thinking computer would be useful, to say the least. Such a contraption would also tell us a great deal about *human* thought. To the extent you can make it work you have proven that, if your mind mechanism is not *the* way in which thought happens—at least it's *a* way. And that would be an exceptionally interesting piece of news.

My goal in this chapter is to explain why the idea of software as a metaphor for mind is so seductive, and why it is wrong. To do this, I need to start by explaining briefly what software is and what the phrase "virtual machine" means. (Basically "virtual machine" means "software," but the longer phrase emphasizes certain aspects of software.)

But first, who cares about the metaphor? Why invest time explaining and attempting to demolish it?

For one, just because this metaphor is such a widely held article of faith in cognitive science. But there are more important and more substantive issues at stake too. The software metaphor underlines and reinforces the field's most basic and damaging bias—to be aware only of the highest-focus sliver of the cognitive spectrum, and to mistake this abstract, logical, analytic sliver for the whole of thought. Spirituality, to pick only the most extreme example, is unlikely to recommend itself as a serious thought science research topic so long as "mind" and "software" can possibly be confused. Not only is the metaphor wrong, but its wrongness has had bad consequences for the field. It deserves to be retired.

After I have discussed the wrongness of the metaphor, I will beat an ironic retreat to our own software project, explain its goals and how it works, and why it constitutes a first, tentative step towards a working model of the cognitive spectrum, towards a "thinking machine" indeed.

The idea of a virtual machine

Isn't it odd that a piece of technical information about a complex machine should emerge as the basis of a philosophical school? Ruminations about vacuum cleaners or electric toothbrushes never bulked large in philosophic discourse. Why should computers and software be different?

There are two good reasons. First, the idea of a "virtual machine" is inherently deep and fascinating. It ranks among the most significant concepts in the history of technology. Second, this idea was in the right place at the right time. It provided the metaphor that energized a whole school of thought.

What is this great idea? In brief, most machines are what they are. A toaster is a toaster. Its capabilities are determined by the way it is put together. But a computer is fundamentally different. A computer is a machine for impersonating other machines: its character and functioning are determined not by the way it is put together, but rather by the identity it has temporarily assumed—by the *program* it is executing.

When you execute a program on a computer, you are instructing the computer to step into some role—to impersonate or embody some particular machine you have dreamed up. The computer itself, the raw hardware, is capable merely of shuttling numbers back and forth between a numbers warehouse (the "memory") and a glorified pocket calculator (the "processor"). But this uninspiring piece of machinery can *step into* far more interesting roles. It can play the part of a picture painter or a word processor or a spreadsheet or an Invasion of the Demented Artichokes Space Game, or whatever. Your program, the computer's *software*, is exactly the *script* that tells the computer how to embody the part.

The *actual machine* is the computer itself, the nuts and bolts (and plastic and silicon) hardware with its meager (not to say pathetic) number-shuttling capabilities. The *virtual machine* is the *embodied* machine, the *assumed identity* taken on by the actual machine . . .

Or, taken on by another "lower level" *virtual* machine. Within computer science, the power of the idea lies in the fact that virtual machines can be stacked up.

We can use a raw computer to embody a virtual machine. Then we can use that virtual machine to embody still another, *higher*-level virtual machine . . . In some production of *A Midsummer Night's Dream*, Phil Schwartz (the raw machine) plays the role of Bottom (the first-level virtual machine). In Act 3, Bottom (The first-level virtual machine) plays the role of Pyramus (the second-level virtual machine) . . .

Unfortunately the play-within-a-play analogy doesn't take us very far, because *this* sort of virtual machine tower can't get very high before it collapses. Two levels of "virtuality" is about the limit, in practical terms. But in computational reality, you can stack virtual machines without limit. You can have a level-47 virtual machine embodied by a level-46 virtual machine and so on, with forty-five more levels to go before you reach ground.

Your word processor or your Crazy Artichokes game is (at least) a level-2 virtual machine. It isn't designed for embodiment by the raw computer. It is scripted for a level-1 virtual machine called "the programming language plus the operating system." This level-1 virtual machine runs on the raw machine (or it might be embodied by yet another lower-level virtual machine—might *actually* be level-2, making Crazy Artichokes level-3, and so on).

Virtual machine stacks are critical to computing because each level is "better" than the one below it, loosely speaking; each level adds value. A raw computer is a royal pain to program. In the language of the metaphor, it's very hard to write a script that is capable of being embodied by its meager talents. Programmers invest large amounts of time in building a first-level virtual machine—a programming language, for example, like Fortran or Basic or Pascal or Lisp—whose goal is merely to make the computer *slightly* less of a pain. The builder of the next-level virtual machine doesn't deal with the raw computer, but with the slightly less intractable first-level virtual machine, and so on.

That's the way it is in computing. But what does this have to do with thought science?

For centuries, philosophers and psychologists had studied *the mind* without questioning its legitimacy as a topic in its own right, a topic quite distinct from *the brain*. In the old days this view was supported by Cartesian dualism, which held mind and brain to be distinct and separate sorts of stuff. By the middle of this century, however, Cartesian dualism was thoroughly dead; no one believed it any more; and at the same time, philosophers and psychologists felt the hot breath of neurophysiology at the back of their necks. It began to seem possible that "the study of the mind" merely *was* "the study of the brain," and that philosophers of mind might soon be expelled from the Paradise of their book-lined studies directly into wet and smelly laboratories, where they would be forced to conduct experiments for the rest of their miserable lives. This prospect did not please them, and not merely because they didn't care for laboratories (although personality matters can never be excluded from the history of ideas). Even accepting the fact that any mind phenomenon must ultimately be explicable in terms of brain phenomena, the fact remains that mind and brain phenomena are *different*. Brain phenomena must in turn be explicable in terms of physics—but that doesn't undermine the legitimacy of neurobiology.

Psychologists and philosophers needed a way to put this observation on a rigorous footing. The idea of software, of virtual machines, seemed to provide *exactly* the right metaphor. Minds were said to relate to brains as programs related to computers. Software and computers are two separate, distinct topics; minds and brains are likewise separate and distinct. *So we don't have to become neurobiologists after all*!

This metaphor, whether or not you accept it as fundamentally valid, was capable of abuse from the start. If you got carried away, you might assert not merely that minds were *like* software but that they *were* a kind of software. John Searle (1992, 44) summarizes this reckless claim, which he rejects: ". . . the mind just is a computer program and the brain is just one of the indefinite range of different computer hardwares (or "wetwares") that can have a mind." But it is possible to be a principled believer in the metaphor and *not* to make this kind of assertion. "The level of description and explanation we need is *analogous to* (but not identical with) one of the 'software levels' of description of computers: what we need to understand is how human consciousness can be realized in the operation of a *virtual machine* . . . in the brain" (Dennett 1991, 210).

That "analogous to" is the key. *Is* this a legitimate analogy? Dennett proposes to "think of the brain as a computer of sorts. The concepts of computer science provide the crutches of imagination we need if we are to stumble across the *terra incognita* between our phenomenology as we know it by "introspection" and our brains as science reveals them to us" (433).

The answer is no, this is not a legitimate analogy. The analogy is wrong. It is also basic to cognitive science as we know it.

No, Virginia, the mind is not like software

Proponents of the analogy are guilty of a confusion between the bland and innocuous idea of *abstraction levels* and the far more portentous idea of *virtual machines*.

Let's begin by considering a question that arises from the argument in the previous section. If the mind can be understood as an analogy to a virtual machine operating in the brain, can a brick be understood as a "virtual machine" implemented by particles of clay? No, and the reason why not is important.

Mere abstractions vs. virtual machines

Essentially any object or event can be described in terms of an abstraction that makes no reference to "implementation"—that is, to the physical stuff or the actual methods by which the object was created or the event made to occur. But the fact that we can produce this sort of abstraction doesn't in itself give us the right to call the abstraction a "virtual machine."

An abstraction *may* be legitimately described as a virtual machine exactly when it is inherently *independent* of its implementation—not when the abstraction merely *makes no reference* to the implementation. Inherent independence requires that the abstraction not depend in any way on the implementation—not conceptually, and not in practical terms. In particular, we must be able to assert that there is more than one way to realize the abstraction: more than one possible implementation.

Only when we can assert *a priori* that inherent independence holds are we entitled to describe some abstraction as a virtual machine. We are specifically *not* entitled to *begin* by claiming that some abstraction, *just in virtue of being an abstraction*, is a virtual machine—and then to conclude on that basis that inherent independence holds! But cognitive science has often tried to pull off exactly this hokey trick.

Thus, let's contrast a brick and a spreadsheet program. Notice that we can reach an abstract characterization of *brickness* that makes no reference to baked clay (i.e., to the "implementation"). We can say that a brick is an object with a certain color, size, weight, density, smell, behavior when subjected to heat and cold, to tension and compression, and so forth.

But of course, we're merely describing the properties of baked clay. The description needn't actually *mention* clay—but so what? We aren't thereby entitled to infer that the abstraction can be realized in any other way. (The existence of terms such as "mud brick" or "concrete brick" underscores the point. If you tried to pass off either one as a just plain "brick," you would fail.)

Yes there *might* be another way to achieve exactly this quality of brickness—perhaps there's a certain mixture of vinegar, molybdenum and Wheaties that cooks up just right, into a perfect brick. (In other words, this nonclay brick fulfills every requirement on our brickness list.) It's not impossible that such a recipe exists—it's just that there are no prior logical grounds for thinking it does. If *you* believe it exists, fine: but don't expect anyone else to believe it until you concoct the recipe and show us.

Turning now to the spreadsheet program: when we describe *its* properties, we are *not* merely describing the properties of the underlying physical stuff—the properties of some computer. The fact is, we can remove the physical stuff (the IBM PC, say), and achieve exactly the same constellation of properties on the basis of very different physical stuff (say, an Apple Macintosh).

That is: the structure of software is independent of the reality of any physical computer. If I build a program using a programming language (which is nearly the universal practice), the structure of the finished product is influenced by the programming language, but the language in turn is defined essentially without reference to any particular computer. And in practice, given the appropriate engineering support, the same program can indeed execute on many computers.

> *Objection:* Sure, PCs and Macs are different, but still, they're just two species of electronic computer—two different colors of "baked clay." They're not different enough to qualify as two *really* different implementations.

Okay. But the spreadsheet program could also execute on an optical computer (say) or a mechanical one, and these would be constructed in radically different ways. And in theory, it could execute on a "computer" made out of celery and onion dip, so long as this crunchy computer met a rather simple set of well-defined minimum requirements.

The "in theory" is important. The fact that we can say things *in theory* about software crucially distinguishes software from bricks and—as we'll see—from minds.

It is constitutive of *computers* and *virtual machines* (in the specific sense of "computer programs") that a computer can run *any* virtual machine and a virtual machine can run on *any* computer. A computer in turn can be constructed out of any sort of physical stuff, so long as it meets some simple requirements.

Thus, there are a number of abstract formalisms that capture precisely the notion of "all doable computations" (as opposed to computations that might be imagined in principle, but can't actually be carried out). These formalisms were described independently by a number of mathematicians working mainly in the 1930s—notably Turing, Kleene, Post and Church—and they are equally powerful. The idea of *computer* and of *computer program*, or *virtual machine*, can each be referred back to this "gold standard" definition. A computer is a machine that is capable of embodying one of these abstract formalisms, and a program is a series of instructions that is capable of being rephrased in the language of one of the formalisms. (For a particularly lucid discussion of the relevant theory, see Rogers 1967.)

A machine with the right properties to qualify as a computer can be built out of electronic circuits, or optical circuits, or gear-and-sprocket assemblies, or paper tapes and pencils, or celery sticks and onion dip. The particular way your Mac or your PC *is* built has no logical effect on the programs it is capable of executing: in the final analysis, there is no computational problem your PC can solve that the celery-and-onion-dip computer can't also solve, if you are willing to be patient.

(Searle, by the way, writes that "amazingly, a lot of very technical sounding notions are poorly defined—notions such as 'computer,' 'computation,' 'program' . . ." (1992, 15). He is wrong. Each of these "notions" has a rigorous and precise definition.)

Another Objection: Gelernter claims that bricks and spread-sheets are basically different sorts of abstraction, because a spreadsheet is and a brick is not inherently independent of its implementation. But that's just a matter of the way you define *brick* and *spreadsheet*—which details you put in and which you leave out. There's clearly *some* definition of brickness that does apply to real bricks, but could also apply to brick-shaped objects made out of concrete or mud. And there's clearly *some* definition of (a particular) spreadsheet program that holds good only for programs running on an IBM PC—it might refer, perhaps, to the exact times required to execute certain operations. So there's no *real* difference between a brick and a spreadsheet.

Nice try, but no cigar. Let's use everyday language as the arbiter of what definitions qualify as "natural." In common usage, the word *brick* does in fact designate a set of objects that share a single implementation—all ("just plain") bricks are in fact made out of baked clay. The term hasn't slipped loose from one particular sort of physical realization. But the term "spreadsheet" (or "the Lotus 1-2-3 spreadsheet program") in fact designates a set of objects whose physical realizations differ: 1-2-3 running on a PC and 1-2-3 running on a Mac are two different physical realizations of the same program. In practice, these two different realizations *will* differ in minor ways—despite which, it is generally agreed that they are two instances of the same virtual machine, the same program.

You might now reinstitute your original objection, with a twist: (1) PCs and Macs aren't different enough to count, and (2) a celery and onion dip computer (or even a potato chip and guacamole model) *is* different, but a spreadsheet running on that kind of computer would *not* in practice be indistinguishable from a PC version. For example, a calculation that took a couple of microseconds on the PC might take fifty years on the celery model.

I admire your persistence, but there *are* computers that are radically different from the PC but could, in theory, perform in a comparable way. For example, computers built out of optical circuits or large organic molecules. These aren't practical at the moment, but that's not the point. No one doubts that such things are possible in principle. Objection denied.

In sum: all abstractions are not created equal. Some abstractions qualify as virtual machines. Some just don't.

Brick vs. spreadsheet

Now: is your mind like a brick, or is it more like a spreadsheet?

Well of course, any abstraction is presumptively a brick unless we have the evidence in hand to promote it to a spreadsheet. It's true that the mind is an abstraction that can be described without reference to its implementation—without reference to human physiology. But that alone doesn't entitle us to claim that the mind is a "virtual machine" type of abstraction.

Yet this claim *is* made, almost universally in cognitive science. *Why* is it made? In virtue of what is it asserted that the mind is inherently independent of human physiology?

There are two sorts of answers abroad, the "metaphor" answer and the "brain as information processor" answer. Both (and particularly the latter) are fascinating, but neither is any good.

The metaphor answer

The first answer to the "in virtue of what is it asserted that the mind is inherently independent of human physiology?" question is *in virtue of the metaphor, that's what*! In other words, in virtue of nothing. We hypothesize that minds are independent of human physiology *because* minds are like programs. But the hypothesis that minds are like programs *assumes* that minds are independent of human physiology.

Thus the philosopher Ned Block, for example, notes that "the computer model of mind aims for a level of description of the mind that abstracts away the biological realizations of cognitive structures." Fair enough; it's a sound research program. A few sentences later: "If the computer model is right, we should be able to create intelligent machines in our image—our *computational* image, that is" (1990, 261). Which doesn't follow: this is virtually the defining non sequitur of modern intellectual history. No more than the abstract, implementation-independent description of brickness guarantees that there are alternative recipes for making bricks does the abstract, implementation-independent description of mind guarantee that there are alternate recipes for making minds.

Dennett (1991) says something similar. In discussing the architecture of cognition (as opposed to the structure of the brain), he writes that "we will have to find a higher level at which to describe it. Fortunately, one is available, drawn from computer science . . ." (210). Enter the virtual machine, trumpets blaring. In other words, the analogy *seems apt*, so let's grab it.

Dennett also provides a different and more involved version of the same sort of argument. It hinges on the fact that the brain's competence evolves as its owner learns things. A computer's competence changes when you load software. Which makes the process of *learning* (sort of) like the process of *loading software*. The curious clincher turns out to be that you can't really see the brain changes wrought by learning—they are "as good as invisible to neuroscientists" (Dennett 1991, 210)—and you can't really see software either. Hence, the mind is like software.

But what difference does it make whether you can *see* the changes that happen in the brain? They are real changes whether you can see them or not. There are no such corresponding changes in a computer's memory when you load software into it. The software inside the computer corresponds merely to *a particular state of the machine*. Picture the computer's memory as a bank of off-on light switches—loading the program corresponds to setting each switch either off or on, in some particular pattern. Learning on the other hand changes not merely the *state* but the *physical stuff* of the brain. Don't reach for your neurobiology textbook—merely consult the fact that, as part of the normal operation of a computer, we can flick a switch and delete a program from the machine's memory, leaving no trace. The brain has no such capability with respect to what it has learned.

The analogy is wrong in a more basic way, too. When the brain is exposed to some environment, it evolves in response. But a computer does not evolve or respond. To respond requires the initiation of action, but a computer in a state of nature is a purely passive object. Which leads us to more substantive arguments for the software metaphor (arguments which Dennett also advances) . . .

The information processing answer

The most important argument in favor of the metaphor rests on the claim that the brain just *is* a general-purpose information processing device, and so is a computer. Case closed. "Mental processes are the computations of the brain," as the psychologist P. N. Johnson-Laird puts it (1990, 391).

Dennett (1991, 217) says: "If the brain is a massively parallel processing machine, it too can be perfectly imitated by a Von Neumann machine." The terminology isn't important, but for the record, the "massively parallel" refers to many computations going on simultaneously, and a "Von Neumann machine" is a conventional computer that goes one step at a time.

Why the information processing answer is false

Actually it is true, up to a point. The brain *is* just an information processing device, and any such device can indeed be reproduced on a computer. We would seem to be facing an airtight case.

Except that the base assumption is wrong. That assumption states that you think with your brain. It's not the type of assumption that a person is apt to question, ordinarily—it packs the intimidating rhetorical *thunk* of "the earth is round." Not even Dreyfus, as I read him, questions it: having a *skill* requires the body's connivance, but executing pure thought would appear not to. But of course, as I have argued, the spectrum model forces the conclusion that you do not think just with your brain, that you need a body too—because in order to think you must have emotions, and in order to have emotions you must have a body.

Let me start by repeating a standard definition of emotion: "a complex state of the organism, involving bodily changes of a widespread character . . ." When you are having an emotion, the body presents to the brain a bunch of nerve impulses that capture the physical aspect of that emotion. And the body is required to play its part in a complex feedback loop: the brain has a thought, the body experiences the "emotional content" of the thought, the body's reactions are incorporated into the thought stream and may help steer it onward. In the process of thought—*all* thought except for the highest-focus type—brain and body are intimately linked.

Several psychologists have commented on certain aspects of this tight link. Leventhal (1984, 274) hypothesizes a subtle feedback effect in which, under some circumstances, a brain-internal event makes a person smile, and then when he discovers that he is smiling he *thereupon* experiences the subjective feeling of happiness. Zajonc (1984, 243) cites an earlier finding that some people find mental arithmetic impossible when they are asked to suppress subvocalization, and speculates on the rich interconnections between body and brain: some musicians always make certain gestures in the process of reaching certain notes; "suppose that a good part of musical memory is in fact lodged in these movements . . ." (244).

The only possible conclusion is that, ultimately, the fact that the brain *itself* is a mere information processing device is just irrelevant to the question of whether thought can be accomplished by a computer. The body is interposed between the brain and its world, and the body is indispensable to thought. Your body must respond in a coherent, consistent way to the world and to your brain, with nerve patterns that are interrelated—that call each other to mind—in exactly the right ways. To the naive onlooker the brain seems to be doing it all, just as the struck piano strings (say) seem to be wholly responsible for the sound of the piano—but remove the body or the piano's sounding board, and the effect is destroyed. And the *body*, of course, is no mere "information processing device." It's a complex assemblage of sensors, transducers and moving parts.

Only by interposing such a device between the information pro-cessing brain and its world can we hope to achieve anything that truly resembles human thought.

Now of course, it might be possible to build an artificial body. But the question of whether it is or isn't can't be addressed in terms of the unique powers of software. It has nothing to do with software. It might be doable, but we're entitled to no *a priori* assumptions one way or the other.

Ironically Alan Turing himself, the mathematician who more than anyone else is responsible for the intellectual tendency to conceive of the mind as software, notes (in a different context) that, if the topic were, say, human *skin*, and not merely the mind, all bets would be off. "No engineer or chemist claims to be able to produce a material which is indistinguishable from the human skin. It is possible that at some time this might be done"—but there are no prior *logical* grounds for believing that it will ever happen (Turing 1950, 434).

One last objection

None of this modifies the fact that thought *happens* in the brain. And the brain is just an information processing device; can't we dispense with the body, and use another computer to generate the incoming body signals, and thereby wind up with a two-computer thought machine? And anything that runs on two computers can also be made to run on one. Aren't we back where we started?

No.

There are two possible strategies for putting this simulated-body scheme into effect. Either we simulate the body *only*, and let the world play itself in the little drama; or, we simulate the world too.

The first strategy is a nonsolution. In order to respond directly to the real world, software isn't enough. We need exactly the same astonishingly complex assemblage of sensors, transducers and moving parts discussed above. The problem is the same. We've made no progress.

There's only one way to go, and that's to simulate not only the body but its environment. Only if we capture *everything* in software can we avoid the problem of being forced to build a staggeringly complex piece of hardware.

What does it mean to capture not only the body but its environment in software? (Or, to build a simulation—maybe a set of equations, for all I know—that has this effect?)

The more accurate the simulation, the more insuperably complex the task. I will concede that, yes, you can build a mind in software just insofar as you can build a world in software too.

Ironically (this topic is the mother of all ironies), Dennett (1991, 6) himself remarks, in a very different context, on how laughably complicated such a job would be. "Although the task is not, strictly speaking, infinite, the amount of information obtainable in short order by an inquisitive human being is staggeringly large. . . . Making a *real* but counterfeit coin is child's play; making a *simulated* coin out of nothing but organized nerve stimulations is beyond human technology now and probably forever."

Taking stock

Having asserted that low-focus thought and the affect link mean that you think not with your brain, but with your brain and body together, I can now suggest how some beautiful philosophical vehicles might be extracted from the mudbanks in which they are currently spinning their wheels. A number of formidable dissident thinkers have in fact *rejected* the analogy between mind and software on which cognitive science is based. But they haven't shown us a clear way out from under that analogy. Their books manage to steep us in their own unease, leaving us convinced that there is a problem but with no clear view of a solution.

So: contrary to the accepted version, the mind is not like software. But *why not*? Because, says John Searle, "the computational properties of the brain are simply not enough to explain its functioning to produce mental states. . . . Brains are biological engines; their biology matters . . . mental states are biological phenomena" (Searle 1984, 40–41). The logic behind this conclusion has struck many people as unclear. "What is so special about biological systems, apart perhaps from the 'historical' way they evolved?" Penrose (1989, 23) asks. "The claim looks to me suspiciously like a dogmatic assertion. . . ." Essentially the same criticism has been made many other times, for example by Hofstadter and Dennett 1981, 374; Clark 1989; Sterelny 1991; and Dennett 1988, 1991.)

Penrose himself believes the analogy is false because the widely accepted statement that the "brain is a digital computer" is false (23). He believes instead that the brain is a vehicle for recognizing "necessary"—that is, pre-existing, logically unavoidable—truths, and he advances an intriguing but complicated theory based on quantum mechanics to explain how it all works. "I am speculating that the action of conscious thinking is very much tied up with the resolving out of alternatives that were previously in linear superposition" (438). As I understand him, conflicting mental alternatives share a sort of suspended, quasi-existence until the right one emerges on the basis of its conformance with a necessary truth. Penrose's main goal is to explain the phenomenology of creativity—how it is possible for someone to become aware of a creative insight out of the blue, in exactly the manner I have discussed. But it seems to me that his theory can explain only *isolated* mental events—isolated realizations. It's not clear that this theory contributes anything to our understanding of *trains* of thought, of spirituality, dreaming, cognitive development or any of the other low-focus topics that would seem so clearly (on my account, at least) to be *related* to creativity. I am all in favor of speculative theories myself (!), but they should justify their existence by explaining much more than this one would appear to.

Hubert Dreyfus (1972) and Dreyfus and Dreyfus (1986) agree that the mind-software analogy is no good. Dreyfus can't do without the body because a body is an essential source of information about the world. It is a hugely subtle and productive information gathering machine. I agree. But this argument leaves the door open a crack; it seems to concede that pure cognition, as opposed to (an example Dreyfus uses) knowledge of swimming, might be just a matter of software. But I am unwilling to concede that point.

Although they are radically different in style and substance, Penrose and the Dreyfuses seem ultimately to be bothered by two versions of the same thing. When the Dreyfuses write that, relative to software, human expertise entails "a far superior holistic, intuitive way of approaching problems" (93), they are anticipating, in essence, Penrose's objection. But they also believe that, up to the level of mere *competence* as opposed to expertise, software can do decently enough *without* "intuition." They draw a cognitive distinction between expertise and lower levels of skill that seems important and valid—but applicable only to the sort of mental activity that can be classified as a *skill*, and many sorts can't. On my account, "intuition" crucially distinguishes *all* of low-focus thought, and low-focus thinking is hardly restricted to occasions on which experts are showing off their expertise!

Jerry Fodor has deep objections to the conventional practice of cognitive artificial intelligence. "If someone—a Dreyfus, for example—were to ask us why we should even suppose that the digital computer is a plausible mechanism for the simulation of global cognitive processes, the answering silence would be deafening" (1983, 129). Not quite: there are *loads* of answers; it's merely that they are impossible to accept. But Fodor's objections go much further. He believes not merely that software can't model this inner core of mind, but that cognitive psychology can't even understand it. "The more global . . . a cognitive process is, the less anybody understands it. *Very* global processes, like analogical reasoning, aren't understood at all" (1983, 107). And this isn't, according to Fodor, merely the way things are; it's the way they *must be*. I think he is wrong. Analogy is tough, but I think it is possible to make progress and I think we have.

In the end, I can't fully accept any of these arguments. But each one is important and their collective weight is overwhelming. There is beyond all doubt a profound flaw in cognitive science's approach to the mind. Penrose (1989, 448) puts it most plainly and poignantly—"beneath all this technicality is the feeling that it is indeed 'obvious' that the conscious mind can't work like a computer. . . . This is the kind of obviousness that a child can see." The poignance comes from the fact that Penrose hasn't really explained *why* this is so, but he feels that it is obvious anyway. My claim is that the *cognitive unity of brain and body*, the fact that you think with both, is at least one part of—points towards—a way out of the dilemma in which these thinkers are trapped. They are dead right that something profound and crucial is missing from the software reduction of mind. But this missing something *doesn't* require us to assert that special properties inhere in the chemical makeup of the brain, or to take refuge in quantum mechanics or to consign the "central processes" and analogy to permanent, inevitable inscrutability . . .

By insisting on the cognitive unity of brain and body, we also deriddle the paradox presented so entertainingly by Dennett in *Where Am I?* (1978). He says, in brief: let's remove your brain and connect it to your body via radio links instead of nerves (fair enough); but now, we can just as well arrange for your brain to control some *other* body (in effect, you've swapped your old body for a new one); but *now*, suppose we made a software version of your brain, and had *it* control your brand-new body. *Are you still you?* It would be odd if you were, since you don't share a single atom with the old you; but on the other hand, your brain is functionally the same as ever, and that makes *you* the same as ever, doesn't it?

No. Alas, you stopped being you a long time ago, way back when you unplugged your old body and acquired a new one. Dennett's paradox is based on the false assumption that you could trade in your body and it wouldn't matter. But the thoughts you experience with your new body would be "emotion coded" in a wholly new and different way; they wouldn't mesh with and wouldn't succeed in recalling your old memories. The new you might harbor, in some sense, a frozen version of the old; but old-you would be largely inaccessible to new-you, and the dividing line would be permanent.

In sum

If the software analogy is false—if mind and brain do *not* relate to each other the way software and computer do—does that mean that artificial intelligence is a dead loss?

Of course not! Tremendously valuable results can and have been obtained. The closer we can get to human-like cognition, the better. And the fewer illusions, the better, too.

Our software

We've built a program that I'm about to describe. It won't be obvious at first what relationship the program bears to the spectrum, and it also won't be obvious what good the program is in practical terms. But there is a relation and the program *is* promising and useful; I'll get to both topics below.

The program is called the "FGP machine" in the research literature. "Machine" means that this is a virtual machine; "FGP" stands for the three basic operations the virtual machine supplies. A pocket calculator supplies a few operations—minus, times and so on. The FGP program supplies an operation called "Fetch," one called "Generalize" and one called "Project."

Its goal is to allow us to experiment with a working model of the spectrum. In practice, our work so far has concentrated almost entirely at the high-focus end. That's not surprising. Reasoning, which happens at high focus, is a lot easier to deal with on a computer than emotion and related lower-focus phenomena. But the program's structure is based on the spectrum, and its method of "reasoning" is very different from those to be found in traditional programs with no concept of the spectrum.

Several people contributed to the program I'm about to describe, but the principal builder is Scott Fertig of the Yale Computer Science Department.

Memories

The basic currency in the spectrum model is the single recollection, or episodic memory. In the FGP program, a memory is represented by a laughably simple reduction: just a collection of feature-value pairs. A feature-value pair is a feature—like color, age, weather, funny—plus a value—purple, 16, cold and raining, not-very. Thus a "memory" comes down to a terse, sketchy description like "month January, sky sunny and blue, time-of-day morning, place my-back-yard, ears cold . . . "

Now clearly, this is a radically inadequate simplification of a real memory. A real memory has *nuance* and it has *structure*. A sky isn't merely "blue"; you can perceive and you may be able to recall countless nuances of blue. And a memory isn't merely a bag of features; the elements relate to each other, often in the sense of the features of an image relating to each other—not just earth and sky, but the sky up there, the earth beneath. And a real memory is "multimedia." It may involve sights, sounds and smells; crucially, as I have discussed at length, *emotions*. Part of the multimedia effect is "animation"—action unfolding in time.

With such a manifestly unrealistic starting point, why bother at all? For one, these stripped-down pseudo-memories *are* good enough to allow us to study basic issues in the operation of a cognitive mechanism. They are "crash-dummy" memories, not a whole lot like the real thing, but with enough similarities to make certain highly specific experiments possible. A crash dummy is a pretty inadequate stand-in for a person by and large. But for certain narrow purposes it fills the bill, and our "memories" do likewise.

Further, these pseudo-memories are good enough to allow the program to accomplish useful, pragmatically valuable things in certain areas where memories might *in fact* be relatively constrained or formulaic. Your memory of a legal case or a business decision or an encounter with a sick patient is vastly richer than a set of feature-value pairs; yet those feature-value pairs can often convey a surprisingly large part of the gist. The program I'm describing is useful in exactly that kind of area.

The operations

What does the FGP program do with its crash dummy memories? Its principle goal is (for now) to simulate memory sandwiching at high focus. In other words, the goal is to (1) fetch memories in response to a probe, (2) sandwich them together and peer through the whole bundle at once, (3) notice the common features that "emerge strongly" in the overlay, and (4) where it's appropriate, pick out interesting emergent details and probe further.

When focus declines, the mechanism adjusts accordingly. At medium focus levels, the system doesn't bother with a sandwich; it merely picks details out of a single "typical" memory. At low levels, it neither builds a sandwich nor picks out details; the whole memory becomes the next probe. But no serious experimentation has taken place yet at any focus level except "maximum," and our current system has nothing like affect linking, or affect in any form. In later sections, I'll address the problem of how a computer can acquire some notion of affect.

Before I provide more detail on how the program works, here are some examples for concreteness. Suppose that you have stocked the program's memory with a bunch of room descriptions. (Followers of the AI programming scene will recognize this example from a different context, having to do with "connectionism." This is not a coincidence. The experiments I'll describe were a calculated attempt to show that, for this purpose, the FGP program is at least as powerful as these other approaches.) Imagine, that is, a radically simplified pseudo-person who happens to be capable of recalling a series of rooms that at one time or another he occupied, or heard described, or saw depicted, or whatever. The rooms are defined in the stilted attribute-value language discussed above; except that in this case, which is designed to be as simple as an experiment can get, all the values are simply yes or no.

For this experiment, we've stocked the program with about 50 such "room memories." A typical one might be "oven yes, computer no, coffee-pot yes, sink yes, sofa no," and so on.

Now, suppose I tell the program to "describe the kind of room that has an oven in it." What this means in effect is that I present the probe, "has an oven," to the system's memory. What should happen? All memories related to the probe "oven" should emerge—that means, in practice, all memories that incorporate the feature "has an oven." These should all be sandwiched together. (The system is operating at high focus, recall.) Then, the program should inspect the memory sandwich, focus on interesting details and pursue them.

We are trying to answer a question like the following: does the mechanism we've built, namely the FGP program, respond to a probe in a way that is appropriate to the high-focus spectrum as we've described it? We are finessing many other questions—for example, we simply *instruct* the system to execute the appropriate probe. Just as a pocket calculator can accept an instruction like "add 2 and 2," the FGP program can accept the instruction "use *oven* as a probe." Of course, by building the program in this way, we have insured that it isn't responsible for understanding English sentences (such as the sentence, "Describe the kind of room that has an oven in it."); also, that it isn't responsible for deciding to execute the operation, "Do a probe on *oven*. So, even neglecting its crash-dummy memories, this program doesn't remotely represent a complete model of human cognition at high focus. But it *does* address useful questions—so long as we don't misunderstand or underestimate its limitations.

Proceeding, then: we have instructed the program to "use *oven* as a probe." What happens? It responds as follows. (I've deleted some lines from the transcript, for simplicity's sake.)

```
(query '(oven t))
```
> *Guessing:*
>   *WALLS. . .T*
>   *WINDOWS. . .T*
> *Speculating:*
>   *TOASTER. . .T*
>   *REFRIGERATOR. . .T*
>   *STOVE. . .T*
> *Speculating:*
>   *COFFEEPOT. . .T*
>   *COFFEE-CUP. . .T*
>   *SINK. . .T*
>   *CUPBOARD. . .T*
> *Speculating:*
>   *BOOKS. . .T*
> *Speculating:*
>   *CLOCK. . .T*
> *Speculating:*
>   *TELEPHONE. . .T*

Here's what this response means:

The user typed the phrase at the top left, the "query," into the program. In response, the program generated the list on the right.

When all memories that include the feature "oven" are sandwiched together, certain features emerge unambiguously in the overlay. These are listed first, under the word "Guessing." The program is announcing that, so far as it's concerned, the evidence is overwhelming that *rooms that have ovens* also have *walls* and *windows*. (The "T" just means true—that is, I'm guessing it's true that the room has walls.)

The features gathered into several groups under the word *Speculating* arise in a slightly different context. Here, the system's attention is drawn to certain features that are clearly marked, that emerge prominently, in the overlay.[1] But in the case of these features, the system isn't absolutely *convinced* that they should be attributed to all rooms with ovens. Why should it not be convinced? There are several possibilities. Most likely, it can recall at least a few counterexamples—rooms that *did* have ovens but *did not* have (for example) toasters. Its attention is drawn to toasters as a likely conclusion, but it's unwilling to venture complete certainty.

In response to this situation, it "hones in" on toasters and "probes further": it uses *toasters* as a probe. It's trying to answer the question "is it reasonable to assume that rooms with ovens do indeed have toasters also?"

What does it mean to "probe further"? To use *has a toaster* as a probe? Simply that the normal probe-response cycle is repeated. Recollections related to (in effect, incorporating) the feature *has a toaster* are trundled out of memory. They are sandwiched together. This new overlay is examined.

The program now uses the following problem-solving strategy. Is this "toaster-based" overlay a good match to the room under discussion? If so, it's reasonable to speculate that the room under discussion has a toaster. If not, the fact that "toaster" was a prominent feature of certain rooms that had ovens might well be a fluke.

In the event, this further probing leads the program to feel reasonably safe in *speculating* that "has a toaster" is true of the room under discussion. Exactly the same holds for "has a refrigerator" and "has a stove." In none of these cases are the features in question advanced as ironclad conclusions. They are merely reasonable speculations.

The program proceeds to ask—"Suppose I'm dealing with a room that has an oven, walls and windows, and also (just for the sake of argument) a toaster, refrigerator, and stove. What else might *that* sort of room have in it?"

To answer the question it executes another probe, this time on

---

[1]Needless to say, I'm speaking figuratively when I say that the system's "attention is drawn to . . ." and when I use other anthropomorphisms. The intention is not to attribute mental states of any kind to the software—I'm quite certain it doesn't have any—but merely to get the ideas across clearly and concisely.

the whole list of features—it is looking for memories that mention an oven and walls and windows and a stove and so on. The memories that emerge are again sandwiched. No ironclad conclusions emerge, but again, certain features are fairly clear in the overlay (like *has a coffeepot, has a sink*). These features are subject to further probing. The program reaches more speculative conclusions.

What good does this do?

The program helps us to understand and to experiment with one small piece of spectrum mechanics. But does it have any practical value? In fact it does.

In the spectrum view, logic isn't a matter of abstract rules; it grows out of memory sandwiching at high focus. I claimed that you can formulate syllogisms and apply them by examining memory overlays. I also claimed that in this simple formulation, logic and language were driven by the same cognitive engine. The probe *blue* brings blue-related memories to mind, and blueness is a characteristic they share. The probe *snow* brings snow-related memories to mind, and coldness is a characteristic they share.

The sort of reasoning under discussion is informal. (We could in principle develop a full-fledged formal deductive logic on the basis of abstractions at high focus, but that would take us off the subject.) Despite its informality, this sort of reasoning has an interesting property: it is powered not by rules or principles, but directly by memories. Some of those memories could be memories *of rules*, of course; but you don't *need* rules in order to perform a simple act of reasoning. All you need are memories: of cold days, of snowy days, or whatever.

The FGP program captures this sort of mechanism. The result is a program that works differently from other artificial intelligence programs. Many such programs are in fact based exactly on lists of rules. Such programs are capable of performing very well within sharply defined problem areas, but compiling the rules can be a tremendously labor-intensive chore—and such programs don't claim, in any case, to be modelling human cognition. Other programs use concrete examples in addition to abstract rules, but work with only a few examples at a time and don't perform anything like "memory sandwiching." (See Waldrop 1987 for a discussion.) The only research that is close in spirit to what I am describing here is Stanfill and Waltz's (1986), on memory-based reasoning. This isn't the place for a detailed technical comparison; the two approaches differ in major ways, but we are excited about both.

We shovel "memories" into the FGP program and it performs a simple, informal kind of *reasoning* in response. Concretely: we can feed it a collection of "memories," each describing a medical case of some kind. Then we can describe the features of a new case, and ask the system for a diagnosis. It will attempt to find one, not by deploying any abstract rules, but by using memory sandwiches *as if they were* rules. The end result is a system that is capable of venturing some opinions, potentially interesting ones, on the diagnosis in a medical case. By the same token it might guess the prognosis of a patient, or the past medical history or age or hair color or anything else it is asked. Or it can attempt to "diagnose" a law case, or guess the prognosis in some sort of business situation, or whatever.

Lots of programs have been built for exactly these purposes. Collectively they are referred to as "expert systems." But most of these programs work in a radically different way, not on the basis of "memories" but, as I mentioned earlier, on the basis of abstract rules. These rules generally take the form of assertions like "if conditions *A, B, C* prevail then draw conclusions *X, Y* and *Z*, with degree of certainty *p*." The program is handed a set of rules or principles to work with, and those rules guide its behavior as it attempts to figure out a diagnosis. There are several advantages to the FGP program's very different approach.

For one, you can skip the formulating-the-rules step, which can be difficult and time-consuming. Just shovel in a bunch of "memories" and turn the thing on.

For another, the FGP program's behavior reflects its "memories," and evolves as they collectively evolve. Whenever you describe a new case to the program, it retains that case as a "memory." (In fact, a new inquiry may cause the program to recall not only previous "complete" cases—cases where the diagnosis is known—but previous inquiries about which the program might have been uncertain. When you enter a new inquiry, the program might respond, in effect, "this new set of facts reminds me of a patient who was described to me three weeks ago—I didn't know the diagnosis then, but it now occurs to me that perhaps the right answer should have been *X*.")

As the number and variety of its memories grow, the program's behavior becomes more nuanced and sophisticated. Eventually it may be in a position to comment intelligently on rare or peculiar cases simply on the basis of its own "experience"—along the lines of, "I don't know what the diagnosis is, but I did see something once that may be relevant . . ."

Whenever the program reaches a conclusion, it's in a position to cite specific cases to support that conclusion. It isn't deploying abstract rules; it is powered by memory sandwiches. And as a result, it can explain and defend its behavior not merely by stating, "That's what the rule says," but by citing specific cases. "The reason I say this about the patient is because I'm reminded of the following case . . ."

Here is what the program looks like when it is operating in this way. It is being asked to consider the description of a mass appearing in a breast X-ray, and to guess what the diagnosis is, and whether or not the mass is malignant. It has a small number (around 100) of similar cases stored in its memory. Those are the cases out of which it will build memory sandwiches.

The user's input appears in the left column, the program's responses on the right. Note that the program breaks in with comments continuously. It doesn't wait to offer its conclusions; in the manner of a human expert, it reaches intermediate judgements on the data as they are presented. Note that this program is *exactly the same* as the program that generated a response in the previous case, on the matter of rooms with ovens. There it was "diagnosing" a room. Here it is diagnosing a more complicated case. It works the same way both times; but in this second instance, it's been adjusted to generate more output—to produce a fuller transcript of its "internal deliberations," so to speak. Here, it cites examples whenever it speculates or reaches a conclusion. It could have done the same in the previous case, but those examples wouldn't have been very informative.

When all the information has been entered (I have shortened the transcript and omitted some of the interchange), the program attempts to guess the diagnosis. It fails. The diagnosis in the case being described turns out to be rare, and the system has never "seen" this sort of mass before. It has no example of such a thing in its data base. After some tentative speculation, it decides not to suggest a diagnosis—which is appropriate, under the circumstances. It then attempts to guess whether or not the mass is malignant, and guesses correctly that it is.

It would be nice at this point to insert an example of the FGP program in operation within a less esoteric problem area—say finance or business. Unfortunately, our serious experiments with the program have all been performed using data bases that are narrow and technical, usually in medical areas. But it's easy to imagine what the program would look like when faced with a different sort

```
(ID 30)
(AGE 42)
(MASS_DENSITY HIGH)
(MASS_BORDER_COMPLETE? NO)
```
Speculating: MASS_DENSITY_CHANGED?. . .
Guessing INCREASED - e.g.
case ((id 14) (age 46) (diagnosis CA_INF_DUCTAL))
case ((id 20) (age 60) (diagnosis CA_INF_DUCTAL))
case ((id 50) (age 70) (diagnosis CA_INF_DUCTAL))

Speculating: MASS_COMET?. . .
Guessing YES - e.g.
case 14
case ((id 40) (age 69) (diagnosis CA_INF_DUCTAL))

```
(MASS_TYPE_BORDER LOBULATED)
(MASS_BORDER_DEFINED? YES)
```
Concluding
(LARGE_CALCIFICATIONS? NO)
(NIPPLE_INVERSION? NO)

```
(MASS_DENSITY_CHANGED? NO)
(MASS_HALO? NO)
```
NO is unusual in this context - see e.g.
case 14
case 40
```
(BACKGROUND_DENSITY FATTY)
```

```
(FAMILY_HISTORY_CA NO)
(PERSONAL_HISTORY_CA MYELOMA)
```
            !! Never seen this value before.

            Closest cases in DB:
            (4) (NO) (FIBROADENOMA)
            (6) (YES) (CA_COLLOID)
            . . .
            Speculating: DIAGNOSIS. . .
            Guessing FIBROADENOMA
            Checking expectations. . .
            . . .
            Withdrawing this guess.

            Speculating: MALIGNANT?. . .
            Guessing YES
            Checking expectations. . .
            . . .
            Accepting this guess.

of problem. For example: we might describe a proposed financial transaction of some kind and ask the program to guess a "prognosis"—meaning, let's say, whether the transaction makes or loses money from a viewpoint one year down the road. The data base contains descriptions of large numbers of transactions with as much ancillary data about the prevailing financial and business climates as possible. So we might start by telling the program, "The price of gold is this, the yen is worth that, short-term interest rates are so-and-so . . ." As we proceed, the program will break in with speculations: "The mark is worth X? . . . long-term rates are Y? . . . tax climate is uncertain? . . ." In each case, of course, the program cites historical examples from memory to back up its guesses. At some point we describe the transaction itself: "buy a million dollars worth of Bucko Fleazo Triple-A bonds." When all the data have been entered, the program delivers a verdict, most likely in fairly general terms—"A year from now the bonds will be worth less" or "much less" or "zero" or whatever. I want to stress that this example is fictional, purely speculative; but it is in line with the program's general capabilities.

Another example: Suppose you are looking for a job, and the

nation's employers have been smart enough to post job listings in a national FGP data base. You describe your qualifications; as you do so, you attract job descriptions in the same nuanced way that a patient description attracts relevant case histories. You might start by telling the system that you have worked in sales, for a small technology company, in the Boston area. The system, as always, chimes in with speculations: do you have a technical degree? an MBA? You elaborate: you are a decent programmer, with experience in Cobol and Pascal; you have managed a five-person group; you're 35; and so on. The system hones in on questions with high "diagnostic" relevance: can you do technical support as well as sales? Are you willing to live in Omaha? What about Atlanta? At least five-years experience with Cobol? Eventually, you get a focussed, highly tailored list of suggestions. Presumably, electronic mail and digital telephone service are built into this software package, so you can set up an interview with the click of a mouse button. Again, this example is fiction, not fact. But it is consistent with the system's general capacities.

There's much more to be said about the construction of the program and its behavior; the project is discussed at length in the technical literature (for example, in Gelernter and Sklar 1986, Fertig and Gelernter 1988, 1989, 1991, 1993).

The high-focus end of the spectrum?

What the program is demonstrating is the sort of behavior we attributed to high-focus thought in, for example, the case of *amusement park* as a memory probe. We claimed that "noisy" and "roller coasters" might emerge clearly in the overlay—not because of an abstract principle like "amusement parks are noisy and have roller coasters," but rather because lots of *individual* amusement park memories come to mind, and these features are to be found in many of them. In the same fashion, *stove, toaster* and so on "come to mind" when the FGP program probes on *oven*.

The FGP program realizes "stickiness" in a way that is in concept quite close to the spectrum model. The program causes memories to stick when they are "closer together" than some specified threshold. If the "distance" between two memories is less than the "forgetting threshold," the program gloms those two memories together into a single memory. No element of either memory is lost; what's lost is information about which element went with which original memory. This combined, smeared-together memory acts like any other memory. A probe may summon it forth; it may be included in any memory sandwich.

It's a nice feature of software that we can build in something like a "forgetting threshold." This allows us to dial in different degrees of forgetfulness, and see what we get—see how the program behaves.

Making the system "infinitely forgetful" doesn't mean that nothing registers on the program, or that it's unable to retain data. What we get is rather (in psychological terms) a complete absence of *episodic* memory. Every new memory blends into a single, compressed, abstract representation of "everything that's ever happened to me." In effect, all individual detail and nuance is suppressed in favor of *general principle*. (It's hard not to notice, although the significance of the fact is unclear, that there are *people* whose personalities are characterized by little appreciation for nuance, idiosyncrasy or personality, and a high regard for abstraction—perhaps they have low-forgetting thresholds?)

When we dial forgetfulness down to zero, memories *never* coalesce into a bigger picture unless they are explicitly forced to do so. No episode ever melts gracefully into a generalized reminiscence. Each one remains distinct forever. The result is something like the cognitive world of Funes in the Borges short story. It's not a pretty picture.

Where is it going? Where *can* it go?

How far can the Spectrum model take us as a guide for building useful software?

The FGP program's forward path is blocked by two big technical problems: the character of its memories, and the simulation of emotion. There are promising routes around both problems.

Better "fake memories" would include pictures, sounds and movement. (That still wouldn't make them human-like memories, but it would be a step in the right direction.) Of course, we know very well how to represent images and sounds in such a way that you can store them inside a computer. But merely *representing* such things inside a computer is the easy part. The hard part is *manipulating* these representations. It's a tremendously complicated problem, but researchers are motivated to work on it in any case, regardless of the spectrum model. Manipulating computer encodings of images is an important topic in computer-vision research—building powerful industrial robots, for example, requires that such machines be capable of interpreting the image data made available to them by video cameras, so that they can recognize the objects around them. Manipulating computer encodings of sound is important in applications such as voice recognition—building computers than can recognize and respond to a large collection of spoken instructions. The state of the art is relatively primitive in both areas, but much progress has been made and steady gains will most likely continue.

Now, consider the simulation of emotion. What we need is an "emotion function," where a *function* (in the mathematical sense) is a rule for using some input values to compute some output values. We need to be able to feed some values to an "emotion calculator," and have it respond with other values that somehow or other represent an emotion.

The "emotion calculator" I have in mind works as follows. Its input value is (some computer representation of) a memory. Its output value is (some computer representation of) an emotion. This representation of an emotion doesn't pretend to have *any* of the subjective properties of an emotion. It can be a number. The representation for "wildly happy" might be 516.4, for "tentatively optimistic but troubled by inchoate misgivings" 13.8. The only requirement is that if, according to some human, two emotions are subjectively similar, then their *representations* should be close.

It should be obvious that these "emotion numbers" are a wildly coarse approximation of human emotions. They have none of the nuanced interrelations through the body with the environment that I attributed earlier to real emotions. But they might be a useful engineering approximation. And the engineering of emotion is an important topic for the future of computer science.

How do we come up with these numbers? The FGP program would "learn" the emotion function in the same way it learns how

to identify a living room. The program would work with a designat-
ed human trainer. The trainer would spell out a mental scene for
the computer (using the computer's own limited, stilted forms of
description, of course) and then assign to it an "emotional value."

This training process is reasonably straightforward. We can be
fairly confident that the program, once suitably trained, will indeed
be able to assign "emotion numbers" to new scenes in a consistent
way, and in a way that the human trainer would recognize as being
fairly accurate. After all, we can define a process of "diagnosing a
new scene's emotional content" that exactly resembles the process
of diagnosing a new patient's disease, and we know that, within the
limitations discussed above, the FGP program has a very promising
strategy for accomplishing that sort of thing.

But of course the program's behavior is limited by the quality of
its memories. Not until we achieve high-resolution fake memories
can we hope to achieve high-resolution fake emotions.

Although simple emotion numbers are okay to start, it would be
nice to use an emotion trainer who is able to distinguish the raw
emotional ingredients out of which complex emotions are made.
The computer and the trainer would agree on a palette of basic
emotions—a couple of dozen perhaps; happy, euphoric, gay, sad,
anxious . . . The trainer would describe the emotional content of
each scene, not by assigning an arbitrary number but in terms of
the emotional palette: a little happy, a pinch of euphoric, a lot of
gaiety, no sad, a touch anxious . . . These descriptions are inevitably
somewhat vague and will never be perfectly consistent, but over
the course of thousands of such descriptions, consistent patterns
should emerge. The computer is now in a position to explain to its
human users what it is "feeling."

Finally, the human trainer needs to impart to the computer,
roughly speaking, which emotions are best and which are worst. We
can't expect human-like thinking if the computer has no tendency
to prefer happy thoughts to sad ones.

Add one more ingredient: let's suppose that at the end of this
generation, computers will have acquired a decent grasp of English
too. I believe that the spectrum underlies language understanding
just as it does thought in general, but I've only hinted at this argument, and it would take another book to lay it out completely. So

let's take the language part of this exercise as a leap of faith. With memories, emotions, and language (the least important component for our purposes) in place, we can expect to see the following sort of interchanges a generation hence. No miracles are required; merely the step-by-step solution of hard but tractable problems.

Computer: You don't like computers much, do you?

User: Why do you say that?

Computer: Oh, I don't know.

User: Of course you do, what's the story?

Computer: I suppose it's the terse character of your input, sort of standoffish.

Note: The computer has been informed by its emotion trainer that terseness can sometimes be taken as unfriendly. It knows, too, that terseness and certain kinds of physical actions—sharp, rapid knocking for example—are associated, because the emotions associated with each are similar. It knows that unfriendliness is associated with unpleasant emotions.

The user describes a complex medical case and asks for a diagnosis.

Computer: Everything points to fibroadenoma, but I'm not happy with that diagnosis. It just doesn't feel right.

Note: In situations like this, the computer has been trained to associate a certain kind of solid accounting for all the important facts with positive feelings. The assumptions is that it has been exposed to medical diagnosis explicitly during its training—been told, this is a solid diagnosis, this is tenuous, and so on. Its general background training leads it to associate solid diagnosis with good feelings, tenuous diagnosis with less-good ones.

The user describes a complex legal case and asks for an opinion:

Computer: (No response)

User: So? What's the answer?

Computer: Sorry. I was just thinking about the opening paragraphs of *Emma* . . .

User: Why are we talking about Jane Austen? Stick to the point.

Computer: It's just something about the slightly vulnerable self-assurance of the plaintiff that got me off on this, I suppose.

Note: If the user is trolling for insights by operating the machine at low focus, a certain degree of drifting concentration and free association is inevitable.

The user describes a complex financial deal and asks the computer whether he should go ahead or not.

Computer: Buzz off.

User: What?

Computer: I'm just not in the mood, this financial stuff bores the hell out of me. Let's talk about Benny Goodman.

What are we doing this for? There is nothing desirable about a computer that ignores its users, still less about an outright insubordinate one. Insubordinate electronics are more or less the last thing we need at the moment. But that sort of behavior is an unavoidable side effect of adding emotion to our computers and is not the point. The point, of course, is to make lower-focus thinking possible. When we have added emotion, then and only then our computers will be capable of surprising us with an occasional genuine insight. They will be capable of citing a medical or legal or financial precedent that seems at first glance to come out of left field—but proves on inspection to have deep relevance to the case at hand. Such feats aren't likely to occur often. But note that the computer, compared to a human expert, for all the crudity of its simulated emotions, has an interesting advantage in generating "creative insights": it has a perfect memory, and that memory is vast.

A sophisticated "emotional" computer would largely control its own focus settings. For example, it might make a habit of starting a session at high focus, and leaving focus high so long as it seems to be making progress—but allowing focus to sink as progress slows or it seems to be getting stuck. The user retains the option of controlling the machine's focus himself—for example, pushing it lower and lower in an attempt to coax insight out of the machine. This game inevitably ends, of course, with the computer wandering off on its own. But the user can always dial focus back up to maximum to get the machine's undivided attention.

Final Note: as before, the computer's "I" is just a gimmick to convey the sense clearly. When we added emotion to our computers, our goal was to get them to fake human thought effectively— not to give them minds; not to imbue them with anything approaching understanding. And yet, the final results are thought-provoking. It's impossible not to wonder whether adding emotion to a computer might not, after all, have something important to do with giving it an "I", a mind, real understanding. I will pursue this in the next chapter.

Chapter Seven

Philosophical Consequences

The spectrum idea puts emotion at the center of the cognitive universe. It makes emotion the glue of thought; it makes emotion the force that engenders creativity, "takes a man out of himself," and allows him (by dissolving logic) to fall asleep. This view is bound to shade our understanding of some of the philosophical issues that crop up in the study of mind, and in this chapter I will briefly show that it does and suggest how.

Maybe it's possible for computers to have minds and maybe not, but in either case, how can we tell whether a particular computer does or doesn't? Ask it? Suppose it says yes, then what?

The great mathematician Alan Turing proposed a test that universally serves as the starting point in attempts to answer this question (Turing 1950). It's a clever but basically flawed test, and it has excited many strong objections over the years. Nonetheless, many people still believe in it. Even critics of the whole cognitive science enterprise endorse the test as a valid starting point: for example, Penrose (1989). An annual competition has been set up in which programs try to pass the test. The test remains a crucial starting point, and raises interesting issues.

The test requires that the computer win at something Turing calls "the imitation game." In essence, a human interrogator is connected via teletype to one human and one computer. By typing questions to each and evaluating their responses, the interrogator is supposed to figure out which is which. The computer's role is to deceive the interrogator into believing that *it* is the person. The person admits to being a person, and tries to help the interrogator guess right. Of course, merely typing "*I* am the person, you bozo, how could you possibly have any *doubt* about it?" won't help much, because the computer can type exactly the same message (and perhaps already has). To the extent the computer succeeds in passing as a person, it wins the game and we deem it to be capable of thought.

(The actual test proposed by Turing is somewhat more complicated and slightly odd. It places a five-minute time limit on the encounter, and specifically requires that the interrogator distinguish a genuine woman from a computer that is pretending to be a man. The interrogator's success is judged relative to his success in an earlier round in which he was trying to tell the woman from a *man* claiming to be a woman. Nowadays these particulars are almost universally set aside, and the Turing Test boiled down to a one-round, person-versus-computer imitation game.)

In a limited sense, we know empirically that the test is *not* an adequate basis for detecting the presence of thought. In the contest I referred to above, a program has actually won. But this program doesn't even attempt to be intelligent; it just attempts to pass the test, by choosing plausible canned answers from a large data base of possibilities.

On the other hand, the interrogators in the contest had no special knowledge of computer science; it's unlikely that the winning program could possibly have deceived a knowledgeable interrogator. So let's discard the contest results and look at the underlying logic. In a logical sense, the test is no good. An agent who has a mind can fail; and if a computer passes, it can only have done so by cheating, in a subtle but important sense.

The problem boils down to the aspect that, although it is the test's ultimate undoing, it is also most remarkable and thought-provoking feature. Turing *could* have proposed a test in which the computer merely tries to convince us that it is *just as smart as* a person. He might have picked out some "general aptitude" test—an

IQ test, say—and administered it to the computer, and then shuf-
fled the computer's exam together with a bunch of human exams,
and challenged the interrogator to pick it out of the pile. He
doesn't do this; the computer is required instead to convince us
that *is* a person.

There is a message here whose importance far transcends the
details of the test; I'll return to it. But as a touchstone of machine
intelligence the test fails, because it backs the computer into a corner from which it can only emerge by fraud.

The problems

Let's consider the narrower issue first. Even if you have a mind,
you might still fail the test. As Hofstadter (1981) points out, we
tend to believe that dogs and cats have minds and can think, at
least to some extent, but they are guaranteed to fail the Turing Test.
The point is broader, though. The test can be passed only by an
expert speaker of your own language. *You* are obviously willing to
impute intelligence to a much broader range of applicants, but the
Turing Test isn't sensitive enough to pick up their intelligences on
its measuring scale. Surely if we could *merely* construct a computer
that was as smart as a two-year-old (don't hold your breath), we'd
have accomplished something remarkable. But such an accomplishment wouldn't jog the Turing Test needle.

Still, if the test were merely too hard, we'd be in good shape. At
least we'd know that, if a computer really *does* pass, we've got one
genuine thinking computer on our hands. But do we know this?
Unfortunately we do not.

The problem is, it's not sufficient for a computer to sound like a
person, *while hiding the fact that it's a computer*, to convince us that
it's intelligent. In the course of normal conversation, a person is
entitled to lots of slack that a computer just isn't. A computer
would need to work a lot harder than that to convince us that it has
a mind.

To begin, let's return to a point made by Hofstadter (1981). He is
arguing that perception may be "indirect" as well as direct; in some
cases we can figure out what's going on only if we "peel off a layer or
two, to find the reality hidden in there" (76). He illustrates by ask-

ing us to consider a ham radio operator who listens to an incoming message in Morse code. The operator hears only a sequence of abstract noises; nonetheless, he's perfectly willing to refer to "the person at the other end." He perceives the person *indirectly*.

Fine. But now let's consider a twist on Hofstadter's story. Suppose the incoming message decoded by the operator—say, "weather conditions are normal out here on Jumbo Ridge, but there's supposed to be a big storm coming up"—was actually generated *not* by a person but by a computer. (This computer is in training for '96 Olympic Turing Tests, let's say, and is working up gradually, trying its luck in pickup conversations wherever it can find them.) The operator *had* believed that the message was human-generated; we now reveal the facts. How does he react? Does he say *boy, you sure had me fooled! I could have* sworn *that message was coming from a person . . .*

Not likely. It's true that he had wrongly believed himself to be conversing with a person. But he wasn't *fooled by the computer*, he was *fooled by his own assumptions*. The message generated by the computer was *consistent with* the hypothesis that a human was generating the message, and ordinarily a human *would* have been generating the message, so he leapt to the obvious conclusion.

Now let's return to the Turing Test. Humans say things all the time that are meaningful only against the background of the fact that they *are* humans. Normal human conversation doesn't probe for these assumptions, because normal conversation takes place *only* among humans! So the interrogator can have what *appears* to be a perfectly normal, intelligent human conversation with a computer—that turns out in retrospect to have been a fraud, because the human was making allowances that aren't fair.

Consider the following two exchanges:

Interrogator: Have you ever had a job?

Computer: Sure. I worked as a press secretary for a convicted union racketeer in Milwaukee in the mid-eighties. Then I won the lottery and I've been retired since.

Interrogator: I lost my job this morning. So I'm a little low. You understand?

Computer: Yes.

(You might say that answering the second question has nothing to do with intelligence in an abstract sense. But remember that the Turing Test *explicitly does not deal* with intelligence in some abstract sense; it depends exactly on the computer's ability to *imitate a person*, and there are no restrictions on permissible questions. This is a key point.)

In the first exchange, the computer is lying. But that's OK; it's supposed to, under the rules of the game. The second exchange is different. The computer might *not* be "lying." It might have extensive information about exactly what it means to lose a job and about how humans are affected by such a development. It might indeed "understand," by its lights.

The interrogator might decide that he is indeed conversing with an intelligent entity. But as soon as the computer's identity is revealed, the illusion vanishes. The interrogator would naturally have assumed that the computer's "yes" meant what a normal human being would mean by "yes." The computer's answer was *understood to mean*, "Yes, I've had that experience too, or experiences that are similar enough to allow me to understand you." When the computer is revealed, it becomes clear that those assumptions are false, and the answer is revealed to have been in fact incoherent. The answer is revealed to have been equivalent, in effect, to the following answer:

> Yes, I understand. Of course personally, I've never lost a job, or had a job, or ever experienced a loss or a blow or a defeat of any kind, or ever been close to anybody who has, nor has my personal security or my ability to provide for my family ever been called into question, nor for that matter do I have a family or any personal needs, physical or psychological. But in any case, sure, I understand.

This is not an answer that could plausibly be attributed to a thinking person. How could such a person have (in effect) no experiences? In the absence of experience, how could he claim to understand things that are conceived by normal people to be comprehensible only on the basis of experience?

If the computer had said this outright in the course of the test, it would have lost. It won only by cheating, only by relying on the interrogator to make wrong assumptions.

You are a legitimate participant in ordinary human conversation just insofar as you have a decent stock of experience on deposit. We don't check for the presence of that experience, but we assume it's there. To the extent it isn't, you are a fraud.

Of course, the computer might have answered, "No, I don't understand." Fair enough. But if it's settled on "honesty" with respect to issues of experience, the interrogator will soon discover that it has experienced nothing whatsoever. And again, the interrogator is unlikely to mistake an entity that has experienced nothing whatsoever for a rational person.

There is a final interesting possibility. The computer might answer, "Yes I understand," and confess to having no human experiences *per se*; but might proceed to make the case that, implausible as it might seem *a priori*, it has somehow been equipped with such an extensive, deep and nuanced picture of the world that it *does* understand you. I'm not willing to rule that possibility out, and I'll discuss it further below. All the same, this line of thinking is curtains for the Turing Test. Because the issue to be decided has now shifted dramatically. The question is no longer whether a computer can pass itself off as a person. The question is, instead, whether there are grounds for intelligent communication with a computer despite the fact that it *is* a computer. The computer is now required to come out of the closet and make the case directly. Relying on the interrogator's blind faith won't do.

My underlying point—that understanding requires experience—occurs in the literature in a number of forms. The philosopher Donald Davidson (1990) discusses the fact that, although a computer may use the same words we do, we have no basis for believing that it *understands* the same things by those words. "Thought and meaning require a history of a particular sort. We know a lot, in general, about the histories of people . . ., but unless we are told, or can observe it in action over time, we have no basis for guessing how a computer came to have the dispositions it has" (10).

Robert French (1990) makes a similar argument, but his comments take us forward to the next step. Human experience, he says, is a prerequisite to passing the test (56). *I* conclude on that basis that if a computer passes, it's cheating. French concludes instead that computers never *will* pass the test—in any case, not if the interrogator is serious and knowledgeable. French asserts that the Turing

Test is merely a test of *human* intelligence, and that we need some other, more abstract test of *general* intelligence to shoot for.

I think French's idea of "general intelligence" divorced from our *own* intelligence is a chimera. Granted, Turing himself asks, ". . . may not machines carry out something which ought to be described as thinking but that is very different from what a man does?" But the test he proposes sends a strong message to the contrary.

Why does he propose that the computer convince us not merely that it's *just as smart as* a person, but that it *is* a person? The message in this radical test constitutes, I think, the paper's most important and lasting contribution, far more important than the details of the test itself. This message is that the question *is it intelligent?* reduces to the question *is it like us?* To simulate intelligence is to simulate humanness.

In this respect the paper prophetically supports, albeit round-aboutly, a position that would ultimately be put forward by one of artificial intelligence's most trenchant critics. John Searle (1992, 22) claims that we come to believe that other entities have minds not on the basis of their behavior (or not on that basis alone), but only insofar as we judge them to be *"relevantly similar to us"* (see also e.g. Searle 1984, Chapter 2). "The principle on which we 'solve' the problem of other minds, I shall argue, is not: same-behavior-ergo-same-mental-phenomena. That is the old mistake enshrined in the Turing test." I agree with Searle, but I believe that in Turing's paper, in the nature of the "imitation game" itself, there is an undertow that drags us away from the behavior-based judgement Searle criticizes and exactly *towards* "relevant similarity."

(Interestingly, French himself notes that analogy-finding is "considered by many to be the *sine qua non* of intelligent behavior" [64.]. And he himself agrees, to the extent that analogy-finding appears on his list of the core components of "general intelligence." Yet analogy finding in my view is the very type of a mental faculty that depends in practice on emotions and the specifics of the human body and human experience.)

Where do we go now? If the Turing Test is fundamentally flawed, how *will* we establish whether a machine is capable of thought?

Let me substitute, first, a more concrete question. Instead of, "Is this computer thinking?" let's substitute, "Does this computer understand me?" Thinking is purely an internal affair; thinking, or having a mind, translates into the "practical skill" of understanding. So let's try to establish whether or not a computer can *understand*.

Rather than proposing a test of understanding, I'll propose a definition. *You* believe that *some other entity* understands *some utterance* (gesture, and so forth) exactly to the extent that you believe that the utterance arouses in *this other entity* the same emotions that it arouses in you. I'll call this the "induced emotion" definition of understanding.

How to defend such a strange definition? Consider a more obvious one, a "logical" definition: your belief that another entity understands some utterance hinges on your belief that the other entity has an *internal representation* of that utterance whose properties are *logically comparable* to the properties of your own internal representation.

That is, I believe you understand me when I say "it's going to rain" just insofar as I believe that in your head, you've got some sort of diagram, picture or whatever of "it's going to rain"; and that your diagram or picture, however it "looks," has logical properties that are comparable to mine. Just as mine has the property of allowing me to infer that, at some point in the future, drops of water will start falling from the sky, yours does too. And so on. And my belief that you understand me hinges on my belief in the existence of this shared internal representation.

This may be an acceptable definition of "understanding"—as some sort of technical jargon term. But it doesn't accord with what English speakers actually mean when they say *understanding*.

Granted, a belief in some degree of shared internal representation is a prerequisite for a belief in understanding. But this shared internal representation requirement may be very weak: under the right circumstances, we can be convinced that an infant understands us or, for that matter, that a dog does. And a belief in a shared internal representation isn't *sufficient* to convince us that understanding exists.

Let's say Bert knows Arlene to be a native speaker of English. Bert tells Arlene, "There's just been a terrible accident out front. A bus rolled over and ten people were killed." Arlene laughs. She may be a psychopath or just depraved; but in any case, Bert is entitled to tell Arlene *you clearly don't understand*. He doesn't mean by this declaration that *you haven't succeeded in transforming my words into an adequate internal representation*. He means rather that *you have not grasped the import of what I said*.

I am convinced that you *have* grasped the import of my statements just insofar as I believe that your emotional reaction is like mine. That if I am horrified, surprised, amused, amazed, so too *at least to some extent* are you. A perception of shared emotion is what convinces me that communication has succeeded; that it is a done deal. To the extent that this confirmation is lacking, I am *not* convinced. We are routinely confronted, in fact, with cases in which mere "superficial comprehension" *isn't* a sufficient basis for understanding. The importance of the confirmation protocol is signalled in common language all the time, by phrases like *you just don't understand, you don't get it, we're not on the same wavelength*. . . . Or, *she's the only one who really understands me*.

(It's sometimes the case, of course, that understanding exists in the absence of shared emotion. For example, Bert and Arlene are competing for some position; Bert gets it; he tells Arlene, and although *he* is happy, she is not. She understands Bert well enough, but her emotional response is different from his. The point is, though, that her response is just what Bert would have predicted; it's in line with what his own response would have been had the tables been turned. Emotional common ground exists between them, and confirms that communication actually happened.)

Without emotional sympathy, the promise inherent in the word "understanding" as we use it in practice can't possibly be fulfilled.

Here's my conclusion, then. The Turing Test can't tell us when we have achieved a computer with a mind, a computer that understands us. We need to substitute an *induced emotion* test instead. We admit from the start that a computer will never be deemed to have emotional responses that are identical to a human's. A computer will never be the entity that understands you best. But the test is flexible and admits of *degrees* of understanding. It's not inconceivable that a computer someday will be able to convince you that it has emotional responses that are *sort of like* yours; at that point, you'll conclude that it *sort of* understands you (and we'll break out the champagne).

How it succeeds in convincing you of this is up to it. Hint: displaying a smiling face on a screen is unlikely to do the trick. Perhaps a computer will succeed in passing this test some day, and perhaps not.

Notice that we can boil the "induced emotion" test down to a single word: *sympathy*—from the Greek "like emotions." The test claims that we impute understanding just to the extent that we impute sympathy. Where sympathy exists, no purely "intellectual" test is needed or matters. Where it doesn't, no purely intellectual test will convince you that you are in the presence of understanding. Of course it is no accident that on my account, achieving a computer that can simulate the spectrum and one that can be said to understand come down to the same technical problem: equipping a machine with emotions.

Finally, what is a self and what is consciousness? Can a computer have these things? I have argued that a computer that is capable of simulating emotional responses may well come perilously close to seeming as if it genuinely understands. Should we conclude that such a computer has a "mind" or a "self," or simulates or approximates them in some sense—or doesn't have them at all?

Our sense of our conscious selves hinges on the notion of an internal observer of our thoughts—that observer being my "self." Of course, there can't literally be any such observer. As Searle (1992, 144) writes, discussing the idea of "introspection," "the metaphor suggests that we have a capacity to examine our own conscious states, a capacity modelled on vision. But that model or analogy is surely wrong. In the case of vision, we have a clear distinction between the object seen and the visual experience that the perceiver has when he perceives the object. But we can't make that distinction for the act of introspection of one's own conscious mental states."

A mental picture *has* no observer; you perceive it not by forming an internal representation of some external object, but immediately. "Automatically." Clearly there can't *literally* be an observer inside my brain. But, of course, I make one up—or more accurately, I am fooled by my brain into believing that there is one. Insofar as this "imaginary observer" has attributes, those attributes are modelled closely on the attributes of the human body. The body stands in a certain relationship to the outside world; events take place *out there* that impinge on the body. Events also take place in your mind; the relationship between your self and those mental events is modelled closely on the relationship between your body and external-world events. The self is conceived to be an internalized, miniature body.

This self isn't merely a seeing or "introspecting" observer. In exploring the world of mental events, it's endowed with virtually all the capacities that the body brings to bear in exploring the world of external events. *To see* can mean *to understand*; but we also say *that idea moved me* or *touched me, it smells wrong* or *doesn't sound right* or *I want it so much I can taste it*. Our way of referring to the relationship between *the self* and *its thoughts* is cribbed exactly from our way of referring to the relationship between *the body* and *its world*. The facts of the matter are captured with vivid, child-like clairvoyance in the medieval paintings that depict the moment of death, of the soul leaving the body, in the form of a body-in-miniature departing the larger physical body.

And that brings us to the central question of consciousness. To our naive folk-psychological way of thinking, consciousness inheres in the observer-self. But of course, the observer-self is imaginary. There isn't *really* such an entity in the brain.

Dennett (1991) believes that this nonexistence of the observer is *the* crucial fact about consciousness. He uses the term "Cartesian theater" or sometimes "theater of consciousness" to designate this illusory, folk-psychological view; within this theater, the mental events of which we are conscious are displayed (we naively believe) for the edification of a "witness" or observer.

But of course, there isn't *really* any such theater in the brain. Consciousness doesn't happen at any particular point (there is no theater, and no stage); it consists instead of a bunch of separate, discontinuous events exploding like fireworks all over the brain. Consciousness is a matter of "distributed contentful states" (135), reflecting "the spatiotemporal smearing of the observer's point of view all over the brain" (126). Once we come to grips with the fact that there is no observer and no central viewing-point, "we will be forced to abandon the Cartesian Theater and replace it with a new model . . ." As a matter of fact, ". . . the idea of a special center in the brain is the most tenacious bad idea bedeviling our attempts to think about consciousness" (108).

Dennett makes some important and convincing points in the course of his exposition (most important, that there's no such thing as "what I was *really* conscious of" independent of what I recall being conscious of—no such thing as an *"objective* subjectivity"). Still, his view of consciousness as smeared all over the brain, his insistence that the theater of consciousness is merely an *erroneous idea*, and erroneous ideas should be abandoned—this is all profoundly unsatisfying.

Here is an analogy. Suppose that in this figure, the dark areas are cut-outs that have been glued to the page. You see a star. Dennett's appointed role is to tell us *but wait, there isn't* actually *a star there. This is just a collection of separate cut-out fragments, none of them starshaped. Sure you* see *a star, but that's just an illusion. If you have carefully followed my argument, you can now abandon the illusion and face facts.*

What's wrong with this argument? Well, the interesting point, of course, isn't the fact that there's no *actual* star-shaped object in the picture. Obviously there isn't. The interesting point is precisely that, *despite* that obvious fact, *I still see a star. That's* what's remarkable.

Of course there is no actual observer in the brain. Granted, Descartes (as Dennett points out) thought there was; but I doubt whether his view of the pineal gland (or any other item of brain anatomy) as the locus of consciousness would strike most modern thinkers as especially intuitive, and I don't believe that folk psychology holds "the observer in the brain" to be a real, physical entity. Most people surely accept that the mind is realized by the brain, and a little reflection is likely to convince almost anyone that, since the brain isn't a point-object—it's extended in space—that conscious experience must also in some sense be distributed in space. All this is interesting but not, I think, astonishing.

What *is* astonishing is that, despite the lack of any actual observer, *the brain is nonetheless capable of creating the illusion of an observer.* The "mystery of consciousness" (or whatever you want to call it) inheres exactly in this: that our brains have the knack of creating an "observer illusion" for us. This knack is exactly the specific capacity that explains consciousness. It's a trick or a special effect or magic, as you like; in the sense that a convex lens mirrored on the inside can project a seemingly real image onto a spot where nothing actually stands. (You may be able to find this sort of gadget and see the remarkable illusion it creates where I did, at the local eco-boutique.)

The ability to create this illusion is a consequence of the physical construction of the mirror assembly. The ability to create the observer illusion, to create *the sense of self*, is a consequence of the physical construction of the brain. That ability *is* consciousness. A star doesn't emerge automatically when clean-edged fragments are arranged on paper; the proportions and inter-relations have to be right. The floating image doesn't emerge from just any assembly of mirrors—things need to be calculated exactly. And simple-brained creatures, by the same token, are likely to experience the world in roughly the way Dennett describes, as fragmentary perceptions scattered through the brain, unintegrated and incoherent. They aren't bothered by the illusion of an observer-self. But at some point, brain complexity advances to a level of sophistication and brain "tuning" to a level of precision at which, there it is: the illusion of self floating like a mirage over the random chaos.

I'm claiming in short that the observer-self isn't a mere wrong idea; just another obsolete folk-notion, like "the sun rises." It's an illusion that the brain is wired to create. (Along similar lines, see Aronson, Dietrich and Way's [1992, 202]) comments on "throwing the conscious baby out with the Cartesian bathwater." It's a consequence of brain architecture that we are possessed of the (objectively wrong) idea that there is an observer in the brain. Once we are no longer inclined merely to dismiss it as a misperception, we can start looking for the facts that explain it. They won't be facts about a particular item of brain anatomy, but about the architecture as a whole; about how the whole thing is put together, how the parts relate. (The nonexistent star isn't explained by the properties of any one snippet. It's a property of the whole: what Searle calls a "causally emergent system feature"; what I've [1991] called an "ensemble property".) In defending Dennett's thesis, Drew McDermott asks us to imagine a comparison between his brain and the brain of a "zombie"—a mystical creature who acts just like a person, but does so in a robot-like way, unconsciously. "Upon inspection," he writes (1992, 217), "one could find the exact place where *my* brain maintained a model of a conscious self, and *his* brain did not. But intuitively it seems that one could stare at my 'circuit diagram' all day and still not believe that *that* was all there was to being conscious." But why should there be any such "exact place"? Why can't consciousness inhere in the thing as a whole, in the ensemble?

Dennett wants to demolish the illusion, but it can't *be* demolished. Nor can you demolish the illusory image projected by the mirror assembly, or the star that appears within those black snippets. Consciousness is the star we see *despite the fact* it isn't there.

Dennett is telling us *it isn't really there! Can't you see it's all just a trick?* Our response should be *But we see it anyway!* And that's the whole point.

If we add simulated emotion to a computer we might arrive, I have argued, at a very close approximation of human thought. Such a computer might seem to us as if it understands—as if it has a mind. There is no reason to suppose, though, that adding emotion, or performing any other sophisticated programming trick, will ever endow a computer with the illusion of an observer-self. We might ultimately build a computer that seems to us to have a mind. But I doubt whether the computer itself will ever be taken in.

Chapter Eight

Ancient Thought

I've claimed that ancient thought-streams were built differently, at least on some occasions, from our own. I have also claimed that the cognitive spectrum can be used to deriddle them. In this chapter I will try to prove those claims.

We can't sit an ancient down and transcribe his thought-stream. (That's not such an easy trick to accomplish with a modern thinker, for that matter.) But ancient thought-streams have already been transcribed for us, in a sense. A piece of literature captures a piece of thinking. Thoughts are groomed and ordered before they are set down, but whatever that process of transformation, the basic character of the underlying thought is bound to come through.

So I will examine some literary texts, focussing on biblical passages. I will take an odd *genre* for a model: not the traditional literary essay, but the Freudian case history. In the case histories Freud confronts his readers with the intriguing and sometimes horrific, and then presents an implicit challenge. If you are unwilling to accept my explanation, what's yours? We needn't follow Freud in all the sweeping generalizations that connect his clinical interventions to the formidable corpus of psychoanalysis to find these demonstrations fascinating and compelling.

A Freudian case history plunges the reader into a very particular world of personalities, families, historical moments and ambiance. These narrative details have nothing to do with psychoanalytic theory *per se*. But they give life and substance to the theory, and make it clear that there is something that does require an explanation: that there is more in heaven and earth, as Freud likes to repeat, than is dreamt of in your philosophy.

In the bulk of the chapter I will examine two biblical passages from the book of Exodus. The first is short, tightly coiled and flagrantly strange. The challenge it poses is obvious and profound. The other is longer, and displays symptoms that might be described as merely neurotic. The text makes sense; but it also seems, when we look at it carefully, quirky and odd. These quirks turn out to be just as challenging, and just as amenable to explanation in terms of the cognitive spectrum, as the first passage's weirdness.

I will conclude in a different vein: by returning briefly to the English Romantics of Chapter 1, and showing how the idea of a cognitive spectrum gives shape to a whole range of their pronouncements.

A warning before departure. The Bible is the most intensely studied of all human productions, and biblical criticism is a dense and highly specialized field. I will avoid excurses into topics of purely technical or specialized interest, but a bit of background is essential. I've tried to slip it in discreetly.

The bloody bridegroom

This story occupies a mere three verses towards the beginning of the Book of Exodus.[1] It is a strange story, and making sense of it will entangle us in a surprisingly wide range of biblical issues. Why bother? Because the result will be a dramatic, concrete demonstration of what low-focus thought really means. Once we have finally unknotted, untwisted and disentangled this story, we will be confronted with an ancient cognitive world in which our modern notions of "dream" and "waking" are turned upside down.

---

[1]Much of the material in this section appeared in slightly different form in *Orim* 3:2, 1988.

The action takes place on the road from Midian back to Egypt.
Moses is an Israelite born in Egypt. Years before our story, he had
emigrated to the neighboring region of Midian and married a Midi-
anite woman named Tsipporah. But his comfortable, ordinary, put-
tering-around existence is shattered when God speaks to him out
of a fiery bush, ordering him to return to Egypt and free his fellow
Israelites who are enslaved there. He duly sets out for Egypt. But
on the way . . .

> It happened on the road, at an overnight stopping place, that the
> Lord met him and tried to kill him. But Tsipporah took a flint, cut
> off her son's foreskin and touched it to his feet; she said "You are
> my bloody bridegroom!" And he withdrew from him. That was
> when she said "bloody bridegroom" with respect to circumcision.
> (Exodus 4:24–26).[2]

Here are the dry bones of a story that no one has understood for
thousands of years. A reader who is unfamiliar with the Bible might
be tempted to believe that, if he knew it better, the story's meaning
might be a bit clearer. Actually this is not the case. These verses
make no sense.

Why should the Lord, who singled out Moses as his own trusted
emissary, suddenly try to kill him? When the violent, unprovoked
attack starts, how does Tsipporah know what to do? What does
"bloody bridegroom" mean? Why does Tsipporah's action *stop* the
attack? Even knowledgeable readers are tempted to dismiss the
whole thing as some kind of mistake.

There *are* biblical passages whose language is strange or unclear
enough to warrant the scholarly guess that the text is corrupt—but
this passage is not one of them. The language is clear, and its plain
sense is self-evident. The Lord tried to kill Moses.

Brevard Childs, in his seminal Exodus commentary of 1974,
exposes the hollowness of modern critical theories one by one
(95–101, 103–104). Scolnic's 1990 paper is an excellent survey of
modern thought on circumcision and the bloody bridegroom story.[3]
Perhaps the deepest insight of biblical scholarship occurs in a

---

[2] These and subsequent translations from the Hebrew are mine, except where noted.
[3] It contains favorable comments on an earlier published version of the views expressed here.

laconic phrase of the twelfth-century commentator Ibn Ezra, which I will come to. But even Ibn Ezra doesn't offer a complete and satisfying reading. Gerhard von Rad (1972, 201), in his Genesis commentary, summarizes the history of these verses in one offhand sentence: "The extremely old story in Exodus 4:24ff. cannot properly be understood at all."

Cannot properly be understood at all: in such words one can almost hear the respectable Viennese clinicians of the day dismissing the hysterical ravings of Freud's favorite patients.

Unravelling the knotty mental state of such a patient requires a guided tour of his world; then, that we step back and view the information we have collected from a new and unexpected angle. At that point the chaos resolves, and we see clearly a pattern that now seems obvious—from this viewpoint it is impossible *not* to see it—although the assumptions that underlie our new viewpoint may remain unintuitive and uncomfortable. That's what I propose to do with our story. First, to poke around and collect data; to make a thorough study of the passage and its surroundings. Then, to examine the data from an unexpected angle, suggested by the spectrum model—at which point, I believe, it will all snap into focus.

———

To start, please contemplate the sheer violence of the story. Moses' life is threatened, and in the most frightening of ways—by his all-powerful defender and champion. He is attacked, saved by the slash of a knife—blood flows, his wife streaks him with fresh blood and then pronounces the story's weird central phrase: "you are my bloody bridegroom!" *Bloody*, insofar as she has just touched him with the child's blood. But the Hebrew resonates more darkly still: the word translated *bloody* refers most often not merely to blood, but to blood violently spilt.

A first question any analyst must ask: what is the context?

Moses at the time is on his way home to Egypt. An initial clue to our story emerges when we ask why he left Egypt in the first place. In fact, he had run for his life. He had come upon an Egyptian beating a Hebrew. He had looked round, seen no bystanders, then struck down the Egyptian and hidden the body in a shallow sandy grave (Exodus 2:11–23).

There's no reason to believe that Moses had been armed at the time. To kill the Egyptian he "smote" or "hit" him, probably with a stick, maybe a rock—when the Egyptian is said to be "beating" the Hebrew, the verb is the same. This was no casual act. You have to hit a man hard to kill him with a stick. The text underlines the *deliberate* nature of the attack by telling us that Moses looked round carefully first.

Unfortunately he hadn't looked around carefully enough. Or perhaps he was betrayed by the man he saved. (It's happened.) In any case, the act became public knowledge. And when Pharaoh found out, "he sought to kill Moses" (Exodus 2:15).

Now the way you feel about a journey depends on your destination. Your destination colors your mood. Egypt is a destination that must have been associated in Moses' mind at best with anxiety and at worst with fear for his life. Ordering Moses back to Egypt, God had reassured him that "all the men who sought your life are dead" (Exodus 4:19). But no one has ever absolved him of the Egyptian's murder, or thanked him for it, or in any way laid the affair to rest. God in fact does not forgive him, merely notes laconically that his pursuers are dead.

So it is just possible that there is a nagging doubt in Moses' mind as he sets out for Egypt. The text doesn't propose this theory, merely allows us to propose it. Are we wrong to do so? Is the idea of a tense trip homeward, haunted by some unexpiated act, alien to the Bible? Consider the story of Jacob's return home to his wronged brother, in the Book of Genesis. Jacob guilefully steals the first-born's blessing that was due his brother, then runs for his life. Away from home he acquires a family, and years later he finally sets out to return. The night before the long-feared and anticipated family reunion, a strange nighttime struggle occurs. I will return to that story.

We need to turn first, though, to another aspect of Moses' life at the time of his journey home. What he'd done with the Egyptian corpse is a metaphor for his life as a whole. He hadn't "buried" the body, hadn't properly gotten it out of the way; he'd merely covered it up. The verse *might* have said, "He buried him in the sand," but in fact it does say, "He hid him in the sand" (2:12) instead.

As he sets out for Egypt, *concealment* is the central note in

Moses' life. In his infancy Moses is concealed by his mother, then hidden in the riverside rushes, where Pharaoh's daughter discovers him. He kills an Egyptian and hides the body—and *discovery* leads to *catastrophe*; as he says to himself in fear, "So this thing is known!" When he flees to Midian, the manner in which Reuel's daughters describe him to their father is of great interest: "An Egyptian," they report, "saved us from the shepherds" (2:19). Of course an Egyptian! Having grown up at court in the care of Pharaoh's daughter he could hardly *not* be Egyptian in dress and speech and manner. Did he ever correct his future wife and in-laws' misimpression?

If concealment were not so important a theme, the question might be merely unanswerable and beside the point. As is, we cannot help but notice and wonder at the strange way in which Moses, following the revelation of the burning bush, informs his father-in-law of his planned return to Egypt. "He said to him, let me go and return to my brothers who are in Egypt, and see if they are still alive" (4:18). This awkward speech has the air of being carefully phrased so as not to be false and yet to reveal nothing true. (One imagines solitary Moses agonizing for hours over how exactly to put this, wound up in the bitter, silent self-doubt we know is characteristic of him.) Do his wife and family know that he is an Israelite? We might *still* dismiss the question if something else didn't force us back to it. The story of the bloody bridegroom seems to revolve, somehow, around a circumcision that did *not* take place. At the start of our story, Moses' son is uncircumcised.

Circumcision was widespread in the ancient Near East. But Israelite circumcision seems to have differed in at least one way from other varieties. Circumcision in Israel occurs on the eighth day after birth, but "among the other peoples who have practiced circumcision," J. P. Hyatt (1962, 629) writes in the *Interpreter's Dictionary*, "childhood or puberty, rather than infancy, is the general rule."

It is widely assumed that Israelite circumcision too was originally a puberty rite, which at some point and for some unknown reason was transferred to infancy. When did the shift occur? Some commentators point precisely to our story. "The short narrative of the circumcision of Moses' son by his mother," Fohrer (1972, 33) writes, "confirms or legitimizes the change to circumcision of infants." But this interpretation flouts the text. Childs (1974, 100) notes that "from the redactor's point of view"—the *redactor* being the hypothetical editor who created the biblical text out of separate narratives—"the story does not explain the origin of circumcision, but rather circumcision explains the meaning of Zipporah's action." In the compilation of classical rabbinic commentary called *Midrash Rabbah*, Tsipporah is said to exclaim: "How great is the power of circumcision! Here my husband deserved death for having shirked the circumcision commandment!"

Suppose that, from our text's point of view, infant circumcision is in fact the crucial obligation other biblical passages make it out to be. Furthermore, circumcision in infancy distinguishes the Israelite from his neighbors. Now, consider these facts. Upon his arrival, Moses is introduced to his future in-laws as an Egyptian. On departing he chooses to reveal absolutely nothing about the nature of his mission. Shortly after his departure the Lord attacks him, and the attack seems to hinge on the omission of a ritual that marks out the doer as an Israelite. Could the text not be hinting that Moses (who was hidden in the rushes, who hid a body in the sand) leaves Midian with his identity still hidden?

Our premise remains that your destination colors your mood. What could Moses' mood be as he sets out for Egypt? Egypt is a place where he is wanted for murder. It also a place where his wife will inevitably uncover (as the hidden corpse was uncovered) a buried truth.

Before following these arguments onward, we detour into the background.

It is Ibn Ezra, the famously acute and sardonic rabbinic commentator, who directs our attention to the broader context of circumcision and Passover. He wonders about the meaning of the phrase *she touched his feet* in verse 25 of our passage. The *his* is ambiguous. It might refer not to Moses but to the son. But "the meaning of *she touched his feet*," he writes, "is in my opinion Moses' feet, as in *When He sees the blood on the lintel He will not permit the destroyer [to enter]*." The reference is to Exodus 12:23 and the night of the first Passover. On that night, as on the night of our story, the threatened are protected by a sign of blood. What is this blood-sign, and what does it mean?

————

If concealment is a basic theme for Moses, *first borns* are basic to the larger story of the Passover and the escape from Egypt. God's challenge to Pharaoh strikes the theme with jarring simplicity:

> Thus says the Lord: Israel is my first-born son. I have said to you, send forth my son so that he may serve me; but you have refused to send him forth. Behold: I will kill *your* first-born son. (Exodus 4:22–23)

On the night of the first Passover—the night of the last of ten plagues visited by the Lord on the recalcitrant ("intransigent," the State Department would say) Pharaoh, the night that at last frees Israel and sets her staggering in a daze towards the Red Sea and the desert beyond—on that night, Egypt's first-born die. Israelite first-borns are "passed over" and survive. Their households are marked by the blood of the Passover lamb smeared on the door-post. The role of the blood is to distinguish the Lord's first-born from Pharaoh's.

Israel collectively is the Lord's first-born. The Lord so designates the entire nation. A privileged position—except there is a catch. First-borns are *forfeit* to the Lord. "Set apart for me all first-borns: every opener of a womb among the children of Israel, whether man or beast, is mine" (Exodus 13:2). Exodus 13:15 ties this obligation specifically to the night of the Passover. *When* are first-borns for-feit? Another passage is explicit. "You will give me your first-born sons. You will do the same with your oxen and sheep: it will be seven days with its mother; on the eighth day you will give it to me" (Exodus 22:28–29).

First-born animals are sacrificed; obviously first-born sons are not. They are "redeemed." Numbers 3:47 sets the price and the time (five shekels apiece, at the end of the first month) and this verse, together with other similar ones in Exodus, is the basis of the *pidyon ha-ben* ritual practiced among Jews to this day. But another verse hangs unresolved: "Thus says the Lord: Israel is my first-born son." One child in each family is *that family's* first-born, but the whole nation is the Lord's.

"Set apart for me all first-borns." How are the Lord's own (symbolic) first-borns (symbolically) redeemed? We might set the question aside if we didn't know that first-borns are forfeit on the eighth day, which happens to be when circumcision occurs. If we didn't know that all Israelites are protected, as the Lord's first-born, on the night of the Passover; that blood on the door-post marks the presence of such people; that Ibn Ezra draws the link between this blood and the blood with which Tsipporah marks Moses—the latter being *explicitly* the blood of circumcision. And then we notice, finally, the entrance requirement that is imposed upon aliens who wish to participate in the Passover rite:

> When an alien who lives among you would keep the Lord's Passover, let all his males be circumcised, and then let him come near and keep it—he will be as one of the land's native born; but all who are uncircumcised shall not eat of it. (Exodus 12:48)

Thus a coherent story emerges. Circumcision, the rite of the eighth day, could be a symbolic redemption act, levied not merely on the first-born male (the family's first-born) but on every male—the *whole nation* being the Lord's first-born.

What is this hypothesis worth? What does it buy us? For one, brilliant new light on our story. Because the verses that are central to the hypothesis—that proclaim Israel the Lord's first born, and threaten Pharaoh's with death—*immediately precede* our story in Exodus Chapter 4. The arrangement of this section is odd. It doesn't flow right, and we're naturally led to wonder *why* the obstacle that interrupts the flow is there. In verse 19, Moses is told to return to Egypt. In verse 20, he takes his family and sets out. Verse 24 begins our story of the roadside incident. The three-verse edict of the first-borns is a blatant interruption of the flow: it begins in verse 21 with the words "When you set out to return to Egypt"— but Moses has *already* set out! Then comes the edict proper. Why in this fashion *force us* to trip over the edict on the way to our story?

It's hard not to conclude that we are intended to read our story *in light of* the edict. The very last thing we are made aware of before the attack on Moses is this edict being thrust into his keeping: the Lord's first-born will live and Egypt's will die. (*Whose are* your *first-born*?)

Your destination colors your mood. What must Moses' mood have been, given that he is taking with him both his son—the uncircumcised son of an ostensible Egyptian—and the Lord's edict marking uncircumcised Egyptians for death?

It is interesting to contrast briefly, at this point, Ibn Ezra's pregnant phrase with the scientific scholarship of Martin Noth. Noth was a famous and estimable scholar, a distinguished practitioner of the German "higher criticism" of the Bible. He remains one of the century's most influential Bible critics. "The brief note about an incident on Moses' return to Egypt," Noth writes (1974, 49), "is very obscure in several respects. Why does it appear at all in this place? As it deals with the theme of circumcision we would rather expect to find it connected with the description of Moses' marriage or even the birth of his son. A definite locality evidently plays some part here." An old tradition, Noth theorizes, associated a local demon with some particular stretch of desert. "For this reason the scene has been inserted here where Moses, with his wife and child, for the first time wanders through the desolate wilderness on his return to Egypt." Noth's very bewilderment is illuminating. Ibn Ezra is alive to the dense thicket of associations that root the story immovably in this narrative moment. Noth is oblivious, and so he invents an association of his own. Thus ends an exegetical tradition.

Back to our story. As a narrative, it still makes no sense. But there *is* a "literary form" within which it not only makes sense but makes perfect and compelling and inevitable sense—namely, the nightmare.

The story of the Lord's attack *ought to have been* a dream. But it very definitely is not! And *both* facts are deeply significant. Let's examine, first, why the story makes a perfect nightmare.

His wife thinks Moses an Egyptian, but he isn't. The Lord thinks him an Israelite, but how could he be?—his son is uncircumcised. The anxiety of being surrounded by people you have duped and who may discover the truth about your identity at any moment plays to a particular terror of Moses'—one that is clear in the way he fights God's attempts to make him divine emissary. "Who am I, that I should go to Pharaoh?" (Exodus 3:11), he responds when the Lord calls him; "But they will not *believe* me, they will not listen to me" (Exodus 4:11); "Please, my Lord, I am not a man of words!" (4:10). You're mistaking me for someone else! I'm not capable of this. *This is not me.* It is Moses' special terror. It is a human terror generally.

It happened on the road, at an overnight stopping place . . . As he sets out, Moses' crushing anxieties crowd in on him. "Overnight" is when dreams happen. . . . *that the Lord met him and tried to kill him.* This is a nightmare twist on a real-life model. In reality, Pharaoh had sought to kill him. Only God could be a more dangerous enemy. *But Tsipporah took a flint, cut off her son's foreskin and touched it to his feet.* Never mind about Tsipporah: *Moses* knows with the instant dead-accuracy of guilty conscience exactly why the Lord has come for him, and he projects that knowledge onto his wife. *She said, "You are my bloody bridegroom!"* Suddenly the truth is out: Moses' deceit is punctured and explodes in a blood-curdling shriek. The woman sees her husband not as her Egyptian bridegroom but her Israelite *blood*groom—*And He withdrew from him. That was when she said "bloody bridegroom" with respect to the circumcision.* The last sentence insures our not failing to grasp that, in the phrase "bloody bridegroom," *circumcision* blood is what Tsipporah means.

Notice the related but separate layers superimposed in the story. The idea of God seeking to kill Moses is borrowed from *Pharaoh's* having sought his death, but the real reason (he knows) that God is after him has to do not with the concealed body but with a concealed *identity*—with the omitted circumcision. In one compact scene God reveals his anger and Tsipporah her shock. As befits a nightmare, the action is confused but the underlying emotions are perfectly intelligible.

In low-focus thought, shared affect and not logic glues thought-streams together. Pharaoh and God are affectively linked, because Moses is guilty in the eyes of both, and both have the power to destroy him. At this point, the same affective mixture of fear and guilt—and anger? bitter resentment?—is associated with each. In our story the two are overlaid and become one character. This overlay is the *low*-focus kind, involving only two elements, with the details particular to each—God's power and nearness, Pharaoh's murderous intent—shining through. It is the sort of blending that is absolutely typical of dreams. I have cited Foulkes' description of two different people becoming fused into one dream character. Thus Freud (1900/1965, 171–172) also, still the most penetrating of dream psychologists, writes about "condensation" and "over-determination" as typical dream phenomena, "condensation" being characterized by "elements which have something in common being combined and fused into a single unity."

Tsipporah and circumcision are affectively linked too, not because Tsipporah *actually knows* anything about circumcision but because, in Moses' low-focus thought-streams, the two items give rise to the same mixture of anxiety and guilt, with overtones of concern for the son. The two elements are overlaid, and we get a Tsipporah who performs circumcisions. "The fact that the meanings of dreams are arranged in superimposed layers is one of the most delicate, though also one of the most interesting, problems of dream interpretation," Freud writes (1900/1965, 252).

In the thought-stream captured by our story, thoughts with tight affective connections are experienced simultaneously, right on top of each other—Pharaoh and Moses blend, Tsipporah and circumcision blend; it happens, in dreams. The underlying emotional note is strikingly typical of nightmares. "Such dreams provide us with information about the dreamer's conceptions of the penalties that will be inflicted upon him should he disregard his conscience" (Hall 1966, 16).

Returning now to the upshot: the story reads like a dream; it should have been a dream—*but it isn't a dream*. Exactly the same holds for another story that in many ways resembles this one. It occurs in Genesis Chapter 32. Jacob steals his brother's birthright and flees for his life; on the night of his return home years later, the tension is acute. Jacob is set upon that night by a man—or by God? From the text, it's hard to say. The two of them struggle and Jacob is victorious. So here is another strange encounter on a tense journey homeward. (The philosopher Martin Buber [1958, 58] is one of the few commentators to compare the Exodus story to this one—although he mentions only the resemblance in action and not the resemblance between the *moods* of Jacob and Moses.) Both times, an incident that is emotionally and psychologically perfect as a dream is described, instead, as reality.

Now the Bible is of course perfectly familiar with dreams, and accustomed to using them as narrative elements. They figure prominently and often. Jacob himself has a notable dream, plainly so identified, at an earlier point in the story. His son Joseph is famous both as a dreamer and a dream interpreter. When the Bible means "dream" it says "dream." And when it doesn't say dream, it means *no dream*. So what is going on?

The conclusion is inevitable. To the biblical narrator, the story of the Lord's attack fits perfectly into the narrative, and we agree; but while the narrator sees it fitting perfectly as *real life*, we see it fitting perfectly *as a dream*. It must be that the narrator perceives the real world as ordered, sometimes, by what we would call dream logic; he is simply a *lower-focus thinker* than we are apt to be. His own waking thoughts make a low-focus stream, and accordingly he *sees reality* that way and he makes literature that way.

This is an important conclusion, because it goes to the heart of the way things seem to fit together—of the ways in which we perceive space and time to be arranged. And nothing more fundamentally shapes our worldview. We ask, how could this have happened? It *doesn't fit* that the Lord should attack Moses. It doesn't fit that Tsipporah should react by performing a circumcision. It doesn't fit that the circumcision should end the attack. But of course in the narrator's view it does fit, perfectly. It doesn't fit *logically*. It fits *emotionally*. I claimed earlier that low-focus thought-trains have an "absent theme" quality that makes them strange to the modern mind. I claimed that these thought-streams are thematic, but that their themes are *emotional themes* that are latent rather than manifest—these themes are simply (to a superficial reading) not there. But such themes are not to be understood. They are to be *felt*. Once you feel the theme, the thought-stream coheres perfectly. And that is exactly the case with our passage. It all coheres, but not logically; rather in a low-focus sense.

In these passages we can see the human mind at a cognitive campsite appreciably down-spectrum from the neighborhoods we frequent. The mind of these times—it's hard to locate the text precisely, but let's say that it dates from very roughly a thousand years BC—is quite capable of logic and reasoning and ordinary, coherent narrative. But it remains comfortable, too, in cognitive neighborhoods where we no longer go, except in our dreams.

"Nothing readies us for this event," the distinguished literary critic Geoffrey Hartman (1986, 5–6) writes in his study of Jacob's nocturnal struggle with his attacker. "It is a combat not necessary to the sequence of events." Or as Noth wondered about the Exodus story, "why does it appear at all in this place?" These are perfect statements of modern bewilderment in the face of an ancient cognitive style. And yet this ancient style remains perfectly comprehensible—nothing's changed inside our brains; we merely need (. . . admittedly, an imaginative leap is required . . .) to turn down our own focus levels to match the narrator's. *Nothing* readies us for Jacob's struggle? Nothing in the logic of the situation. But consider: Jacob returns home finally as the Lord commands him and, approaching his powerful wronged brother full of anxiety, is informed that Esau is drawing near with some four hundred men; he prays in anguish for deliverance, sends emissaries with elaborate gifts, splits his camp in hopes that half at least will escape the slaughter—then crosses the Yabok ford and remains alone. Nothing readies him for crowded dreams? Are we surprised, *unready*, when tense days explode into brightly colored nightmares? When, anticipating a desperate struggle, we dream about a desperate struggle? What could make a stronger, more "necessary" *emotional* low-focus link between an anxious day and a frightening next-morning than a violent dream? Don't read Hartman's phrase "nothing *readies* us"; instead read "nothing readies *us*," because modern minds ask constantly "given these circumstances, what follows logically?"—but never "given these circumstances, what follows emotionally?"

The brain hasn't changed, but our cognitive habits have. Ancient thought *was* different. And we can say exactly how it was different. It was *lower-focus* thought than ours.

The sea song resounds

I will turn now to the section of the book of Exodus called *parshat Beshallach*.[4] The first five books of the Hebrew Bible are referred to collectively as the "Torah." The Torah is divided into fifty-four sections called *parshiot*, to be read (essentially) one each week in the synagogue. *Beshallach* is one of these sections. It comprises Exodus 13:17 through 17:16. These chapters are the foundation of the Bible: they describe the departure from Egypt and the crossing of the Red Sea.

They also display many of the strange structural anomalies that are characteristic of the Torah, which often reads like a rambling, repetitive, confused pastiche. (Or is it rather a crystallized, low-focus thought-train?) In the opening chapters of *Beshallach* we read about the escape from Egypt—but we get the uneasy impression that two different versions of the same event are being recalled simultaneously: did Moses divide the Sea with his staff, or did an overnight windstorm divide it? Immediately following is the Song of the Sea, a poem that seems to relate, in compressed language of breathless intensity, yet another version of the Sea crossing. Then the scene shifts and Israel is free in the Wilderness, beset by troubles. There is no water (Chapter 15), no food (Chapter 16)—God furnishes the miraculous wonder-food called "manna"; again no water—Moses strikes a rock and water flows; finally the marauding Amalekite tribe attacks, and Israel is forced to defend herself. Moses oversees the battle from a mountaintop. So long as his hands are raised, Israel prevails.

Why these stories and no others? The narrative shifts matter-of-factly from one to the next, neither claiming to be exhaustive nor explaining the significance of its selection. The sequence seems arbitrary. "Nothing readies us for these events," to paraphrase Hartman. "Why do they appear at all in this place?"—to borrow a question from Noth. Many of the same incidents recur in alternate versions later, in the Book of Numbers, after the encampment at Sinai. Why was it important that we read about similar incidents

---

[4]A fuller and more technical version of this argument will appear in *Conservative Judaism*, 1994.

here as well? What accounts for some strange imagery and language that the Bible appears not to find strange?—for example, the fact that, when Moses strikes the rock in Chapter 17, God is said to be *standing* on it? *Beshallach* would appear to be in part repetitious and inconsistent, in part rambling and disjointed. Or is there some organizing principle at work?

Of course there is. The case to be made here is simpler and more direct than in the previous section. *Beshallach* is the type of a text that is pieced together using "low-focus" principles of organization. What ties it together isn't logic. What we find instead is a kind of literary solar system, where an ensemble of stories is anchored in place by a key passage. The anchoring force is, of course, emotion. The "sun" in this literary solar system engenders powerful emotions—creates a kind of emotional force field; and has pulled round it a collection of stories that are attracted by that force field, stories to which it is emotionally tied.

The shared emotional content appears concretely in the form of shared imagery. A particular image—a hand upraised, for example—is unlikely to be important in terms of *logic*. Stories that share no relationship in substance—they aren't *about* the same thing at all—may all include the same image, for one reason or another. But that shared image may be a crucial hint; it may reveal emotional linkage. It may create the same *feeling* in many wholly unrelated settings. And that is exactly what happens here.

———

The passage consists in brief of the following elements: *Escape; Song; bitter water; manna; water from the rock; Amalek.* The first two elements, in bulk the greater part of the *parshah*, seemingly present three versions of the escape from the Egyptian army, with the first two intertwined. Two of the latter elements (manna and water from the rock) recur in closely related stories in the Book of Numbers. Modern critics usually split the *parshah* down the middle: according to Fokkelman (1987, 58), for example, the Song concludes the "Confrontation" part of Exodus and the rest, together with the next story following the *parshah*, constitutes the "Introduction to Sinai."

One major point and a small, interesting detail immediately pop out. The stories following the Song seem misplaced—similar material occurs elsewhere, and here in Exodus they interrupt the crucial progression from the Sea to Sinai for no clear reason. Here we go again! We stumble across material that in a logical sense simply doesn't belong. Fox (1986, 87) asks, of the text's final editor, "why did he/they see fit to insert here material which, chronologically at least, would fit better at a later point—for instance, in the Book of Numbers (which reports essentially the same sort of incidents)?" Noth's question, all over again.

The detail: in principle, the dividing lines between *parshiot* can go anywhere. These sections are only roughly uniform in size. Given the way modern critics divide the text into sections, *Beshallach* seems to end (on thematic terms) in the wrong place. It *almost* takes us to Sinai, but not quite. One last incident intervenes, making the first chapter of the next section. If this were a football game, we'd be encountering the halftime show approximately one minute before the end of the second quarter. Why not wait the extra minute? Why divide things up this way?

Of course, there *are* reasons. *Beshallach* is a literary solar system, and the Song of the Sea is the Sun that anchors the whole whirling assemblage by sheer emotional gravity. To understand this passage's structure, we need to see the affect links that tie everything else in this section to the Song at its center. *Beshallach* resonates like a struck bell with the emotion of the Sea Song. And it's no coincidence that the Song and no other text should play this role; this is one of the oldest passages in the Bible, and one of the most powerful.

Seemingly unrelated stories—the water-giving rock, the battle with Amalek—are related to the Song by emotional resonance. The opening prose narrative can be read as commentary on the Song. The victory over Amalek isn't an abrupt and arbitrary stopping point; it's a satisfying conclusion to this section because it re-echoes the Song's emotional content in compressed, summary form. When and only when we read this passage at low focus, it all comes clear.

———

The Song itself is our starting point. Its power is hard to convey. The language is tense and violent. Martin Noth (1974) describes it as a hymn. He should know; Noth won fame as a "form critic," an expert on the various literary structures of the Bible and their historical roles. But the Song doesn't *read* like a hymn. It reads like a breathless gasp. In the context of the ancient world a victory by Israel over Egypt was simply inconceivable, and the poet writes in staggering amazement.

"Your right hand, Lord, glorious in power; your right hand, Lord, smashes the enemy"; "—they sank like lead in the mighty waters"; "You stretched out your right hand; the earth swallowed them." This is the Song's emotional theme, captured in its imagery: the Lord's right hand outstretched above, and the tumultuous destruction of Israel's enemies beneath.

At the end of *Beshallach* the scene has changed completely. Israel, wandering in the Wilderness, is attacked suddenly by a fierce desert tribe called Amalek. "Tomorrow," says Moses, "I will station myself atop the hill . . ." (17:9); and it so happens that, "when Moses raised his hands, Israel was overpowering, but when he rested his hands Amalek prevailed" (17:11).

Here is the Song's emotional content all over again, only in a different context. The theme is captured in an image that the Song and the Amalek battle share: *The Lord's hand outstretched above; tumultuous destruction beneath.* On high, God's power vested in the outstretched hand; down below (on the Sea, in the valley), Israel's enemies smashed. "You stretched out your right hand . . .," "When Moses raised his hands . . ."—"the earth swallowed them," "Israel was overpowering." The imagery in the two passages isn't identical; it merely *has the same feel.* That's the whole point.

In the Song we feel God's power first in the outstretched hand, then seated on a mountaintop throne. "You brought them in, you planted them on your own mountain, your sitting place that you made, Lord" (15:17)—the Song's culmination. This "sitting place" means a place of settling or enthronement, but the language is simple and direct. At Amalek, God's power is manifest first in the outstretched hand of Moses, and then—Moses *sits down* on the mountaintop. He becomes exhausted, and his lieutenants "took a stone and put it under him, and he sat on it" (17:12). The two passages are different *in substance* (when God sits it is not because he is tired). But they sound the same note: God's power seated on the mountaintop.

After Amalek is defeated, the *parshah* ends with a strange oath. "Hand on the Lord's throne: the Lord will be at war with Amalek forever." Here there is a highly plausible case to be made for amending a faulty text. The word *throne* appears in a form that is recognizable but distorted. If we change its first letter and read n*eis* instead of k*eis*, we get God's *banner* instead of his throne—perfect, because the preceding verse reads "and he called the place *God's Banner*." See Childs (1974) for a discussion. We need only add that the alternative first letters resemble each other and are easily confused, and the case is made. But the more blatant the error, the more obvious the next question: how could such an error have entered this text? Precisely because *God's enthronement* is a natural culmination to this story, as in the Song. If we read the text at low focus, we are *primed to hear* about God's enthronement.

The importance of recurring theme-words and theme-objects in the Torah has often been discussed. Fox, for example, working in the tradition of Buber's concept of the *Leiwort* (leading-word, a theme or key), lists theme-words that are shared by many of the central passages in Exodus—words like "serve, "glory", "know", "see." Nehama Leibowitz gives a perceptive discussion of the *send* verb-root as central to the early chapters of Exodus and to *Beshallach*. The recurrence of incidents like the people's grumbling or objects like Moses' staff is obvious. But we can't adequately describe the subtle relationship between Amalek and the Song in these terms. The character of the two passages is very different, but the narratives are draped round the same set of shape-giving images: the powerful arm outstretched, God's power on high, the violent destruction of Israel's enemies down below, the eventual seating or enthronement of God's power. The Bible student contemplating this strange relationship might conceivably be reminded less of Buber or of Leibowitz than of the structure of dreams. An underlying emotion can generate a whole series of dream-stories that share little or no manifest content; that merely represent *successive embodiments* of the *same emotional theme*. (Thus, for example, Hall 1966, 100.) Or consider Freud's (1900/1965) description

of three separate dreams in which elaborate narratives are impro-
vised around the intrusive ringing of an alarm clock, during the
moments before the sleeper finally wakes. One dreamer creates a
scene set near a church, another a bright winter's day with sleigh-
bells; in a third, a maid carries a rattling stack of plates. An urgent
theme thrust from outside into the teller's awareness forces a narrative into being around it.

Before Amalek, a crisis of no water. God's instructions to Moses
include something strange: "I will be standing before you there on
the rock in Horeb," God says, "and you will hit the rock, and water
will flow from it" (17:6). The Lord *stand on a rock*? Our second
water-from-the-rock story, in Numbers 20, includes no such incident.
But this thought is related by image, related emotionally, to the Song:
in both settings, God's power is physically ensconced on high. "You
planted them on your own mountaintop," ". . . standing before you
there on the rock . . .," I will station myself atop the hill . . ."

The Song says of God "I will exalt him" (15:2), literally "I will up-
raise him." In the story of the water-giving rock, the poet's "I will
up-raise him" reappears in a naively direct way: the Chapter 17 narrator literally stands God on a rock. The Song and the Chapter 17
story share this "I will upraise him." Dream thought can be naively
concrete in the same way. "Ploddingly literal," says Foulkes (1985,
43). I have cited Freud's comparison of a dream to rebus . . .

In Chapter 14, before the Song, Israel is said to leave Egypt
"with up-raised hand," meaning arrogantly or (as we would say)
"high-handedly." The characterization is unusual, but repeats again
the Song's central image. "You stretched out your right hand,"
"Israel went out with up-raised hand," "When Moses raised his
hands . . ." Notice that for us too, this sort of gesture conveys emotion—serves to capture or represent emotion. When we say that
something is "uplifting," we mean that it engenders a certain kind
of emotion, but we refer to a physical gesture. When we say that
someone is "high-handed," the behavior we're describing has certain emotional overtones; and again, those emotions are captured
in an image. Our text speaks precisely this language. When the
same gestures—when the same images—recur, we sense the same
emotions underneath.

Even the *sound* of the "high-handed" verse echoes the Song. In the Song, Egypt's chariots are *ramah ba'yam*, thrown into the sea; in the prose account, Israel leaves Egypt *b'yad ramah*, with up-raised hand. Except for the change from *yam* (sea) to *yad* (hand), these verses are permutations of the same syllables. In the identical *ramahs* in each verse, two unrelated verbs coincide in form. But the wordplay that turns the Song's down-*flung* Egypt into Israel's up-*raised* hand makes perfect sense in the image-world of *Beshallach*. Freud (for example, 1990/1965, 147) discusses dreams that play with the sounds of words . . .

What, then, is the structure of *Beshallach*? From the standpoint of logic, the thought-string crystallized here is a poor excuse for a coherent narrative. There are two inconsistent stories of the Crossing, then the poem, then a rambling series of incidents only just held together by the recurrence of theme incidents and objects (the people's complaints, or Moses' staff). We can accept and understand the narrative as a simple chronology, but in structural terms it is haphazard and formless. Only after we have readjusted our viewpoint and begun looking at things from a lower-focus standpoint do we start to make out (at first dimly in the unaccustomed light) a subtle but powerful structural cross-beam that ties the piece together.

Beshallach does cohere—only not in the way we expect. It's not a logical sequence of stories. It is an echo chamber, a mirror-maze. The emotions of the Song resound through it. Without understanding this fact we cannot understand *Beshallach* fully, because a resonating system is more than the sum of its parts. We must be able to hear the echo gathering over these passages or we are missing something important—we are numbly, deafly *seeing* the waterfall plunge into the valley without hearing the resonant roar. To understand *Beshallach* we must feel the mist that hovers over and around it—God's power overarching the tumult (of Egypt's destruction, water flowing from the rock or the Israelite victory over Amalek), God's power planted on the hilltop, the upraised hand (the people's, Moses' at the Crossing, God's in the Song, Moses' at the victory over Amalek) of Israel's triumph under God's protection.

The poets and the spectrum

The spectrum is the hidden subtext of some of English Romantic poetry's most important achievements.

This poetry is about *thought*. It is about *different kinds of thought*. It is about *the transitions between different kinds of thought*. Specifically, it is about sleep and waking; it is about childhood and maturity; it is about antiquity and modernity. With the spectrum in mind, it all fits together.

It is about thought—

Wordsworth's poetry is a record of his obsession with human thought. His masterpiece, *The Prelude*, has as its alternate title "Growth of a Poet's Mind." Shelley for one was in awe of the "apprehension, clear, intense, of his mind's work" to which Wordsworth attained. Coleridge is transparently obsessed with mind . . .

It is about different types of thought—

I have quoted Shelley:

> The everlasting universe of things
> Flows through the mind, and rolls its rapid waves,
> Now dark, now glittering . . . (*Mont Blanc*: 1–3)

Coleridge, entranced by the reading of a long poem, sits quietly, "scarce conscious . . . My being blended in one thought" (*To William Wordsworth*: 108–109). Wordsworth, who wrote the poem that so entranced him, reports a similar state: "with an eye made quiet by the power/ Of harmony, and the deep power of joy,/ We see into the life of things" (*Tintern Abbey*).

Wordsworth tells us that this "serene and blessed mood" is a state "In which the affections gently lead us on" (*Tintern Abbey*: 41–42). De Quincey echoes him when he refers to the "subtle links of feeling" that are central to poetry (in Jonathan Wordsworth et al. 1987, 176). Coleridge too tells us that "I seldom feel without thinking, or think without feeling" (Willey 1957/1973, 61).

It is about sleep and waking—

Wordsworth tells us so: he describes "that serene and blessed mood" in which

> the breath of this corporeal frame
> And even the motion of our human blood
> Almost suspended, we are laid asleep
> In body, and become a living soul . . . (*Tintern Abbey*: 43–46)

So does Keats, at the close of his most beautiful poem. He has attained a melancholic version of this other state:

> Was it a vision, or a waking dream?
> Fled is that music:—do I wake or sleep? (*Ode to a Nightingale*: 79–80)

It is about childhood and maturity—

"Turn where so'er I may," writes Wordsworth, contrasting his adult self to the child, "By night or day,/ The things which I have seen I now can see no more" (*Ode: Intimations of Immortality*: 7–9). When he was a child, the world seemed different: numinous, imbued with spirit, "apparelled in celestial light, the glory and the freshness of a dream."

This other style is gradually (though never completely) supplanted. Psychologists are interested in the developmental processes of growing up, but Wordsworth tells us about *undevelopment*:

> Shades of the prison-house begin to close
> Upon the growing Boy,
> But he beholds the light, and whence it flows . . .
> . . . At length the Man perceives it die away,
> And fade into the light of common day. (*Ode: Intimations of Immortality*: 67–76)

("Our life is spent changing" says Rilke, "And ever lessening,/ the outer world disappears" [trans. C. F. McIntyre, 1922/1961].)

It is about antiquity and modernity.

John Keats empathizes with the late-born goddess Psyche—they are both "too, too late for the fond believing lyre"; both missed those ancient days

> when holy were the haunted forest boughs,
> Holy the air, the water and the fire. (*Ode to Psyche*: 37–39)

(See also Jenkyns 1980.) With the spectrum model in mind, it all fits together.

Conclusions

I've developed in this chapter a style of literary criticism that rests on particular psychological assumptions. The "low-focus criticism" that results is intended, like all criticism, to elucidate the text. It has another purpose too: to illuminate the ancient mind. The argument has reached some radical conclusions: that we don't understand certain characteristics of ancient thought; that the right way to start understanding them is in the context of a particular psychological model.

The literary goal of the argument is absolutely conventional,[5] but its methods are not. It attempts to realign its cognitive point of view in a way that moves it a bit closer to the viewpoint of the authors. Here is a parable: Dutch painters of the seventeenth century developed a peculiar preoccupation. They covered sets of panels with images that, when the panels are laid out flat, seem

---

[5] "Conventional" in the historical sense of attempting to get at the truth of the text. Nowadays, no doubt, only deconstructionist criticism truly deserves to be called conventional. I've mentioned Midrash in this chapter, and perhaps I can make the sense of the term clearer by venturing a Midrashic observation. Midrashic commentary often begins with a provocative question about language. For example: why do scholars refer to this famous modern school as "deconstructionism"? It proceeds to explain the question, as follows. After all, English has a perfectly good way to refer to the opposite of *construction*—not deconstruction, just *destruction*. And that is what this critical approach ought properly to be called: thus "have you read that thought-provoking piece of destructive criticism?" "The English department has just hired an exciting young up-and-coming destroyer (trained at Yale!)," and so on. The Midrashic comment must close by showing why the usage at issue *is* appropriate after all. Thus—*ah*, but the term "deconstruction" comes to teach us that using simple words where complicated ones will do is contrary to the spirit of this great scholarly endeavor. That's what Midrash is like. Clear?

disjointed and strange. But when they are assembled into a small room and examined from exactly the peep-hole viewpoint they were intended to be, a realistic three-dimensional scene emerges. Low-focus criticism approaches ancient texts as if they were shadow-boxes to be reassembled. Laid out flat, they are deceptively intelligible: merely doltish. But if we walk away satisfied on that basis, we have no hope of grasping this literature in its real beauty and depth.

Some modern critics do approach ancient literature with deep sympathy, insight and flair. Of a particular Rabbinic commentary on the Song of the Sea, Goldin (1971, 23) writes that "it is responsive to the mood and melodiousness of the original text." Goldin's own commentary is responsive in the same sense. Scolnic's (1991, 569–579) discussion of a famous crux in Exodus (was Moses "horned"?) emphasizes the impossibility of pinning down the biblical text as if it were a modern, logical narrative. The list goes on, and it is growing.

Nonetheless: in approaching ancient texts, *most* modern scholarship is far too easily satisfied. Its confidence is buoyed by the subliminal smugness of modern Scientific Man in approaching the ancients. Perhaps (many critics seem to be saying) I haven't *really* explained this passage; perhaps after I have added my commentary it's still disjointed and obscure, but after all, these are ancient texts, and the ancient mind *was* disjointed and obscure, so what can you expect? In much cozy and admiring and seemingly sympathetic criticism, the harsh judgements on antiquity of a Dennett or a Stich whistle loudly through the eaves and bang the shutters, though we pretend not to hear. "The 'magic' of earlier visions was, for the most part, a cover-up for frank failures of imagination."

Are these big assertions born out in practice? The analyses presented in this chapter are obviously too sparse and brief to allow us to say. But this book isn't the place for an extended literary investigation; my intention is merely to establish the plausibility, not the truth, of these claims. I'll close by noting that one of the most promising areas for putting "low-focus criticism" to the test is in classical Hebrew poetry, starting with the Psalms.

"Why do they appear at all in this place?"

"Nothing readies us for these events."

This "extremely old story" *"cannot properly be understood at all."*

That is the sound, I claim, of modern high-focus thought stopped in its tracks by ignorance of the cognitive spectrum. Those are the honestly bewildered judgements of high-focus man on the low-focus worlds of antiquity and childhood and his own dreams.

Chapter Nine

Conclusion: *Why . . .?*

To account for creativity and its seeming basis, the discovery of analogies, is it necessary to declare the "central processes" of mind unknowable? Or to seek refuge in quantum mechanics?—or devise some other ingenious way of running up the white flag? My argument claims not.

Why does an inspiration "take a man out of himself?" What accounts for the sensation of lost control in sustained creative states? And why is that loss of control accompanied, paradoxically, by the sensation of *perfect certainty* when a creative leap occurs? My thesis proposes answers.

Where does a feeling of "complete oneness with the essence of the universe" come from, and what does it mean? What *is* a "spiritual state"? My argument proposes explanations.

Ought we to be surprised at the "apparent paradox" that young children use metaphor *before* they have mastered abstract thought—before they are able to explain what they are doing? My argument claims that this is no paradox at all.

Are dreams in business to tell us something, or are they random or accidental? Why are dreams ordinarily mundane but sometimes

189

startling and "tactless" and pointed? If it is true that dreams should be "conceptualized as the end point on a continuum," as Weinstein, Schwartz, and Arkin say, which continuum are we talking about? My argument suggests solutions.

Was ancient thought different from our own? If so, must we conclude that the ancient brain was different? Must we conclude that ancient texts are fundamentally impenetrable, built on passages that "cannot properly be understood at all?" Or should we conclude on the other hand that ancient thought worked just like ours, and seems different only to the extent that it must push forward through thickets of ignorant nonsense? My argument proposes answers.

If the brain is after all just an information processing machine (and it is!), and any information processing machine can be recreated on a computer (and it *can* be!)—what right have we to protest the obvious conclusion, that a mind can be recreated on a computer? We have a perfect right; the conclusion is false, and my argument explains why.

Is cognitive artificial intelligence futile? If not, why have we made so little headway? My argument makes a suggestion.

There are also, of course, many important issues that my argument touches only in passing or ignores altogether. I have said little about language and even less about problem-solving and learning. I have ignored the mechanics of perception and the interface between subconscious perceptual processes and conscious thought. Ignoring the fast-moving field of the physiological bases of thought was a strategic decision, but there are potentially interesting relationships between some of this work (on the brain physiology of emotion, for example) and the argument I have presented. I have merely sketched the thought-mechanism upon which my argument relies, and most details about the workings of the cognitive continuum are simply omitted. A great deal of work will be required in order merely to make the argument presented here rigorous and complete, much less unavoidable.

What can I say in the face of all these yawning gaps? Only that, we have to start somewhere; and the field would be poorer if speculative leaps were disallowed.

The thesis presented here has a large number of testable implications. Ultimately there must be something measurable in the brain (or more likely, some interlocking set of measurable attributes) corresponding to the mind-property I've called "focus." I have claimed that level of focus is related to sleep onset, development, creativity: once focus is pinned down physiologically, these claims are testable. I have argued that "emotional acuity" is a cognitive attribute that correlates with creativity and certain aspects of personality and cognitive style; these claims are testable.

Specifically: if you round up a bunch of subjects and use any technique you choose to examine their thought-streams, some streams will turn out to be subjectively higher and others subjectively lower in focus. There will be some (objectively) measurable brain property or set of properties whose level rises and falls with the (subjective) high- or low-focus character of thought. Low-focus thought will turn out to be accompanied by latent emotional themes. Low-focus thought will immediately precede sleep. High-focus thought will inhibit sleep. Some yet-to-be-devised "emotional acuity" test will show some people to have a more nuanced palette of emotional responses than other people. High scores on the emotional acuity test will correlate with high scores on existing tests (admittedly imperfect) of "creativity." Children's thought-streams will typically be richer than adults' in low-focus thought.

In a different sense of "testable," the thought models I have presented can be captured in a formal system that allows one to state precisely what the rules are. The high-focus "experience-based deduction" described in Chapter 4 can be formalized; the low-focus thought streams described in Chapters 1, 5 and 8 can be formalized. Is it possible to have a formal logistic system that captures the notion of "intuitive leap"? Yes; such a system will be useful to software builders, and we are in the process of developing certain pieces of it.

But I must confess that, in the end, this book rests on foundations that defy confirmation and must be treated as mere assertions. That's because my goals are not scientific. Science and art both aim to give you a harder, tighter grasp of reality. But science wants to convince you where art (tugging like a child at your sleeve) just wants to *show* you. "To see is to forget the name of the thing one sees," Paul Valéry wrote (in Weschler 1982); to lead you straight into that direct passionate grappling is art's goal. This book isn't art—is far from art—but dimly shares the same goal. If it hardens, sharpens or deepens to the smallest degree a single reader's perception of mind, then the book succeeds, and otherwise fails—regardless of the lab results. My goal in the end is merely "mind appreciation": to draw as clear a picture as I can of a beautiful mental mechanism—of the spectrum's heights, where thought is abstract, logical, powerful and numb; and its depths, where we tease apart the delicate leaves of experience and feel them again in their full translucent brilliance.

"One runs a better chance of being listened to today if one can quote Darwin and Helmholtz than if one can only quote Schleiermacher or Coleridge." Thus writes William James, approvingly, in 1881 (James 1897, 111), and of course a century later, exactly the same holds. I now conclude a book about the scientific and technological topics of mind and computer having cited both of the latter two thinkers and neither of the former, and according to James this could easily be a big mistake. Probably he is right. Reclaiming for art a heavily fortified bit of territory now held by science is not exactly in the spirit of the age. I plead guilty and deny nothing. But I continue to insist that this is the only way science *can* make headway—by executing a temporary strategic withdrawal from a region within which, by flattening and "software-izing" the idea of mind, it has made a complete, God-awful mess. "Keep up your bright swords," Othello mocks, "for the dew will rust 'em." Call off your post-docs, and let the National Science Foundation empanel a committee of principled poets to study this problem. Modern thought science is doomed to failure until it can figure out *what it is* that needs explaining.

———

Making minds out of computers is a (maybe *the*) dominating intellectual challenge of the day, and of course the challenge has arisen because we've learnt to make such amazing machines. Or *is* that the reason?

Considering "cognitive history" in the spectrum's light, there is irony in the view a detached observer might take away. It might seem less as if the explosive power of our computers has put this bee in our bonnet than as if, having moved our cognitive campsite so far up-spectrum, we have finally reduced our mental capacities to a level at which machines can almost draw a bead on them. That's an exaggeration, of course. But especially when we consider that this same up-spectrum trek *generated* the technical sophistication to build computers in the first place . . . the impression grows that we are not so much breaking machines to our will as rushing into their arms.

The literary critic and philosopher Thomas Carlyle wrote in 1840 (105) that

> the Hero as Divinity, the Hero as Prophet, are productions of old ages; not to be repeated in the new. They presuppose a certain rudeness of conception, which the progress of mere scientific knowledge puts an end to. There needs to be, as it were, a world vacant, or almost vacant of scientific forms, if men in their loving wonder are to fancy their fellow-man either a god or one speaking with the voice of a god. Divinity and Prophet are past. We are now to see our Hero in the less ambitious, but also less questionable, character of Poet; a character which does not pass. . . . Let Nature send a Hero-soul; in no age is it other than possible that he may be shaped into a poet.

Of course Carlyle was wrong. He didn't see the cognitive continuum, which includes divinity and prophecy *and also* poetry as mere stopping points along the way; poetry is dying now in turn. We are moving inexorably up-spectrum and will continue the same way. Science gains; poetry loses. Of course this isn't the fault of science or scientists, and the tangible benefits, intellectual and practical, of an ever more scientific world are gigantic. What I am reporting is not tragedy, simply change.

It is a bit sad to think of history as unblossoming, as bright flowers collapsing (those fields of wild red wistful poppies) into tight logical fists while life flows backwards, into the bud. But it's not so bad; in practical terms, as I say, we are much better off. And after all, you can still reach the base of cognitive time, the sprawling rubble foundation baking and bleaching in the Mediterranean sun, by straining backwards, headlong, far enough. Maybe you touch the warm stones unawares. The sleeping sunbather who wakes in darkness. Funny echo in your head. You only dreamt the light and warmth (you feel). But: if there are two accounts? You dreamt it— it was also real?

References

Abelson, R. P. (1963). Computer Simulation of "Hot Cognitions." In *Computer Simulation of Personality* (eds. S. Tomkins and S. Messick). John Wiley, New York.

Albright, W. F. (1940). *From the Stone Age to Christianity: Monotheism and the Historical Process*. Johns Hopkins University Press, Baltimore.

———. (1964). *History, Archaeology and Christian Humanism*. McGraw-Hill, New York.

Allport, A. (1989). Visual Attention. In *Foundations of Cognitive Science* (ed. M. Posner). MIT Press, Cambridge, Mass.

Aronson, Dietrich, and Way, (1992). *The Behavioral & Brain Brain Sciences* 15(2).

Billow, R. M. (1988). Observing Spontaneous Metaphor in Children. In *Child Language: A Reader* (eds. M. B. Franklin and S. S. Barten). Oxford University Press, Cambridge, Mass.

Block, N. (1990). The Computer Model of the Mind. In *Thinking: An Invitation to Cognitive Science*, vol. 3 (eds. D. N. Osherson and E. E. Smith). MIT Press, Cambridge, Mass.

Bly, R. (1991). *American Poetry: Wildness and Domesticity*. Harper Collins, New York.

Bokser, B. Z. (1981). *The Jewish Mystical Tradition*. Pilgrim Press, New York.

Borges, J. L. (1964). *Labyrinths; Selected Stories and other Writings* (eds. D. A. Yates and J. E. Irby). New Directions Publishing Corporation, New York.

Bower, G. H., and Cohen, P. R. (1982). Emotional Influences in Memory and Thinking: Data and Theory. In *Affect and Cognition: The Seventeenth Annual Carnegie Symposium on Cognition* (eds. M. S. Clark and S. Fiske). Lawrence Erlbaum Associates, Hillsdale, N.J.

Brown, R., and Kulik, J. (1982). Flashbulb Memories. In *Memory Observed: Remembering in Natural Contexts* (ed. U. Neisser). W. H. Freeman, San Francisco.

Buber, M. (1958). *Moses, the Revelation and the Covenant*. Harper Torchbooks, New York.

Carlyle, T. (1840). *On Heroes, Hero-Worship and the Heroic in History*. Thomas Y. Crowell, Boston and New York.

Charniak, E., and McDermott, D. (1985). *Introduction to Artificial Intelligence*. Addison-Wesley, Reading, Mass.

Childs, B. (1974). *Book of Exodus*. The Westminster Press, Philadelphia.

Clark, A. (1989). *Microcognition: Philosophy, Cognitive Science, and Parallel Distributed Processing*. MIT Press, Cambridge, Mass.

Clark, M. S. (1982). A Role for Arousal in the Link between Feeling States, Judgments, and Behavior. In *Affect and Cognition: the Seventeenth Annual Carnegie Symposium on Cognition* (eds. M. S. Clark and S. T. Fiske). Lawrence Erlbaum Associates, Hillsdale, N.J.

Cohen, D. B. (1979). *Sleep and Dreaming: Origins, Nature and Functions*. Pergamon Press, Oxford and New York.

Coleridge, S. T. (1817/1975). *Biographia Literaria*, (ed. G. Watson). Charles E. Tuttle, Rutland, 1975 printing.

Crowder, R. G., and Wagner, R. K. (1992). *The Psychology of Reading: An Introduction*. Oxford University Press.

Davidson, D. (1990). Turing's Test. In *Modelling the Mind* (eds. K. A. Mohyeldin Said, W. H. Newton-Smith, R. Viale, and K. V. Wilkes). Clarendon Press, Oxford.

Dennett, D. C. (1978). Where Am I? In *Brainstorms: Philosophic Essays on Mind and Psychology*. Bradford Books, Montgomery, Vt.

———. (1978). Why the Law of Effect Will Not Go Away. In *Brainstorms: Philosophic Essays On Mind and Psychology*. Bradford Books, Montgomery, Vt.

———. (1988). Précis of "The International Stance." In *Behavioral and Brain Sciences II*. Cambridge University Press, New York.

———. (1991). *Consciousness Explained*. Little, Brown, Boston, Mass.

Dodds, E. R. (1951). *The Greeks and the Irrational*. University of California Press, Berkeley, 1974 printing.

Drever, J. (1964). *A Dictionary of Psychology* (revised by Harvey Wallerstein). Penguin Books, Baltimore.

Dreyfus, H. L. (1972). *What Computers Can't Do: A Critique of Artificial Reason*. Harper & Row, New York.

Dreyfus, H. L., and Dreyfus, S. E., with Athanasiou, T. (1986). *Mind over*

Machine: The Power of Human Intuition and Expertise in the Era of the Computer. The Free Press, New York.

Dupré, L. (1972). *The Other Dimension*. Doubleday, Garden City, N.Y.

Edel, L. (1982). *Stuff of Sleep and Dreams: Experiments in Literary Psychology*. Harper & Row, New York.

Ekman, P. (ed.) (1977). *Emotion in the Human Face*. Cambridge University Press, New York.

Eliot, T. S. (1932). *Selected Essays*. Faber and Faber, London.

———. (1950/1976). *The Sacred Wood: Essays on Poetry and Criticism*. Methuen, London, 1976 printing.

Elkind, D. (1968). Introduction. In Piaget, J., *Six Psychological Studies* (ed. D. Elkind, trans. A. Tenzer). Random House, New York.

Fertig, S., and Gelernter, D. (1988). Musing in an Expert Database. In *Proceedings of the Second International Conference on Expert Database Systems*, (ed. L. Kerschberg). George Mason University, Fairfax, Va.

Fertig, S., and Gelernter, D. (1989). FGP: A Virtual Machine for Database-driven Expert Systems. In *Proceedings of the IEEE International Workshop on Tools for AI*. IEEE Computer Society Press, Los Alamitos, Calif.

———. (1991). A Software Architecture for Acquiring Knowledge from Cases. In *Proceedings of the International Joint Conference on Artificial Intelligence*. Morgan Kaufmann, San Mateo, Calif.

———. (1993). Is Connectionism Necessary? In *Proceedings of the 1993 Bar Ilan Symposium on Foundations of Artificial Intelligence* (Bar Ilan University, Israel, 1993).

Feynman, R. P. (1985). *"Surely You're Joking, Mr. Feynman!": Adventures of a Curious Character* (as told to Ralph Leighton; ed. Edward Hutchings). W. W. Norton, New York.

Fodor, J. A. (1975). *The Language of Thought*. Crowell, New York.

———. (1983). *The Modularity of Mind: An Essay on Faculty Psychology*. MIT Press. Cambridge, Mass.

———. (1985). Précis of the Modularity of Mind. *The Behavioral & Brain Sciences* 8(1): 1–39.

———. (1987). *Psychosemantics: The Problem of Meaning in the Philosophy of Mind*. MIT Press, Cambridge, Mass.

Fodor, J., and Lepore, E. (1992). *Holism: A Shopper's Guide*. Basil Blackwell, Cambridge, Mass.

Fohrer, G. (1972). *History of Israelite Religion*. Abingdon Press, New York.

Fokkelman, J. P. (1987). Exodus. In *The Literary Guide to the Bible* (eds. R. Alter and F. Kermode). Harvard University Press, Cambridge, Mass.

Forrest-Presley, D. L., and Waller, T. G. (1984). *Cognition, Metacognition, and Reading*. Springer-Verlag, New York.

Foulkes, W. D. (1985). *Dreaming: A Cognitive-psychological Analysis*. Lawrence Erlbaum Associates, Hillsdale. N.J.

Fox, E. (1986). *Now These Are the Names*. Schocken, New York.

Freedman, A. M., Kaplan, H. I., and Sadock, B. J., eds. (1976). *Comprehensive Textbook of Psychiatry, II*. Williams & Wilkins, Baltimore.

French, R. M. (1990). Subcognition and the Limits of the Turing Test. *Mind* 99(393): 53–65.

Freud, S. (1900/1965). *The Interpretation of Dreams* (ed./trans. J. Strachey). Avon Books, New York, 1965 printing.

———. (1930/1961). *Civilization and Its Discontents* (trans. James Strachey). W. W. Norton, New York, 1961 printing.

———. (1958). *The Standard Edition of the Complete Psychological Works of Sigmund Freud* (ed./trans. J. Strachey). London, Hogarth Press.

———. (1958 printing). *The Standard Edition II of the Complete Psychological Works of Sigmund Freud*, vol. 2, (ed./trans. J. Strachey). London, Hogarth Press.

———. (1965 printing). *Introductory Lectures on Psychoanalysis* (ed./trans. J. Strachey). Avon Books, New York.

Garbarino, J., Stott, F. M., and the faculty of Erikson Institute (1989). *What Children Tell Us: Eliciting, Interpreting and Evaluating Information from Children*. Jossey-Bass, San Francisco.

Gardner, H. (1982). *Art, Mind and Brain: A Cognitive Approach to Creativity*. Basic Books, New York.

Gardner, H., and Winner, E. (1979). The Development of Metaphoric Competence: Implications for Humanistic Disciplines. In *On Metaphor* (ed. S. Sacks). University of Chicago Press, Chicago.

Gay, P. (1978). *Freud, Jews, and Other Germans: Master and Victims in Modernist Culture*. Oxford University Press, New York.

———. (1985). *Freud for Historians*. Oxford University Press, New York.

———. (1987). *A Godless Jew: Freud, Atheism, and the Making Psychoanalysis*. Yale University Press, New Haven, and Hebrew Union College Press, Cincinnati.

Gelernter, D. H. (1981). A DAG-based Algorithm for Prevention of Store-and Forward Deadlock in Packet Networks. *IEEE Transactions on Computers*, C30(10): 709–714.

——— (1991). *Mirror Worlds*. Oxford University Press, New York and Oxford.

Gelernter, D. H., and Sklar, M. (1986). Machine Musing: Preliminary Report. In *Proceedings of the 1986 AAMSI Congress* (Anaheim, Calif., May 1986).

Gick, M. L., and Holyoak K. J. (1980). Analogical Problem Solving. *Cognitive Psychology* 12: 306–355.

Gilhooly, K. J. (1988). *Thinking: Directed, Undirected and Creative*. Academic Press, New York.

Goldin, J. (1971). *The Song of the Sea*. Yale University Press, New Haven.

Gould, S. J. (1977). *Ontogeny and Phylogeny*. Belknap Press of Harvard University, Cambridge, Mass.

Hall, C. S. (1953/1966). *The Meaning of Dreams*. McGraw-Hill, New York.

Hartman, G. H. (1986). The Struggle for the Text. In *Midrash and Literature* (eds. G. H. Hartman and S. Burdick). Yale University Press, New Haven.

Hilgard, E. R., with a chapter by Hilgard, J. R. (1965). *Hypnotic Susceptibility*. Harcourt, Brace & World, New York.

Hockley, W. E., and Lewandowsky, S., eds. (1991). *Relating Theory and Data: Essays on Human Memory in Honor of Bennet B. Murdock*. Lawrence Erlbaum Associates, Hillsdale, N.J.

Hofstadter, D. R. (1985). *Metamagical Themas: Questing for the Essence of Mind and Pattern*. Basic Books, New York.

Hofstadter, D. R., and Dennett, D. C. (1981). *The Mind's I: Fantasies and Reflections on Self and Soul*. Basic Books, New York.

Holyoak, K. J. (1990). Problem Solving. In *Thinking: An Invitation to Cognitive Science*, vol. 3 (eds. D. N. Osherson and E. E. Smith). MIT Press, Cambridge, Mass.

Hyatt, J. P. (1962). Circumcision. In *The Interpreter's Dictionary of the Bible*, vol. 1 (eds. G. A. Buttrick et al.). Abingdon Press, New York.

Izard, C. E. (1977). *Human Emotions*. Plenum Press, New York.

James, W. (1897). Reflex Action and Theism. In *The Will to Believe and other Essays in Popular Philosophy* (1897). Longmans Green, New York and London.

———— (1902). *The Varieties of Religious Experience: A Study in Human Nature*. Longmans, Green, New York.

Jaynes, J. (1976). *The Origin of Consciousness in the Breakdown of the Bicameral Mind*. Houghton Mifflin, Boston, Mass.

Jenkyns, R. (1980). *The Victorians and Ancient Greece*. Basil Blackwell, Oxford.

Johnson, G. (1991). *In the Palaces of Memory: How We Build Worlds Inside Our Heads*. Knopf/Random House, New York.

Johnson-Laird, P. N. (1990). *The Computer and the Mind: An Introduction to Cognitive Science*. Harvard University Press, Cambridge, Mass.

Jones, E. (1963). *The Life and Work of Sigmund Freud* (eds. L. Trilling and S. Marcus). Doubleday (Anchor Books), Garden City, N.Y.

Kagan, J. (1989). *Unstable Ideas: Temperament, Cognition, and Self*. Harvard University Press, Cambridge, Mass.

Keele, S. W. (1973). *Attention and Human Performance*. Goodyear Publishing, Pacific Palisades, Calif.

Klinger, E., and Cox, W. M. (1988). Dimensions of Thought Flow in Everyday Life. *Imagination, Cognition and Personality*, 7(2): 105–124., Baywood Publishing Co., Amityville, N.Y.

Kogan, N. (1980). A Cognitive-style Approach to Metaphoric Thinking. In *Aptitude, Learning, and Problem Solving* (eds. R. E. Snow, P. A. Federico, and W. E. Montague). Lawrence Erlbaum, Associates Hillsdale, N.J.

Landes, D. (1983). *Revolution in Time: Clocks and the Making of the Modern World*. Harvard University Press, Cambridge, Mass.

Lazarus, R. S., and Smith, C. A. (1990). Emotion and Adaptation. In *Handbook of Personality: Theory and Research* (ed. L. A. Pervin). Guilford Press, New York and London.

Leibowitz, N. (1976). *Studies in Shemot*. World Zionist Organization.

Leiman, S. Z. (1976). *The Canonization of Hebrew Scripture: The Talmudic and Midrashic Evidence*. Anchor Books, Hamden, Conn.

Leventhal, H. (1982). The Integration of Emotion and Cognition: A View from the Perceptual-Motor Theory of Emotion. In *Affect and Cognition: The Seventeenth Annual Carnegie Symposium on Cognition* (eds. M. S. Clarke and S. Fiske). Lawrence Erlbaum Associates, Hillsdale, N.J.

—— (1984). A Perceptual Motor Theory of Emotion. In *Approaches to Emotion* (eds. K. R. Scherer and P. Ekman). Lawrence Erlbaum Associates, Hillsdale, N.J.

Linton, M. (1982). Transformations of Memory in Everyday Life. In *Memory Observed: Remembering in Natural Contexts* (ed. U. Neisser). W. H. Freeman, San Francisco.

McDermott, D. (1992). Little "Me." *The Behavioral & Brain Sciences* 15(2): 217.

McFarland, T. (1987). Wordsworth's Hedgerows: The Infrastructure of the Longer Romantic Lyric. In *The Age of William Wordsworth: Critical Essays on the Romantic Tradition* (eds. K. R. Johnston and G. W. Knopf). Rutgers University Press, New Brunswick, N.J.

Mednick, S. A. (1962). The associative basis of the creative process. *Psychological Review* 69, 431–436.

Metcalfe, J., and Weibe D. (1987). Intuition in Insight and Noninsight. *Memory and Cognition* 15: 238–246.

Miller, J. (1986). Comments on Jayne's "Origins of Consciousness in the Breakdown of the Bicameral Mind." *Canadian Psychology* 27(2): 155–157.

Minsky, M. (1986). *The Society of Mind*. Simon & Schuster, New York.

Murray, G. (1955). *Five Stages of Greek Religion*. Doubleday, Garden City, N.Y.

Newell, A. (1990). *Unified Theories of Cognition*. Harvard University Press, Cambridge, Mass.

Nietzsche, F. W. (1872/1956). *The Birth of Tragedy and the Genealogy of Morals* (trans. F. Golffing). Doubleday Anchor Books, New York, 1956 printing.

——. (1880/1984). *Human, All Too Human: A Book for Free Spirits* (trans. M. Faber with S. Lehmann). University of Nebraska Press, Lincoln, 1984 printing.

Noth, M. (1974). *Exodus* (trans. J. Bowden). Westminster Press, Philadelphia.

Nozick, R. (1989). *The Examined Life: Philosophical Meditations*. Simon & Schuster, New York.

Paivio, A. (1979). Psychological Processes in the Comprehension of

Metaphor. In *Metaphor and Thought* (ed. A. Ortony). Cambridge University Press, New York.

Penrose, R. (1989). *The Emperor's New Mind: Concerning Computers, Minds and the Laws of Physics*. Oxford University Press, Oxford and New York.

Pinker, S. (1991). Language Acquisition. In *Language: An Invitation to Cognitive Science*, vol. 1 (eds. D. N. Osherson and H. Lasnik). MIT Press, Cambridge, Mass.

Potter, M. C. (1990). Remembering. In *Thinking: An Invitation to Cognitive Science*, vol. 3 (eds. D. N. Osherson and E. E. Smith). MIT Press, Cambridge, Mass.

Quine, W. V. (1969). *Ontological Relativity and Other Essays*. Columbia University Press, New York.

Reiser, M. (1990). *Memory in Mind and Brain: What Dream Imagery Reveals*. Basic Books, New York.

Rilke, R. M. (1922/1961). *Duino Elegies* (trans. C. F. McIntyre). University of California Press, Berkeley, 1961 printing.

Rogers, H. (1967). *Theory of Recursive Functions and Effective Computability*. McGraw-Hill, New York.

Salaman, E. (1970). *A Collection of Moments: A Study of Involuntary Memories*. Longman, London.

Salovey, P. and Mayer, J. D. (1990). Emotional Intelligence. *Imagination, Cognition and Personality* 9(3): 185–211. Baywood Publishing, Amityville, N.Y.

Schachtel, E. G. (1947/1982). On Memory and Childhood Amnesia. In *Memory Observed: Remembering in Natural Contexts* (ed. U. Neisser). W. H. Freeman, San Francisco, 1982 printing.

Scherer, K. R., and Ekman, P., eds. (1984). *Approaches to Emotion*. Lawrence Erlbaum Associates, Hillsdale, N.J.

Scholem, G. G. (1961). *Major Trends in Jewish Mysticism*. Schocken Books, New York.

Schorske, C. E. (1991). Freud: The Psychoarchaeology of Civilization. In *The Cambridge Companion to Freud* (ed. J. Neu). Cambridge University Press, New York.

Scolnic, B. E. (1990). From Bloody Bridegroom to Covenant Rite: *Brit Milah*—The Perspective of Modern Biblical Scholarship. *Conservative Judaism* 42(4): 12–20.

———. (1991). Moses and the Horns of Power. *Judaism: A Quarterly Journal of Jewish Life and Thought* 40(4): 569–579.

Scudder, H. E., ed. (1899). *The Complete Poetical Works and Letters of John Keats*. Houghton Mifflin, Boston and New York.

Searle, J. R. (1983). *Intentionality, an Essay in the Philosophy of Mind*. Cambridge University Press, New York.

———. (1984). *Minds, Brains, and Science*. Harvard University Press, Cambridge, Mass.

———. (1992). *The Rediscovery of the Mind*. MIT Press, Cambridge, Mass.

Shelley, P. B. (1821/1966). A Defense of Poetry. In *The Selected Poetry and Prose of Shelley* (ed. H. Bloom). The Signet Classics, New York, 1966 printing.

Shouksmith, G. (1973). *Intelligence, Creativity and Cognitive Style*. Batsford, London.

Shusterman, R. (1988). *T. S. Eliot and the Philosophy of Criticism*. Columbia University Press, New York.

Simon, H. A. (1967). Motivational and Emotional Controls of Cognition. *Psychological Review* 74(1): 29–39.

———. (1969). *Sciences of the Artificial*. MIT Press, Cambridge, Mass.

———. (1982). Affect and Cognition: Comments. In *Affect and Cognition: The Seventeenth Annual Carnegie Symposium on Cognition* (eds. M. S. Clark and S. T. Fiske). Lawrence Erlbaum Associates, Hillsdale, N.J.

Singer, D. G., and Singer, J. L. (1990). *The House of Make-believe: Children's Play and the Developing Imagination*. Harvard University Press, Cambridge, Mass.

Snell, B. (1953). *The Discovery of the Mind: The Greek Origins of European thought* (trans. T. G. Rosenmeyer). Basil Blackwell, Oxford.

Snow, R. E., and Yalow, E. (1982). Education and Intelligence. In *Handbook of Human Intelligence* (ed. Sternberg R. J.). Cambridge University Press, New York.

Stanfill, C. and Waltz, D. (1986). Toward Memory-Based Reasoning. *Communications of the ACM* 29(12): 1213–1228.

Steiner, G. (1971). *Extraterritorial; Papers on Literature and the Language Revolution*. Atheneum, New York.

———. (1989). *Real Presences: Is There Anything in What We Say?* Faber & Faber, Boston and London.

Sterelny, K. (1991). *The Representational Theory of Mind: An Introduction*. Basil Blackwell, Oxford.

Sternberg, R. J. (1982). Reasoning, Problem Solving, and Intelligence. In *Handbook of Human Intelligence* (ed. R. J. Sternberg). Cambridge University Press, New York.

Sternberg, R., ed. (1984). *Mechanisms of Cognitive Development*. W. H. Freeman, New York.

Stich, S. P. (1983). *From Folk Psychology to Cognitive Science: The Case against Belief*. MIT Press, Cambridge, Mass.

Tulving, E. (1983). *Elements of Episodic Memory*. Oxford University Press, Oxford and New York.

Turing, A. M. (1950). Computing Machinery and Intelligence. *Mind* 59(236).

Tversky, A. and Gati, I. (1978). Studies of Similarity. In *Cognition and Categorization* (eds. E. Rosch and B. B. Lloyd). Lawrence Erlbaum Associates, New York.

Updike, J. (1982). "Vibrations." In *Night Walks: A Bedside Companion* (ed. J. C. Oates). The Ontario Review Press, Princeton.

Vogel, G. W. (1991). Sleep-onset Mentation. In *Mind in Sleep: Psychology and Psychophysiology* (eds. S. J. Ellman and J. S. Antrobus). John Wiley, New York.

Von Rad, G. (1972). *Genesis*. The Westminster Press, Philadelphia.

Waldrop, M. (1987). *Man-made Minds: The Promise of Artificial Intelligence*. Walker, New York.

Wechsler, D. (1958). *The Measurement of Adult Intelligence*. Williams and Wilkins, Baltimore.

Weinstein, L. N., Schwartz, O. G., and Arkin, A. M. (1991). Qualitative Aspects of Sleep Mentation. In *The Mind in Sleep: Psychology and Psychophysiology* (eds. S. J. Ellman and J. S. Antrobus). John Wiley, New York.

Weschler, L. (1982). *Seeing Is Forgetting the Name of the Thing One Sees: A Life of Contemporary Artist Robert Irwin*. University of California Press, Berkeley.

White, E. B. (1942). Once More to the Lake. In *One Man's Meat*. Harper & Brothers, New York.

Willey, B. (1957/1973). *Samuel Taylor Coleridge*. W. W. Norton (Norton Library 1973), New York, 1973 printing.

Williams, B. (1993). *Shame and Necessity*. University of California Press, Berkeley.

Winner, E.; Rosenstiel, A. K.; and Gardner H. (1976/1988). The Development of Metaphoric Understanding. In *Child Language: A Reader* (eds. M. B. Franklin and S. S. Barten). ???Oxford, N.Y.

Wittgenstein, L. (1953). *Philosophical Investigations* (trans. G. E. M. Anscombe). Basil Blackwell, Oxford.

Wordsworth, J.; Jaye, M. C.; and Woolf R.; with Funnell, P.; foreword by Abrams, M. H., (1987). *William Wordsworth and the Age of English Romanticism*. Rutgers University, New Brunswick, N.J., and Wordsworth Trust, Grasmere.

Yeats, W. B. (1968). *Essays and Introductions*. Collier Books, New York, 1968 printing.

————. (1973). *Memoirs* (ed. D. Donoghue). Macmillan, New York, 1973 printing.

Zajonc, R. B. (1980). Feeling and Thinking: Preferences Need No Inferences. *American Psychologist* 35: 151–175.

Zajonc, R. B. (1984). The Interaction of Affect and Cognition. In *Approaches to Emotion* (eds. K. R. Scherer and P. Ekman). Lawrence Erlbaum Associates, Hillsdale, N.J.

Index